Arsenio Rodríguez and the Transnational Flows of Latin Popular Music

In the series

STUDIES IN LATIN AMERICAN AND CARIBBEAN MUSIC

edited by Peter Manuel

Arsenio Rodríguez

and the Transnational Flows of Latin Popular Music

DAVID F. GARCÍA

TEMPLE UNIVERSITY PRESS
Philadelphia

Temple University Press
1601 North Broad Street
Philadelphia PA 19122
www.temple.edu/tempress

Published 2006
Printed in the United States of America

∞ The paper used in this publication meets the requirements of the American National Standard for Information Sciences—Permanence of Paper for Printed Library Materials, ANSI Z39.48-1992

Library of Congress Cataloging-in-Publication Data

García, David F.

Arsenio Rodríguez and the transnational flows of Latin popular music / David F. García.

p. cm. — (Studies in Latin American and Caribbean music)

Includes bibliographical references (p.), discography (p.), and index.

Contents: Feeling son montuno : issues and theoretical approach — I was born of Africa : Black consciousness and Cubanidad. Formative years ; Reclaiming Africa ; Adore her as Martí did — Negro y macho : Arsenio Rodríguez's conjunto and son montuno style. The early septetos and conjunto, 1926–1944 ; Contratiempo and the emergence of the son montuno feel ; Placing the emergence of son montuno — Who is who in mambo? Migrating to New York City ; I sell rhythm! The political economy of son montuno and mambo ; The pueblo pueblo of El Barrio and the Bronx — Remembering the past with El Ciego Maravilloso. Arsenio Rodríguez in Chicago, Curaçao, and Los Angeles ; Nostalgia, exile politics, and the pre-salsa milieu in New York City ; Final performances and death — Salsa and Arsenio Rodríguez's legacy. We were disciples of Arsenio ; Son montuno and salsa aesthetics — Conclusion : remembering Arsenio Rodríguez/remembering son montuno.

ISBN 1-59213-385-1 (cloth : alk. paper) — ISBN 1-59213-386-X (pbk. : alk. paper)

1. Rodríguez, Arsenio. 2. Musicians—Cuba—Biography. 3. Popular music—Latin America—History and criticism. I. Title. II. Series.

ML410.R63235G37 2006
781.64092—dc22
[B] 2005058042

2 4 6 8 9 7 5 3 1

For Rose, Benicio, and Adriana Gabriela

And in memory of Raúl M. Travieso (1920–2001),
who welcomed me into his home and shared with me
his many memories of his beloved brother

Contents

Preface

THREE FACTORS LED ME to pursue research on Arsenio Rodríguez and his music. First, Dr. Robin Moore, who was my teacher at the University of California at Santa Barbara (1995–96), introduced me to the name and music of Arsenio Rodríguez. He also informed me of both his importance to Cuban and Latin music history and the lack of research on particularly the latter part of his career and life. Second, the compilation *Cuban Counterpoint: History of the Son Montuno* (Rounder CD 1078), produced by Morton Marks, was the first CD I bought that contained recordings by Arsenio's conjuntos. I was especially drawn to his 1966 recording of "Para bailar el montuno" (To Dance Montuno) for its melodic lyricism, funky bass line, and distorted *tres*. Third, the first person I made contact with and interviewed was Raúl Travieso, Arsenio's brother, whose encouragement was the decisive factor in convincing me to pursue research on Arsenio's life and music.

I feel that detailed musical analysis and the analysis of the interrelationship of music and dance have been largely absent in recently published social histories of Latin popular music. Also rare are critical biographies of important Latin musicians. Therefore, from the start of my research, I sought to understand the social and especially the musical aspects of Arsenio's importance. Hence, I have analyzed Arsenio's extensive recorded repertory, focusing on his son montuno style as it developed and persisted from 1940 to 1968. Although his recorded repertory forms the backbone of my musical analysis, I draw especially on the accounts of musicians, dancers, and other constituents of the dance music milieus in which Arsenio operated to gain insight on the musical, dance-related, aesthetic, social, and historical significance of his son montuno style. The observations of musicians, in particular, helped me identify and focus on the underlying musical principles and procedures that accounted for the innovativeness of his style in the 1940s and its continuing distinctiveness throughout the 1950s and 1960s. And the terms that musicians, dancers, and others used to describe or distinguish his style from the styles of his contemporaries led to a more concrete understanding of the social resonance that Arsenio's music had in the various local dance music milieus in which his conjuntos performed.

My primary source for data comes from the more than eighty interviews I have conducted with more than fifty individuals (see the

Bibliography). My most important contact was Arsenio's youngest brother, Raúl Travieso, with whom I conducted eleven formal interviews in addition to the numerous informal conversations we had at his home and on the phone. The questions that I prepared for all of the interviews were intended to gather factual data regarding dates, places, and names relevant to the interviewees' own experiences and their relationship to Arsenio and issue-oriented data regarding the interviewees' thoughts on the trajectories of Arsenio's music, musical career, and life and his importance to the history of Cuban and Latin popular music. I thank all of these musicians and dancers for agreeing and taking the time to be interviewed. This book would not have been possible without their assistance.

In addition to these interviews, I also consulted interviews conducted by other scholars and historians who graciously provided me with either their transcripts or audio and video copies of their interviews (see the Bibliography). The most significant interview I have consulted is one that was given by Arsenio with Colombian radio disc jockey José Luís Logradia in Los Angeles in 1964. A copy of this interview was given to me by Raúl Travieso. I also found two other interviews given by Arsenio that were published in Havana's *Bohemia* magazine and San Juan's *El Imparcial* newspaper (see Cubillas 1952; Nieves Rivera 1952). In all of these three primary sources Arsenio discusses various aspects of his music and career, from which I quote throughout the chapters of this book.

To substantiate and cross-reference the data collected from these interviews, I referred to government documents such as Cuban and U.S. censuses; U.S. State Department records; and local governmental studies of Havana, Matanzas, the Bronx, and East and South Central Los Angeles; documents from Musician's Union Local 802 (New York City) and 47 (Los Angeles); and especially newspapers and magazines published in Curaçao, Havana, San Juan, New York City, Los Angeles, and Miami. And to compile his discography, I consulted various sources including the BMG Archives and the American Federation of Musicians, Local 802, Recording Department. Last, I have obtained photographs of Arsenio and his conjuntos from private collectors; these sources have also been helpful in documenting the names of band members, the dates of their membership, and the places where Arsenio and his conjuntos performed.

Finally, I have collected almost all of Arsenio's original recordings. In addition I have acquired recordings by his predecessors and contemporaries whose musical contributions are also significant to the history of Cuban and Latin dance music and thus relevant to my musical analysis. I have also consulted with private record collectors, some of whom have furnished me with cassette copies of those recordings made by Arsenio (mostly the 78s he made with RCA Victor in Havana during the 1940s and 1950s), which have not been rereleased on CD. Finally, I have obtained noncommercial recordings made by Arsenio that are archived at the Center for Folklife Programs and Cultural Studies Archive of the Smithsonian Institution.

The purpose of the musical examples is not to present a definitive representation of the music as heard on the recordings but rather to demonstrate important features expounded on in the text. For instance, the subtle palm and fingertip strokes of the bongó and tumbadora (conga) players' left hands, which are mostly inaudible on the recordings, are notated with slashes. The more audible attacks are notated with a notehead (for open-tone attacks) and an X (for slaps). Many of these attacks as well as many notes in the other parts (i.e., voices, trumpets, tres, piano, and bass) correspond with the steps of the Cuban *son*'s basic footwork. I have identified these notes, attacks, and steps with numbers that correspond to the basic steps of the son's footwork. It is important to also emphasize that the notation of the footwork is primarily to indicate relationships between the music and basic movement or pulse in the dance. It obviously does not indicate other features of the dance, which I do discuss in descriptive terms in the text. Finally, I have transcribed all of the brass and reed parts in C to facilitate easy reading. I hope that this book on Arsenio Rodríguez will be one of many soon-to-be published works that gives balanced attention to social history, musical style, and dance while also focusing on individual historical figures.

I would like to thank those who assisted me in my research at the following institutions. In New York City: American Federation of Musicians, Local 802; BMG Archives; Centro Archives, Hunter College; New York Public Library, Mid-Manhattan Library; New York Public Library for the Performing Arts; New York Public Library Science, Industry and Business Library; Raices Archive, Harbor Conservatory for the Performing Arts; Robert F. Wagner Labor Archives of the Tamiment Institute Library, New York University; and Schomburg Center for Research in Black Culture. In Havana, Cuba: Archivo Nacional de Cuba; Biblioteca Nacional José Martí; Centro de Investigación y Desarrollo de la Música Cubana; Museo de la Danza; and Museo Nacional de la Música. In Los Angeles: Los Angeles Public Library, Central Library and University Research Library, University of California at Los Angeles. In Washington, DC: Center for Folklife Programs and Cultural Studies Archive, Smithsonian Institution. In Miami: Cuban Heritage Collection, University of Miami and Steve and Dorothea Green Library and the Cristóbal Díaz Ayala Collection of Cuban and Latin American Music, Florida International University. In New Jersey: Institute of Jazz Studies,

Rutgers, The State University of New Jersey. In Curaçao: Archive Nashonal and Fundashon Biblioteka Públiko Kòrsou. I would also like to thank Alfred Publishing, Emusica Entertainment Group, Hal Leonard Corporation, and Hall of Fame Music for graciously granting permission to reprint excerpts of music and lyrics from their respective catalogs.

I had many teachers, colleagues, and friends facilitate and guide my research and writing for the past nine years. They include Peter Manuel, Juan Flores, Steven Blum, Robin Moore, Tim Carter, David Carp, Raúl Fernández, Cristóbal Díaz Ayala, Jaime Jaramillo, and Richenel "Muz" Ansano. I also thank the Music Department and Office of the Vice Chancellor for Research and Economic Development at the University of North Carolina at Chapel Hill for the postdoctoral research fellowship (2003–4) that helped me complete the book.

Finally, thanks to my children, Benicio and Adriana Gabriela, to my mother and father, and especially to my wife, Rose, for giving me the much-needed support and all-important love that make the long hours researching and writing possible and worth it!

Introduction

ARSENIO RODRÍGUEZ (1911–70) was one of Cuba's most important composers and musical innovators of the twentieth century. Since the late 1930s, Arsenio's music has continued to make an indelible impact on a broad range of musical styles from the Caribbean and Latin America to West and Central Africa and beyond.[1] In the early 1940s Arsenio created the *son montuno* genre with his innovative *conjunto* ensemble, and by the 1950s Benny Moré, Ernest "Tito" Puente, and other Cuban, Puerto Rican, and Latin big band leaders had adopted the son montuno genre into their repertories, bringing it to a broader international audience. Contemporary musicians readily admit to the significant impact the music of Arsenio and his successors has had on their approach to performing Cuban and Latin dance music. As Cuban composer, pianist, and bandleader Adalberto Álvarez has stated: "If I've had to regularly resort back to these masters it's because in the conception of the rhythm, of the *sabor* [taste, feel], in the secrets of son montuno, it was all in Benny, in Arsenio, in Chappottín, and for those who want to play this type of music they must drink from these fountains" (Padura Fuentes 1997, p. 179).[2] Salsa composer and pianist Enrique "Papo" Lucca of Puerto Rico's La Sonora Ponceña has similarly stated: "There's Arsenio Rodríguez, Chappottín, Benny Moré, [Orquesta] Aragón, [Conjunto] Casino; whoever wants to start playing the music has to start with that music, because if you don't start with that I don't think the schooling will be complete" (ibid., p. 159). And Latin jazz and salsa musician Eddie Palmieri continues enthusiastically to study Arsenio's recordings (Christopher Washburne, personal communication).

In addition to inspiring composers, arrangers, and musicians, Arsenio's music has been performed and rerecorded by musicians of various musical backgrounds, most recently by the Afro Cuban All Stars, Manuel "Guajiro" Mirabal, and Rubén González of the internationally famous *Buena Vista Social Club*. In fact, González performed and recorded with Arsenio's conjunto in Havana from about 1945 to 1946. In the liner notes to his CD *Chanchullo* (World Circuit/Nonesuch 79503-2), González is quoted as saying: "[Arsenio] taught me many things; to always think about a solo before playing it, never to play the same thing twice and never depart from the rhythm." Experimental jazz guitarist Mark Ribot has recorded two CDs of Arsenio's music reworked for a jazz combo.[3] In

Curaçao his son montuno style has inspired a revival since the late 1960s known as "comeback," which includes son montuno—based Curaçaoan popular dance music. His music has even made a mark on Senegalese, Malian, Angolan, and Congolese popular music, if not directly then via the recordings of Cheo Marquetti, Johnny Pacheco, Ramón "Monguito" Quián, Eddie Palmieri, and others.[4] For example, Orchestra Baobab from Senegal rerecorded Arsenio's 1950s hit "Hay fuego en el 23" (There's a Fire at 23rd) for its 1979 LP *Gouygui de Dakar* (Succes 79).

Despite the broad and profound impact his music has had on several generations of musicians throughout the Cuban and Latin music world, Arsenio's own career was characterized by an ongoing series of musical and professional contentions and resolutions, struggles and negotiations, failures and successes. In 1935, internationally popular orchestras and musicians began to record his compositions, some of which contained coded critiques of slavery and its legacy of racism. He began his own recording career in 1940 with his group Arsenio Rodríguez y Su Conjunto, and by 1942 he had established a transformational style of Cuban son music known as son montuno, which would play a key role in the subsequent developments of mambo, *pachanga*, boogaloo, and salsa. His conjunto's popularity reached its apex by the mid-1940s throughout Cuba, but especially among the black working class of Havana. Between 1950 and 1952 he made frequent trips to New York City, where he organized another conjunto, Arsenio Rodríguez y Su Conjunto de Estrellas, which was made up of mostly Cuban and Puerto Rican musicians of color and with whom he performed and recorded regularly. The Conjunto de Estrellas even performed in San Juan, Puerto Rico, in 1952. He decided to stay in New York due to personal matters as well as deteriorating social and political conditions in Havana.

Through the first half of the 1950s Arsenio continued to compose, record, and lead his conjunto, which performed regularly in New York's most prominent Latin music dance halls alongside internationally popular mambo big bands, such as those led by Dámaso Pérez Prado, Tito Puente, Pablo "Tito" Rodríguez, and Frank "Machito" Grillo. However, Arsenio found it elusive to attain international recognition for his role in the development of the mambo. Nevertheless, as in Havana, his conjunto remained active in and had a significant impact on the local musical life of the Puerto Rican and Cuban communities in East Harlem and the South Bronx. The conjunto also performed for the largely Puerto Rican community in the north side of Chicago for several months in 1958 and again in 1962. In 1960 his conjunto toured extensively throughout Puerto Rico and performed in Curaçao in the Netherlands Antilles where his conjunto and son montuno style had been extremely popular since the 1940s.

In the first half of the 1960s, a younger generation of musicians and entrepreneurs emerged in New York City's Latin dance music milieu to popularize pachanga, which drew much of its musical features from the son montuno genre. Yet Arsenio's conjunto, most of whose members were now middle-aged, performed sparingly. Arsenio moved to Los Angeles in late 1964 where he attempted to create a niche for himself with a new conjunto, which consisted of Cuban, Puerto Rican, and Mexican musicians. But once again, his performances were largely relegated to peripheral locales, especially in East Los Angeles. In 1966 he returned to New York and reformed his conjunto as the nascent salsa industry was set to recast much of the Cuban conjunto music of the 1940s and 1950s, including Arsenio's recordings, into new instrumental formations. However, he and his conjunto continued to be conspicuously overlooked by early salsa promoters and record producers. In addition his alienation from the large community of Cuban political exiles in Miami and the Northeast, due to existing racial tensions and his own suspicion of all Cuban political orientations, accounted in part for his career's demise. He returned to Los Angeles in mid-1969 to resume performing until his death on December 30, 1970. Ironically, within two years of his death, salsa record labels Fania and Tico Records released two LPs in tribute to Arsenio, posthumously recognizing his magnitude in the development of salsa. In 1999 the International Latin Music Hall of Fame inducted Arsenio for his formative contributions to Latin popular music, including mambo and salsa.

"Feeling Son Montuno": Issues and Theoretical Approach

This book is the first scholarly work to document and analyze Arsenio Rodríguez's career and music. I am particularly interested in addressing the conflict in his volatile professional career and his music's long-term significance to Cuban and Latin popular music history. Although Arsenio's recorded repertory and son montuno style shaped transnational musical trends—from mambo in the 1940s and 1950s to salsa in the 1970s—his own professional viability beyond local music cultures in the Caribbean and the Cuban diaspora remained tenuous throughout his career. To help address this divergence, I focus my analysis by following three approaches: first, situating his conjunto and son montuno style within the distinct social, musical, and historical contexts of Havana, New York, Los Angeles, and elsewhere throughout three decades; second, distinguishing his importance to local music cultures in the Caribbean and the United States from his difficulties in the international popular music industries; and finally, focusing on the role that race, identity, and politics had in shaping his music and the trajectory of his musical career both locally and within the transnational realm of Cuban and Latin popular music. All three can be subsumed under a broader transnational approach, which for reasons I will explain shortly, addresses various interrelated areas of Arsenio's music, performance career, and identity.

Son Montuno as Musical, Social, and Historical Text

Though the number of social histories of Latin American popular music genres are increasing, not enough documentation and theoretical attention is being given to the intimate and complex relationships that historical figures such as Arsenio fostered with local communities within larger urban settings. Here, the notion of *pueblo pueblo* (people people), as developed by Juan Flores and others, is especially helpful in differentiating local cultures whose musical histories are often subsumed under the broader moniker of national (e.g., Cuban or Puerto Rican) or transnational (e.g., Latin) popular music repertories. As Flores explains, the purpose in doubling the term pueblo pueblo is to

> provide a necessary marker of specification or qualification. It is a sign of internal difference and contradiction, and of the abiding need to address the questions, "*Which* people?" and "*Which* popular culture?" With the hegemonic meaning of the term *popular culture* so identified with global media culture and communication, some specification of the time or site of the popular becomes indispensable. (Flores 2000, p. 24)

Certainly, the radio and recording industries played and continue to play an important role in the dissemination of Arsenio's music and the shaping of his legacy, from his early career on Cuban radio to the rereleasing of much of his recorded repertory on CD. In addition to his nickname, *El Ciego Maravilloso* (The Marvelous Blind One), which was coined by a Cuban radio disc jockey in the early 1940s, Arsenio continues to be proclaimed by Cubans and others as *una gloria de la música cubana* (a glory of Cuban music), which attests to his status as a national figure. During his lifetime, he depended on the popular music industry, mostly through royalty payments, for his livelihood. These aspects of his career and legacy, however, account for only part or one layer of his importance. In studying the ways in which his contemporaries described his music's significance, we also learn of the social impact his music had on various local communities in different historical periods. Hence, in Havana in the 1940s, musicians and dancers described his style as *negro* (black) and *macho* (masculine) and distinguished it from the *estilo blanco* ("white" style) of other Cuban conjuntos. In New York, Los Angeles, Chicago, and

Curaçao in the 1950s and 1960s, however, musicians and dancers described his style as *típico cubano* (traditionally Cuban) and *auténtico* (authentic).

In viewing these terms as part of broader social discourses, Arsenio's son montuno style may therefore be likened to a sonic palimpsest, or what Ronald Radano called a "soundtext" (see Radano 2003, pp. 2–3), of the musical, dance, and social histories of particular communities and groups of people. As I will show, the crystallization of Arsenio's style in Havana in the early 1940s was directly tied to a broader flowering of black working-class social clubs whose social events were organized around the performance of music and dance. What is particularly significant is the ideologically informed differentiation of Cuban conjunto styles of the 1940s in which Arsenio's "black style" embodied and signified a central marker of racial and class difference. On the other hand, for first-generation Cuban and Puerto Rican immigrants in New York, Los Angeles, and Chicago, the characterization of his style as típico cubano and auténtico suggests that his style engendered at once a sense of nostalgia for their respective homelands and cultural resistance to "modern" or Americanized Latin music styles, such as the mambo, which was aggressively marketed and disseminated locally and internationally by the North and Latin American popular music industries. Finally, Curaçaoans' characterization of Arsenio's style as típico cubano involved a similar sense of nostalgia, yet one that was rooted in a unique cultural and musical past centered on the history of Curaçaoan migrant workers in Cuba.

The personal recollections of those whom I interviewed for this book emanate from their unique lived experiences of performing with Arsenio's conjunto and dancing to his music. It is especially significant that many described his son montuno style as having a unique *feel*, whereas others emphasized that understanding his style required *feeling it with the body*. As Veit Erlmann has argued, the meaning of music resides not in its content but rather in its performance, whereby the sensory experience of playing and dancing becomes the integral component of musical meaning (see Erlmann 1996, pp. 186–87). As such, these recollections, in all their differences and contradictions, ground the meanings of Arsenio's music in the local musical histories of communities for whom his conjuntos performed. These recollections and meanings also suggest that no matter the time and place his conjunto and music represented an alternative to those musical repertories and styles associated with dominant classes and ethnic groups. It is my focus on the differences of his music's meanings in time and space that will contribute to the specification and qualification needed in the historiography of Cuban and Latin popular music and culture. In addition, with the issues of race, class, age, and musical style being especially significant to these communities, I hope to move the scholarly debate on salsa in particular beyond the issue of ethnic or national ownership by adopting a more historically and especially musically informed analytical approach.

Popular Music and Contemporaneity

In tracing Arsenio's career dating from the 1930s through the 1960s, this book provides an alternative account to the conventional narratives of the development of mambo and salsa. These historical narratives are fundamentally structured linearly in terms of time and space, whereby the development of these styles has been neatly organized into successive stages of stylistic evolution. As a consequence, these conventional narratives recognize Arsenio's musical contributions of the 1940s as constituting important antecedents to the crystallization of mambo and salsa, while ignoring his ongoing musical activities and contributions in the 1950s and 1960s. Instead, the focus continues to be placed on those such as Tito Puente, Machito, Pérez Prado, Eddie Palmieri, and others whose respective styles are said to constitute the "modern" flowerings of mambo and salsa. In short, the historical narratives of the mambo and salsa obfuscate the contemporaneity that in fact Arsenio shared with these "modern" mambo and salsa innovators until his death in 1970.

Attention to coevalness, as Johannes Fabian notes, "militates against false conceptions of dialectics—all those watered-down binary abstractions which are passed off as oppositions [e.g., traditional versus modern]... What are opposed... are not the same societies [or musical repertories] at different stages of development, but different societies [musical repertories] facing each other at the same Time" (Fabian 1983, p. 155). Indeed, Arsenio's contemporaries as well as Cuban and Latin music scholars have drawn extensively on the dualism of "traditional" and "modern" for various purposes. For instance, writers have emphasized jazz-inspired voicings, chord progressions, and instrumentation in mambo and salsa as rationale for characterizing these repertories as "modern" and distinguishing these from their "traditional" Cuban and Puerto Rican antecedents.[5] Similarly, Arsenio's contemporaries, especially those who experienced his music outside of Cuba, characterized his style as típico and auténtico to distinguish it from the "modern" (read "Americanized") styles that were developed by Pérez Prado, Puente, Machito, and others. As Erlmann has discussed, the constructed nature of "tradition" allows musicians and others to make sense of their immediate social and musical conditions via images of the past (see Erlmann 1991, pp. 10–14).

One inconsistent aspect in characterizing Arsenio's style as típico rests in the fact that he did make changes, however temporary and subtle, to his conjunto's instrumentation and overall sound beginning in the 1950s in accordance with commercial expectations. Another inconsistency involves limiting Arsenio's relevance on salsa music to those salsa musicians like Johnny Pacheco, whose early recorded repertory consists mostly of rerecorded Cuban originals. In fact, Pacheco's pastiche-like treatment of Cuban conjunto styles, in which he reinterpreted Arsenio's son montunos in the style of La Sonora Matancera, transcends musical, social, and historical fidelity. Hence, *típico* in these instances resonates little with historical continuity and stylistic fixity but more with the ways that forms and values have been linked together in discourse and in recordings to substantiate the immediate goals of writers and musicians in the present.

This book brings Arsenio and the local settings in which his conjunto performed into the historical present of mambo and early salsa. It does this by privileging the voices of his contemporaries not as a homogenous authentic voice unaffected by mass media culture and ideological conditions but rather as evidence of the internal difference and contradiction that has always characterized the complex histories of Cuban and Latin popular music. As Flores notes, the idea of popular culture is often directly equated with the offerings of the culture industry and no longer of "the people," adding that "the notion of 'traditional' as distinguished from 'modern' popular culture explicitly projects the community-based, expressive variant into a past tense, and cedes to the mass-mediated experience the crucial space of contemporaneity" (Flores 2000, pp. 18–19). In short, the perspectives of those interviewed for this book regarding Arsenio's musical significance reveal a much more varied and contested history as to the relationship between son montuno, mambo, pachanga, boogaloo, and salsa and the local music cultures of Cubans, Puerto Ricans, and others in the Caribbean and United States.

Arsenio's African Diaspora

In focusing on the glaring discrepancy in Arsenio's profound musical importance and his volatile professional career, this book also shows how issues of race, class, age, image, and identity significantly shaped his career and the workings of the Cuban and Latin popular music industries. Studying the lyrical content of his songs as well as the difficulties he encountered professionally brings the issue of race in particular to the forefront. For example, Arsenio's many references to Africa, his African heritage, and the persistence of racism in his songs and performances bring into focus the myth of racial democracy and *mestizaje*, as far as these ideas have been claimed as the basis of national identity in Latin American nations, including Cuba, as well as the distinguishing factors in race relations between the United States and Latin America.

It is often claimed by some scholars of Latin American (broadly defined to include the Caribbean) and Latino studies that the concept of race and the history of race relations in the United States and Latin America were and continue to be distinct. Besides what is often perceived as the benevolent treatment of slaves and the lack of official discrimination, the celebration and extent of racial and cultural miscegenation or mestizaje in Latin America has been especially emphasized as distinguishing its more tolerant attitudes toward its populations of color from the more segregated and violent history of race relations in the United States (see Helg 1995, p. 6). Numerous Latin American musical traditions that developed from Amerindian, African, and Iberian sources have served as particularly effective symbols of this process of mestizaje and national identity (see Moore 1997). Yet while complex processes of hybridization have indeed accounted for Latin America's cultural richness and racially diverse populations, the rhetoric of mestizaje paradoxically has involved the persistent reiteration of racial difference and, more important, maintains strong notions of white supremacy (Brock 1998, p. 18).

Peter Wade, for example, has shown that the classic Spanish-African-Amerindian triad is constantly adduced when Colombian music and national identity are discussed (Wade 2000, pp. 65–66). Wade also points out that in talking about mestizaje "black and indigenous people are seen as the eventual repositories of true tradition..., but as a result [of the contradiction between mestizaje and the persistence of African-derived or Amerindian cultural traditions and ways of life] they can be seen as both backward and authentic" (ibid., p. 66). In his comparative analysis on the treatment of racial hybridity in the literary traditions of the United States and Latin America, Carlos Hiraldo acknowledges that "a hierarchy that is not as clearly defined as the U.S. racial hierarchy remains to stratify people in Latin America according to the desirability of their racial phenotypes" (Hiraldo 2003, p. 3). Hiraldo adds that the rampant racial miscegenation in Latin America has been taken naively as evidence of a benevolent racial past (ibid., pp. 22–28). Despite the ideals of mestizaje, Cuba's social construct of race, as Aline Helg notes, has historically tended to show a two-tiered system—whites and *raza de color*, consisting of mulattoes and blacks—similar to that of the United States (Helg 1995, p. 3).

Arsenio clearly understood and commented on the pervasiveness of racism, making no distinction in the plight of black people based on cultural, national, or historical boundaries as he eloquently stated in "Aquí como allá" (It's the Same Here as It Is over There): "En África y en el Brasil / igual en Cuba como en Haiti / igual al Sur que en Nueva York / el negro canta su dolor" (In Africa and in Brazil, the same in Cuba as in Haiti, the same in the South as in New York, the black man sings of his pain). Furthermore, Arsenio's outspoken pride in both his African heritage and Cuban national identity represented a counterdiscourse to Cuba's dominant ideology of a national identity born of the process of mestizaje. It also challenged Cuba's myth of racial equality, which was constructed on the theme of male racial fraternity in nationalist wars, making "it blasphemous for Afro-Cubans to proclaim both their blackness and their patriotism" (Helg 1995, p. 7). Simply put, Arsenio projected an empowered sense of double consciousness, whereby his blackness and *cubanismo* were distinct, coexistent, and hence antagonistic to the tenets of mestizaje and Latin America's myth of racial brotherhood and equality.

Notwithstanding the complex differences in the history of slavery and race relations in the United States and Latin America, it is my opinion that scholars from both regions have privileged these differences while overlooking the rather obvious capacity of the ideology of racial supremacy and ever-present threat of racial terror to transcend national and cultural boundaries. Given Arsenio's commentary on the plight of black people throughout the Americas and Africa and his own firsthand experience of racism in Havana, Tampa (Florida), New York, and elsewhere, I draw on the concept of the African diaspora whose theoretical underpinnings transcend national boundaries and highlight the very transnational history of slavery and racism that Arsenio critiqued throughout his career (see Gilroy 1993). A transnational perspective on Arsenio's racial and national identities has significant theoretical implications on the issues of race as well as ethnic and national identity as treated in Cuban, Latin American, and Latino studies.

At the same time, however, it is necessary to specify to what degree Arsenio's identification with the transnational black struggle translated into actual participation on his part in and assimilation of, for example, African American popular music and culture. To address this, we should consider the black Latino immigrant experience in the United States, which continues to be underresearched.[6] Extremely scarce is the historical literature on the black Cuban immigrant experience prior to 1959. One notable exception is the memoir *Black Cuban, Black American*, written by Evelio Grillo, a black Cuban who grew up in Ybor City, Tampa, in the 1920s; attended all-black colleges in New Orleans and Washington, DC; and served in an all-black regiment of the U.S. Army during World War II (Grillo 2000). Kenya Dworkin y Méndez, writing in the introduction, describes Grillo's memoir as an "intimate account of his costly but effective triumph over racial and ethnic ambiguity and disempowerment—a journey from Afro-Cubanness to African-Americanness" (ibid., p. viii).

Not unlike Grillo, black Cuban musicians Mario Bauzá, Machito, Mongo Santamaria, and others escaped their doubly marginalized status—within the white Cuban and Latino community of New York as well as within the broader American society—by assimilating into the jazz music world.[7] According to Grillo, however, black Cubans who decided not to assimilate at least partially into African American society faced a stark reality living in the Latino barrios of New York.

> Our choices became clear: to swim in black American society or drown in the Latin ghettoes of New York City, never to be an integral part of American life. This is why the experience of black Cubans who joined with black Americans is so different from that of black Cubans who remained loosely tethered to the white Cuban [or in general Latino] society. (ibid., p. 12)

Although Grillo's characterization appears to be accurate for black Cubans living in the United States before 1959, Celia Cruz also transcended racial barriers through her musical, business, and, most important, political shrewdness; her outspoken condemnation of Fidel Castro resonated with the predominately white Cuban exile population who responded with genuine affection for Cruz throughout her career in the United States.

On the other hand, Arsenio remained loosely tethered to the almost all-white dominated Latin and North American popular music industries while never making a concerted effort to appeal musically or politically to an ethnically and racially diverse audience. Moreover, his blindness and stocky physical stature hardly met the image of the exotic white or light-skinned Latin lover that has continued to circulate through the popular culture industries of the United States and Latin America. Nevertheless, although the lives of Arsenio Rodríguez, Mario Bauzá, Machito, Mongo Santamaria, Celia Cruz and other black Cubans in the United States took on divergent trajectories, each had to confront and negotiate the same issues of racism and identity that have sustained the Afrodiasporic experience.[8] It is my contention that the issues that have shaped the experiences of black Latino immigrant musicians in the United States and their music remain to be defined, analyzed, interpreted, and brought to bear on the limitations that have characterized the analytical and interpretive scope of both Latino studies and African diaspora studies. In examining Arsenio's music, career, and life, this book provides valuable insight into the difficulties and local alliances that black Cuban and other musicians of color encountered and forged in the socially stratified, hierarchically structured, and ethnically diverse dance music milieus of the Caribbean and the United States, thereby expanding our understanding of the music and experiences of the African diaspora.

Outline

This study of Arsenio Rodríguez and his music introduces us to people, places, musical styles, and ideas that have either been inadequately treated or overlooked altogether. It is woven from the memories of his family, friends, peers, and contemporaries, sometimes quoted, sometimes paraphrased, clustered around the chronology of his exceptional musical career and life. Ultimately, it looks at Arsenio through his musical, professional, and personal relationships, regarding them as prisms of local histories that have otherwise been overshadowed by his more internationally recognized contemporaries and colleagues such as La Sonora Matancera, Dámaso Pérez Prado, Tito Puente, Celia Cruz, Johnny Pacheco, and many others. In short, this biography is as much a history of the local Cuban and Latin dance music milieus of Havana, New York, Los Angeles, and other cities as it is of Arsenio himself.

Chapter 1 explores the complex contours of Arsenio's racial and national identities as he expressed these in his lyrics and music throughout his career. His racially conscious songs are particularly significant because of the scope of his critique encompassing slavery, colonialism in Africa, and the persistence of racism throughout the African diaspora. Chapter 2 documents the formation of Arsenio's first conjunto in the early 1940s and analyzes the importance of his son montuno style, focusing on the impact it had on both the transformation of Cuban music, including the emergence of mambo, and the flowering of a black working-class consciousness and dance music milieu in Havana. The increasingly complex and contested history of the mambo in the early 1950s is further explored in chapter 3. It discusses Arsenio's contention for recognition as the creator of the mambo, which he expressed on stage and in the print media, while also documenting the impact that his repertory had on local Cuban and Puerto Rican residents of East Harlem and the Bronx, who differentiated their music culture from what the Palladium and mambo mania symbolized.

Chapter 4 contends that despite the significant wane in his commercial appeal by the late 1950s, Arsenio remained popular among local audiences in disparate places such as Puerto Rico and Curaçao as well as among the aging first-generation of Cuban and Puerto Rican immigrants in Chicago, Los Angeles, and New York. It also focuses on the different types of nostalgia that Arsenio and other Cuban musicians inspired during the 1960s. Chapter 5 explores Arsenio's contribution—aesthetic as well as musical—to early salsa music as performed and recorded in New York. It also shows that Arsenio and his son montuno style continue to symbolize musical authenticity for mostly first-generation salsa musicians of New York. The book concludes by outlining various dimensions of Arsenio's legacy, including the different repertories and local music cultures in which his music and style still thrive.

1 "I Was Born *of* Africa": Black Consciousness and *Cubanidad*

IN 1960 ARSENIO recorded "Yo nací del África" (I Was Born of Africa) for his LP *Cumbanchando con Arsenio (Fiesta en Harlem)* (SMC-1074). The lyrics of this song express the core of Arsenio's racial identity. In the verse section he rejects his Spanish surnames while speculating as to what his true African name and ethnicity might be. He then resolves his uncertainty in the *montuno* (call-and-response) section by embracing his African and Congolese heritage: "Yo no soy Rodríguez / yo no soy Travieso... tal vez soy Lumumba / tal vez soy Kasavubu / yo nací del África / ¡sí! ¡África!... yo soy el congo / tú eres mi tierra / mi tierra linda" (I'm not a Rodríguez / I'm not a Travieso... maybe I'm a Lumumba / maybe I'm a Kasavubu / I was born of Africa / yes! Africa!... I am the Congo / you are my homeland / my beautiful homeland). But Arsenio does more than merely claim Africa and the Congo as his homeland.

In fact, he reclaims the tropes of Africa and the Congo, which historically stood for cultural and racial inferiority and backwardness, and redeploys them as viable and enviable entities of identity. He expresses this sentiment by signifying on the Republic of the Congo's independence in 1960 from Belgian colonial rule when he lists Kasavubu and Lumumba—Joseph Kasavubu was the first president (1960–65) of the Republic of the Congo, and Patrice Lumumba was its first prime minister (1960–61)—as his possible "real" names. He also signifies on the trope of Africa in the title "Yo nací *del* África" (I Was Born *of* Africa), in which he affirms his African identity as having been "born" from the legacy of colonialism, slavery, and the ideology of white racial supremacy.

Throughout his career, Arsenio expressed in his lyrics a transnational or Afrodiasporic perspective on issues of race and black identity. He contested the racist significations of Africa and blackness and decried the persistence of racism throughout the Americas and Africa. He also expressed his *cubanidad* (Cuban identity) as well as his aspirations for peace and national reconciliation for Cuba. In effect, Arsenio affirmed his African heritage and Cuban identity as coexistent yet distinct rather than as a *mestizaje* or synthesis as, for example, his compatriot and Cuban national poet Nicolás Guillén expressed in many of his poems. In "El apellido" (My Last Name), for example, Guillén also reflected on Cuba's ancestral ties to Africa, but in the end he affirmed his own racially mixed background and desired a Cuban national identity that was also "mulata" or racially mixed (Benítez-Rojo 1996, pp. 126–30; White 1993, pp. 60–62).[1]

This chapter situates Arsenio's racial and national identities within the contexts of the *afrocubanismo* cultural movement of the 1930s, the Cuban revolution of the 1950s, and both the civil rights movement in the United States and African independence from colonial rule in the late 1950s and 1960s. By celebrating his African heritage and Cuban nationality while condemning racism in Cuba and throughout the Americas, Arsenio directly challenged Cuba's and in general Latin America's ideological contradiction, which historically has posited both the democratic principle of racial equality and the superiority of racial and cultural "whiteness" (see Helg 1995, pp. 6–7). In addition he rejected the dominant Western value system, which through centuries of slavery and colonialism defined African and African-derived cultural traditions of the Americas as backward, immoral, comical, and repulsive. It is through the veracity of Arsenio's Afrocentric and patriotic songs that we can appreciate what lay at the core of his sense of self.

Formative Years

Dorotea Rodríguez Scull (d. October 29, 1956) had fifteen children, fourteen boys and one girl.[2] Raúl Travieso, Arsenio's youngest brother, could only remember the names of six siblings. Of these six the first three, Julio (b. 1902), Aurelio (b. 1906), and Ignacio Arsenio (b. 1911), were born in the small rural town of Güira de Macuriges in the municipality of Bolondrón in the interior of the province of Matanzas.[3] Arsenio's father, Bonifacio Travieso (d. 1933), worked in the fields of Bolondrón as a farm worker. (Sometime in the 1930s Arsenio adopted Rodríguez, his mother's maiden name, as his stage name to avoid the awkward name Travieso, which in Spanish means "mischievous" or "naughty.") By the time Arsenio was four years old (1915), the family had moved to the large agricultural and sugar municipality of Güines, in the south coast of the province of La Habana.[4] They rented a small two-bedroom house in the barrio of Leguina where Arsenio's last three siblings were born: Estela (b. 1915), Israel "Kiki" (b. 1917), and Raúl (b. 1920). In addition to Bonifacio, there were other family members who worked in Güines's agricultural and sugar industries. For example, Dorotea's brother Yingo worked as a truck driver for a North American exporter, transporting produce from Güines to the docks of Havana and Matanzas, where it was later shipped to the United States. Arsenio's older brother Aurelio worked in the Centro Amistad, a large sugar plantation.

Several years after moving to Güines, Arsenio suffered a tragic accident that eventually left him totally blind. The accident occurred when the youngster mischievously poked a mule on the backside with a stick, causing the animal to deliver a violent kick to the boy's head. It is unclear exactly how old Arsenio was when the accident occurred. His daughter Regla believes that he was around seven or eight years old (c. 1918), whereas his brother Raúl remembers that he was around twelve years old (c. 1923). It is certain, however, that Arsenio was old enough to remember having sight. Just as tragic were the inadequate medical resources in Güines, which otherwise might have saved his left eye, which was removed, and his sight in his right eye.[5] As a result of this tragedy, he and younger brother Kiki initiated an extraordinarily close bond that would last for the rest of Arsenio's life. In his pain and fear, Arsenio turned to the music that penetrated his darkened world. And the traditions that formed his musical upbringing were those most associated with African-derived rural musical culture in central western Cuba.

Rural Beginnings

Slavery in Cuba officially ended in 1880, a mere thirty-one years before Arsenio's birth.[6] There were two periods in the decades leading to the abolition of slavery that saw the introduction of an extraordinary number of African slaves. Forty-seven percent of the total number of slaves who were brought to the island during the entire nineteenth century was introduced between 1821 and 1840. Another large number of slaves were introduced between 1851 and 1860, 73 percent of whom were concentrated in the interior of Matanzas and La Habana. Güines and Matanzas were two of the nine provinces with the largest slave populations, the majority of which were rural slaves.[7] It has been estimated that in the nineteenth century the ethnic composition of Africans in this part of Cuba was predominately Congo (35 percent), followed by Lucumí or Yoruba (23 percent), Gangá (13 percent), Carabalí (9 percent), and Macuá (4 percent) (Guanche 1996, pp, 61–62).[8]

These figures support Arsenio's many assertions that his African ethnicity was Congo.[9] As he stated in 1964, "My family [and] I come from the Congo. So as a child I knew many things that my grandfather taught me and many other things that I no longer practice" (Rodríguez interview 1964). In Güines, Dorotea's father, who died before Arsenio had his accident, most likely taught him the beliefs of Palo Monte, a religious system that was introduced by the Congo in Cuba.[10] He must have learned Palo Monte from his father as well, who was also a practitioner.[11] Arsenio was also immersed in Congo-derived secular traditions such as *yuka* and *rumba*. On days off, his uncle Yingo borrowed his North American boss's truck to take Arsenio and Kiki on regular trips throughout the interior of Matanzas to participate in rumbas. These were festive and often spontaneous reunions that took place in homes, cafés, street corners, and parks and featured couple and solo dancing accompanied by drummers and vocalists. The young boys learned how to play *tumbadoras* or conga drums in Matanzas from legendary *rumberos* such as Malanga, Mulence, Roncona, Cesario, Tanganica, and Andres Baró,[12] as well as in Leguina, Güines, which was also known for its famous rumberos (Orovio 1985, p. 15). They also learned the similar but older drumming tradition known as *yuka*, which was especially associated with the rural interior areas of Matanzas (León 1984, p. 71).

In Leguina the young Arsenio absorbed other African-derived sacred and secular traditions. A neighbor of theirs who was a *santero*, a practitioner of the Yoruba-based Santería religion, hosted an annual celebration for Changó (or Santa Barbara) on the fourth day of every December. These celebrations, which would sometimes last for more than two days, were attended by people from near and far. Finally, Arsenio engrossed himself in *son* music by learning to play the *marímbula* (a large box resonator with tuned metal tongues that are plucked), the *botija* (an earthenware vessel whose side hole was blown into and whose top hole was covered and uncovered by the hand), and the *tres* (a traditional Cuban guitar with three double-coursed strings). The marímbula and botija were used to provide bass accompaniment by early rural and urban son groups.[13] Arsenio learned to play on a marímbula that older brother Julio made out of a wooden guayaba crate. He learned to play the botija at rural festivals known as *guateques*. Finally, he first learned to play the tres from Victor González, a well-known tres player in Güines. But he was forced to continue on his own after González became too ill to continue giving the young boy lessons.

Urban Migration

In the early morning hours of October 20, 1926, the western half of Cuba was struck by a powerful and deadly hurricane. It began its path of destruction over the southern island of Isla de Pinos (renamed Isla de la Juventud in 1978), crossing into the southern part of the province of La Habana, directly over Güines. Three days after the hurricane hit, news from Güines reported that in the city industrial and public buildings were completely destroyed or suffered considerable damage. The situation in rural Güines was even more distressing, as the following reporter described: "What is certain is that Güines . . . bears a new and rough blow. It remains in misery, and hundreds of its inhabitants will go hungry. . . . Today, many *güinero* families find themselves without a livelihood"

(*Diario de la marina*, October 23, 1926). Among these families whose homes were destroyed and whose circumstances were uncertain were the Traviesos. Luckily, Arsenio, Kiki, and their uncle Yingo were on one of their trips to Matanzas when the hurricane hit. Several days later, they returned to rejoin the family. The Traviesos and many other homeless families were temporarily housed in schools and other public facilities that withstood the powerful hurricane. Soon after, Bonifacio and Dorotea decided to move the family to Marianao, near the capital of Havana. Marianao was also hit hard by the hurricane, the damages of which totaled about 4 million pesos. Los Hornos, Pogolotti, Los Angeles, Buena Vista, and other working-class sections of the city suffered the worst damages (Inclán Lavastida 1943, p. 149). Despite the destruction, however, the family's best opportunity for living a better life seemed to be in Marianao, which was the fastest-growing city in the province of La Habana. Older brother Julio had already been living and working in Marianao before the rest of the family arrived.

From 1926 through the 1930s Arsenio and his family lived in several working-class *repartos* (wards) in Marianao. The family first settled in Los Hornos, in the barrio of Quemados, where the fifteen-year-old Arsenio did not have to go far to meet famous black son musicians. For example, the family lived several blocks away from Felipe Neri Cabrera, the singer and maraca player with the popular black son group Sexteto Habanero. This son group had returned from New York City, where they made twelve recordings for RCA Victor in September 1926, about one month before the hurricane. Raúl remembers that he, Arsenio, and Kiki regularly observed Habanero's rehearsals from the window of Cabrera's home. In one occasion Kiki told the musicians that Arsenio played tres and wanted to learn more. The musicians obliged his request and invited Arsenio to play. After, Raúl remembers the following: "When we left, Arsenio told us, 'my brothers, I'm going to play better than [Carlos Godínez].' My other brother asked him, 'Why do you say that?' [Arsenio] 'You know why? Because he plays only two chords and more chords can be played on the tres. I'm going to play more than he does'" (Raúl Travieso interview June 19, 1996). Evidently, Arsenio's interest in breaking the mold took root early in his life.

Shortly after this time, the family moved north of Los Hornos to the reparto of La Serafina, which was also in the barrio of Quemados. It was here that Isaac Oviedo, tres player and director of Sexteto Matancero, heard people talk about a young, blind tres player who had recently arrived from Güines.[14] Oviedo met Arsenio and subsequently gave him several lessons on the tres. Exactly what impact, if any, Oviedo had on Arsenio's style of playing tres is difficult to determine. It is safe to say, however, that Oviedo's predilection for both tres solos (his were the first to be recorded) and unconventional chord progressions appealed to the young musician (see Ávalos 1991, p. 18, and 1995, pp. 21–22). Arsenio and his brothers would also walk to nearby Pogolotti, a reparto in the barrio of Redención, where another famous black son group, Septeto Boloña, frequently performed at the *sociedad* (social club) Club Casadores.

In all likelihood, Arsenio's encounters with these black son musicians and their music had a profound impact on the teenager in terms of his musical interests and identity. In the first place, these musicians incorporated aspects of sacred and secular Afro-Cuban cultural traditions in many of their recordings of the late 1920s and early 1930s. Second, opportunities for economic and professional gain opened up to them as a result of their success as recording artists. For example, Septeto Habanero's popularity grew as they became established performers in exclusive nightclubs and *encerronas* (or exclusive parties in private residences of wealthy white politicians and business leaders) (see Moore 1997, pp. 94–101). Hence, for Arsenio, playing and composing music was not simply one of the very few occupations available to a blind, black working-class individual. It was also a promising means by which he could achieve artistic and personal recognition. He undoubtedly was aware of the social challenges he faced. But as his musical accomplishments reflect, he was committed to overcoming what might have seemed to be insurmountable odds. By 1937, at the age of twenty-six, Arsenio Rodríguez would indeed become a commercially successful composer beginning with his *afrocubano* "Bruca maniguá."

Reclaiming "Africa"

In July 1969, Arsenio, along with his brother Kiki and Cuban bassist Luís Salomé, performed at the Festival of American Folklife in Washington, D.C. The program in which he was scheduled to perform was titled "Black Music through Languages of the New World." (The circumstances of this event and Arsenio's participation in it are discussed further later.) Arsenio began by introducing himself and his music:

> Good afternoon ladies and gentlemen . . . I am Arsenio Rodríguez, the composer of many songs, principally African, which you have heard. I composed all of those *afros* that you used to hear Miguelito Valdés sing, "Bruca maniguá," "Fufuñando," and "Adiós África," which Xavier Cugat recorded, and many songs which are sung all over the world, all of which have an African influence from my heritage.[15]

Arsenio's characterization of his music as African certainly resonated with the theme of the program and the broader political and social environment of the 1960s, marked by the civil rights movement in the United States and the black power movements throughout the African diaspora.

Through the 1930s in Cuba, however, recognizing one's African heritage with pride and praising the African contribution to the nation were largely condemned as tantamount to harboring antiwhite racist and unpatriotic sentiments (Helg 1995, p. 7). In addition, many black Cuban intellectuals denigrated African-derived cultural traditions, such as the Afro-Cuban religions Santería and Palo Monte, as backward and antithetical to the ideals of mestizaje (cultural and racial miscegenation) and *superación* (racial uplift). As we will see, Arsenio reversed many of these myths' cultural signs in much of his music from the late 1930s through poetic techniques that in other Afrodiasporic traditions have been characterized as signifyin(g).

Repetition with a Difference: The Afrocubanos, 1937–40

In the nineteenth and early twentieth centuries, social Darwinism and positivism provided the ideological framework in which Cuban intellectuals reflected on race and Afro-Cuban culture (Helg 1995, p. 16; Hagedorn 2001, pp. 177–78). For instance, in his earliest work Cuban anthropologist Fernando Ortiz drew from the social Darwinian roots of his training in criminology in racializing the notion of crime, whereby he identified the "superstitions, organizations, languages, dances," and, ultimately, the "African psyche" of black Cubans as the most grievous vices of Cuba's races and of Cuban society in general (Hagedorn 2001, pp. 175–77). The cure, according to Ortiz, was to "civilize," that is, "de-Africanize," Cuba's black population beginning with its expressive cultural traditions. Indeed, in the first two decades of Arsenio's life, action was taken by the Cuban government to repress forms of African-derived Cuban traditional practices (see Moore 1997, pp. 229–32). Such measures often incited racial violence against black practitioners of Afro-Cuban religions (Helg 1995, pp. 238–9; Hagedorn 2001, p. 190).

Paradoxically, beginning in the 1920s, a group of Cuban artists, poets, and composers led a cultural movement known as *afrocubanismo* that supported modernist interpretations of Afro-Cuban folkloric traditions for the sake of defining a new Cuban national culture (see Moore 1997).[16] As these artists increasingly drew from Afro-Cuban traditions for their modernist works, black intellectuals in particular became more critical of afrocubanismo artists, whom they saw as exploiting "decadent" cultural traditions and therefore contradicting and threatening the goals of mestizaje and superación. The fact that the exponents of afrocubanismo were primarily white middle-class intellectuals and artists probably stimulated more resentment and suspicion on the part of their black critics. No other black writer was more emphatic in his or her rejection of Afro-Cuban traditions and the tenets of afrocubanismo than Alberto Arredondo, who in the pages of *Adelante* (*Onward*), a black middle-class magazine, evoked the ideals of mestizaje and superación in his critiques: "It is logical that what began to be known as 'Cuban music' during the colonial era, was a mix of African and Spanish rhythms, although the marked improvement of the former continued to get stronger" (Arredondo 1938). By the 1930s Fernando Ortiz himself had also embraced the tenets of mestizaje when he defined Cuban culture as an *ajiaco* (stew) that had been produced by the "disintegration" of the ajiaco's basic elements (Spanish and African) into a new "mestizaje de razas" and "mestizaje de culturas" (Hagedorn 2001, p. 192).[17]

Arsenio's afros or *afrocubanos*, as he called them, seemingly evoke all the ambiguity, contradiction, and tension that defined the discourse on race and national identity in Cuba at this time. In 1937 Orquesta Casino de la Playa, an all-white Cuban jazz band, and its lead vocalist, Miguelito Valdés, a Cuban of mixed heritage, became the first group to record "Bruca maniguá" (Witch from the Bush), Arsenio's first and most recognized international hit.[18] The basic musical form of Arsenio's afrocubanos consists of four sections: introduction, verse, bridge, and *montuno*. The introduction, verse, and bridge sections are marked by the *tango-congo* rhythmic pattern, whose song form of the same name became a conventional genre of the Cuban *zarzuela* (light opera) beginning in the early 1910s. The afrocubano's concluding montuno section is marked by a basic son rhythmic structure.

The predominant characteristic of Arsenio's afrocubano songs, however, is its textual portrayal of black slaves and nineteenth-century plantation life. Arsenio did this by setting the text in "Africanized" Spanish, commonly referred to as *bozal* speech, and by introducing conventional black character types of the Cuban popular theater. These familiar signs of black difference and inferiority became popular in the minstrel-like portrayals of blacks in nineteenth-century Cuban *bufos* or comic theater (see Moore 1997, pp. 42–52). A closer examination of his afrocubanos, however, reveals that in redeploying these dominant signs of blackness Arsenio engaged in a parody of a parody, a reversal of received racist conventions, or what Henry Louis Gates Jr. has referred to as "repetition with a difference" (Gates 1988, pp. 106–10).

Although its stylized form became especially common in Cuban popular theater in the nineteenth century, the Africanized Spanish that had been created by newly arrived African slaves remained prominent in the speech of practitioners of Palo Monte well into the twentieth century.[19] As linguist John Lipski notes, the speech of *bozales* or African-born slaves formed as a hybrid structure consisting of a Spanish (or pidgin Spanish) morpho-syntactic frame with an African lexical core. Hence, much of the vocabulary used by bozal speakers or Palo Monte practitioners consisted of "Congo" or Ki-Kongo lexical items (Lipski 1993, pp. 18–19, 103). In contrast, slave songs in bufo productions and zarzuelas, though superficially alluding to Afro-Cuban imagery, in all likelihood lacked African lexical items and, more significantly, proverbs actually used by practitioners of Palo Monte and other African-derived religious systems of Cuba.

Regardless, Afro-Cuban oral traditions and speech were unintelligible to most listeners of Cuban popular music, especially Casino de la Playa's core audience, which consisted of tourists and the white Cuban elite in Havana. Arsenio's afrocubanos, therefore, were received as consisting of familiar tropes of black difference, primitivism, and inferiority. Although Arsenio's opening verses introduce the conventional black character type and imagery, a transformation in representation occurs in the bridge section, for example, of "Bruca maniguá" in which the slave condemns the *mundele* (Ki-Kongo for "white man") or slave owner: "Mundele con bafioté / siempre tan garchá / etá po mucho que lo ndinga / siempre tá matratá / ya ne me cabá / bafioté füirí" (The white man with his hostility / he's always deceiving / he's saying many things I don't understand / he always mistreats me / he's killed me / with his abuse).[20] In "Ven acá Tomá" (Come Down Tomás) the black protagonist aspires to one day own a small plot of land, warning the *mayoral* (slave overseer) of his impending escape: "Yo quiere que te acueda / lo que yo te tá decí / ma que yo me va de aquí ¡Mayorá!" (I want you to remember / what I'm going to say to you / look, I'm leaving this place, slave overseer!). In both excerpts, the black protagonists' outspoken criticism of and confrontational stance toward their oppressors break with the conventional representation of particularly the comical "negro bozal" or pretentious "negro catedrático" character types of the Cuban popular theater. Additionally, by inserting Congo lexical items within a "Spanish syntactic frame," the bozal speech in "Bruca maniguá" reflects a more accurate representation of nineteenth-century African speech in Cuba than its strictly parodied form in early twentieth-century zarzuelas.

Arsenio also uses proverbs associated with Palo Monte and other traditional passages with Congo lexical items. "Adiós África" (Goodbye Africa) contains several such passages, the first verse of which follows: "Ahora mimo yo tá llorá / po que me tá recordá / como nego me trae / de África" (Today I'm crying / because I am remembering / as a black man they took me / from Africa). Later in the montuno section, the protagonist, speaking the line "ya son las hora" (it is time), orders his "ganga" (the cauldron where the spirit that the *palero* "owns" resides) to resolve his problems.[21] The line "quien rabo mono 'mara mono" (he who ties the monkey's tail will be tied by the monkey) is a traditional Palo Monte proverb, which warns that any deception or ill will toward somebody on your part will have negative ramifications.[22] The literal translation of the line "ahora sí que casilla 'garra coronise" is "Now my bird trap works." But in this context, *casilla* (pigeon-hole) represents the ganga" and *[a]garra coronise* (to grasp a Cornish hen) signifies the mystical power of the ganga. The word *kiyumba* refers to an animal or human skull, which was used for Palo Monte rituals, but is no longer practiced (Castellanos and Castellanos 1992, p. 391). Finally, *Kindimbyola*, which is spoken by Miguelito Valdés toward the end of the recording, was the name of a powerful ganga, which is well-known among paleros. There are subtle translations of other words that also refer to the ganga, such as *caravela* and *kimbisa* as heard in "Yo son Gangá" (I'm a Gangá).[23] Also, the spiritual sources residing in the ganga are often ridiculed by Palo Monte priests, as in the lines "¿Qué dinga bobo? ¿Qué kuendá?" (What are you saying, idiot? When is it going to grow?), to provoke the ganga's mystical power.

Arsenio's afrocubanos demonstrate not only the extent of his knowledge of Palo Monte spirituality but also his critique of the discourse on African inferiority and atavism as (1) manifested in racist representational tropes in Cuban popular culture and (2) implied in the ideology of mestizaje (read: racial and cultural "progress").[24] The ideals of mestizaje, in particular, directly marginalized rural and urban lower- and working-class black Cubans, like Arsenio and his family, who were deeply rooted in African-derived cultural traditions of Cuba. As he countered in the afrocubanos, these traditions of his youth, though representing a "primitive" era for most of the white Cuban elite as well as black intellectuals, continued to be a vital and powerful aspect of his music and life. In another song from the late 1930s, a *conga* titled "Todos seguimos la conga" (We All Follow the Conga), Arsenio restated his critique, but this time explicitly:

> Ya la conga está tocando / por el Prado va / con un baile vengo 'rrollando / todos van de 'tras / y despues muchos critican "Es un antigüedad" / cuando suena los tambores / con ese ritmo y como pasa / repiquetiando su sonido / nacido de África / cuando suena los cencerros todos van a 'rrollar.
>
> (Now the conga is playing / down Prado [Street] it goes / while dancing I come rolling / as everyone follows behind / and later many people criticize "this is an ancient custom" [i.e., atavistic] / when the drums sound / with that rhythm and how it passes by / playing its sound / born in Africa / when the bells sound everyone goes rolling.)

The full effect of Arsenio's strategic revision, however, was borne out in his utilization of the all-white Orquesta Casino de la Playa and in the misreading of his afrocubanos by Casino de la Playa's audiences. As was the case in many elite cabarets in Havana, New York City, and elsewhere in the late 1930s, white musicians and performers presented stylized versions of Afro-Cuban carnival music, known as the conga, which included the use of the conga drum (known as *tumbadora* in Cuba), itself signifying racist stereotypes of African primitivism. Felipe García Villamil, a high-ranking practitioner of Palo Monte, Santería, and Abakuá explained that black Cubans (including himself) resented the often capricious appropriation of Afro-Cuban music by many white composers. He suggests that many even participated in sacred ceremonies to use musical elements in their popular and art compositions.

> This would often upset us because of . . . racism and that whole mess. They wrote arrangements and the majority of those who sang them were white. Also, they gave the impression that they didn't understand what they were singing, which they sang anyway according to what they felt. . . . There were many white Cubans that were mixed up in the religion in order to use the music [for their orchestras]. (García Villamil interview, January 1998)

Although García Villamil did not specify, his criticism may readily be directed to the Cuban popular music industry as a whole as well as afrocubanismo art composer Amadeo Roldán, for example, who was known to frequent Santería and Abakuá ceremonies for musical inspiration (see Moore 1997, p. 203).

In contrast, Casino de la Playa's recordings and performances of Arsenio's afrocubanos represent a strategic reversal of the long history of white appropriation and exoticization of black culture. As he recounted in 1964, Arsenio actively instructed Casino de la Playa's vocalist Miguelito Valdés on how to sing the lyrics: "[Miguelito] hadn't sung afrocubanos. I had to teach him the words . . . [because] the lyric in 'Bruca maniguá' is African, from the Congo" (Rodríguez interview 1964). "Bruca maniguá" as well as "Fufuñando" and "Adios África" were eventually recorded by Xavier Cugat and other internationally famous figures, thereby introducing Arsenio and his music to unsuspecting international audiences. As the Palo Monte proverb "quien rabo mono 'mara mono" goes, Arsenio indulged these audiences with racist fantasies of black inferiority only to infuse the songs with African lexical items and rhetorical aspects of Afro-Cuban oral traditions, condemning slavery and its legacy of racial injustice.

"No Spanish! African! African!"

Throughout his career Arsenio continued to denounce racism and express his identification with the black diasporic experience. It is important to note that in 1947 he had visited Tampa, Florida, lodging in the segregated section of the city, on his way to New York City (see chapter 3). Three years later, in Havana, Arsenio's conjunto, with his sister Estela singing lead, recorded "Aquí como allá" (It's the Same Here as It Is over There), in which he indirectly references his experience with racial bigotry in the American South. In the verse section Arsenio writes of the pain and inequality that blacks in the South as well as Africa, Brazil, Cuba, Haiti, New York, Argentina, Mexico, and Venezuela experience and sing about in song. In the montuno section he emphasizes the shared experience of pain and inequality sung by black people "here" and "there," that is, of the African diaspora. Although he experienced the peculiarities of racial segregation in the South, Arsenio makes clear here the transnational history of slavery and experience of racism shared among black people of the Americas and Africa.

He also composed songs that directly addressed or signified on sociopolitical events specific to particular areas of the African diaspora. In "Yo nací del África" (I was Born of Africa), as discussed at the beginning of this chapter, he signified on the Republic of the Congo's independence in 1960 from Belgian colonial rule by expressing his own rejection of (or independence from) the legacy of slavery and Spanish colonialism (in the form of Spanish surnames) in Cuba. He restated his African and Congo identity in "África canta y llora" (Africa Sings and Cries), which Miguelito Valdés recorded accompanied by Machito's orchestra in 1963 (Tico 1098). Stylistically, "África canta y llora" is an afrocubano, marked by the tango-congo ostinato pattern that is heard throughout the recording. Instead of portraying the imagery of the Cuban colonial plantation and slavery, however, Arsenio discusses the end of European colonial rule in Africa. Most important, he again contests the racist image of the "happy African" playing the drum by praising Africans' yearning for and achievement of political independence: "Decían que no sabía añorar / más que al tambor / ahora todos tendrán que apreciar / tu gran valor / . . . Ahora te toca reir / se terminó tu sufrir / y yo me siento feliz" (They said that you yearned / for nothing but the drum / now everyone will have to appreciate / your great value / . . . Now it's your turn to laugh / your suffering has ended / and I feel happy).

While living in New York City in the early 1960s, Arsenio composed two songs in which he reflected on the continued injustices that blacks were suffering. In "La democracia" (Democracy) he asks, "Si ya las cosas han cambiado / y hay derechos de igualdad / ¿por qué yo soy descriminado? / si todo el mundo somos igual / ¿la democracia donde esta? / nos falta mucho pa' llegar" (If things have changed / and there's equal rights / then why am I discriminated against? / for everyone is equal / where's the democracy? / we have a long way to go).[25] In "Vaya pa'l monte" (Go to the Mountain), which his conjunto recorded in 1966 for his LP *Viva Arsenio!* (BLPS-216), Arsenio again articulates an African diasporic sensibility in pointing out that blacks whether in Carolina, Puerto Rico, or New York City continue to have to fight for better work and living conditions.

Clearly, Arsenio sensed the growing frustration in the poorly enforced or altogether ignored civil rights laws that were passed in the United States in 1957, 1960, and 1964 as well as the disproportionate amount of unemployed and poverty-stricken African Americans. Indeed, several months after Arsenio recorded "La democracia," in summer 1964, riots erupted in African American neighborhoods in New York City, Jersey City, and Chicago. And on August 11, 1965, eight months before the recording of "Vaya pa'l monte," riots erupted in the African American areas of south Los Angeles, including Watts. At this time Arsenio was living nearby, in Exposition, while performing every Saturday night at the Paramount Ballroom in East Los Angeles (see chapter 4). It is uncertain whether or how often he performed any of these songs live. What is clear, however, is that Arsenio shared a deep empathy for and expressed a broad identification with the African diasporic struggle against racial discrimination and colonialism.

In July 1969 Arsenio and Kiki traveled to Washington, DC, from Los Angeles to participate in the Smithsonian Institution's third Festival of American Folklife. Arsenio was invited to participate by the festival director, Ralph Rinzler, who originally conceived of the festival and brought it into being in 1967 (see Abrahams 1995; Gagné 1996). Rinzler was described as having a "clear idea of how to bring great tradition-bearers together with the larger public audience by finding within their work the vitality of their cultural inheritance and the genius of the individual artist operating within that tradition" (Abrahams 1995, p. 325). Although he worked mostly with Anglo and African American musicians and craftsmen, his interest in tradition bearers did include those from other regions of the Americas. He first came into contact with Arsenio in May 1964, when he recorded Arsenio and Kiki performing Cuban and Afro-Cuban folkloric music. The session, which probably took place in Kiki's apartment in the South Bronx, included performances of son, *bembé*, *yuka*, and other folkloric Afro-Cuban music, as well as "La democracia."[26]

Five years later, in 1969, Rinzler, now the director of the Festival of American Folklife, engaged Bernice Reagon, former member of the Freedom Singers, to organize a program of black music for the festival.[27] Reagon conceived of a program that would celebrate the shared aesthetics of black music as performed and sung by African Americans of the former English, French, and Spanish colonial regions of the Americas. She titled the program "Black Music through Languages of the New World." Because of his work with Arsenio in 1964, Rinzler recommended Arsenio to Reagon as the strongest representation of black music of the "Spanish-speaking" New World. Altogether, Arsenio and Kiki, along with Cuban bassist and longtime friend Luís Salomé, performed three times during the festival. They performed music from the Palo Monte, Santería, and Abakuá repertoires as well as Cuban secular folk music. In addition, Reagon invited the Ardoin Family and Canray Fontenot, who were zydeco musicians from Lafayette, Louisiana, and several African American groups, including Ed, G.D., and Lonnie Young; fife and drum performers from Como, Mississippi; and the Moving Star Hall Singers.

Arsenio's second performance, which took place in the evening of July 5 at the main stage (see Figure 1.1), opened with an impromptu collaboration with Reagon singing the spiritual "One More Time," and Arsenio accompanying her on tres, making for a poignant Afrodiasporic moment. Then, in introducing Arsenio, Kiki, and Salomé, Reagon shared the following thoughts with the audience: "It's very strange for me to be in the company this afternoon of about five or six black people, all of whom were from Cuba, all of whom could tell me about their different gods.

FIGURE 1.1. The Rodríguez Brothers, Festival of American Folklife, Washington D.C., July 5, 1969. *Left to right:* Arsenio Rodríguez, Kiki Rodríguez, and Luís Salomé. *Source:* Photographer unknown; photograph courtesy of the Center for Folklife and Cultural Heritage, Smithsonian Institution.

These are people who say, 'I'm African, and I know it.' The Rodriguez Brothers!"[28]

Reagon's impression of Arsenio had been shaped not only by Rinzler's recommendation but most directly from a conversation she and Arsenio had through an interpreter. When she first met Arsenio at the festival, Reagon explained to him her concept of the program, telling him that his music was to represent black music sung in Spanish. According to Reagon, Arsenio ardently responded, "No! No! No Spanish! Lucumí! African! African!" (Reagon interview 2004). His clarification, as Reagon pointed out, instantly transformed her in terms of her own early career as a young scholar of black history and culture as well as her conception of the program: "It opened up in my mind what was American and also what we knew or thought we knew about what existed and what did not exist" (ibid.). In planning the program, Reagon had not considered including musical traditions sung in African-derived languages of the New World, such as Congo and Lucumí. Arsenio, however, instructed Reagon that these traditions still existed and, most important, they were living and not reified African traditions of a bygone era. As Reagon explained, "Arsenio Rodriguez was *very clear* that he was teaching me. And it was not long, it was not oppressive. It was just very clean and he did it in his textured voice that I really recognized because that's the way my father preaches and that's the way my father would talk" (ibid.).

Despite the ideological and political shifts Africa (the trope and continent) would undergo throughout the twentieth century, Arsenio always maintained his admiration for the cultural and historical values it imparted throughout the African diaspora. Indeed, throughout his career Arsenio drew from the African-derived musical and oral traditions of his youth not only for musical and lyrical material but for critical purposes. In the 1940s he composed son montunos, such as "No hay yaya sin guayacán," "Dundunbanza," and "Soy el terror," whose lyrics also drew from the Cuban Congo and Palo Monte oral traditions (see chapter 2). In addition to his African heritage, Arsenio also reflected on his Cuban identity and expressed his patriotism in song. As Cuban Alfredito Valdés Jr. (who performed with Arsenio's conjunto in the early 1960s) succinctly stated, "Arsenio, being a direct descendant of Africans, *siempre lo dijo en su música* [always said it in his *music*]. He always acknowledged that he was *cubano* and that he was *afrocubano*" (Alfredo Valdés interview 2001).

"Adore Her as Martí Did"

In his patriotic songs, Arsenio expressed his concerns regarding contemporary political and social matters that affected *all* Cubans. From the time he began his professional career as a musician and composer in the late 1920s to his final visit to Havana in 1957, Cuba underwent frequent periods of political instability and economic hardship. One of his earliest politically oriented songs was "Pobre mi Cuba" (My Poor Cuba), a *lamento guajiro* that was published in 1935 and first recorded that same year by Septeto Machín in New York City. Arsenio wrote this song during two difficult and overlapping periods in Cuba, the dictatorship of Gerardo Machado (1928–33) and the Depression. During the dictatorship, strikes, violent labor demonstrations, and acts of brutal government repression became common. Furthermore, with the onslaught of the Depression in October 1929, the Cuban economy entered into extreme crisis, resulting in unemployment for hundreds of thousands and desperate living conditions, especially for the country's poor (Moore 1997, pp. 77–78).

Fittingly, in "Pobre mi Cuba," Arsenio describes the hardship of the guajiro or rural peasant farmer, whose cacao, tobacco, and sugarcane crops are either worthless or ruined. It is important to note that this song was published and recorded after the fall of the Machado dictatorship, considering that the government was known to send into exile composers whose material was suspected of being subversive.[29] Arsenio's conjunto recorded it more than a decade later in 1951 in Havana. Unfortunately, Cuba's economic and political situation was once again unstable and primed for a dictatorship. In 1950 Arsenio's conjunto recorded "El que no tiene no vale" (The One Who Has Nothing Is Worth Nothing), which was composed by Arsenio's trumpet player, Félix Chappottín. The song's verses describe the social stigma of not having money as the refrain answers with "¿Cuanto tienes? ¿Cuanto vales? / Nada tienes. Nada vales" (How much do you have? How much are you worth? You have nothing. You're worth nothing). It concludes with the equally cynical advice: "Asi es la vida / asi es el mundo / no hay que pensarlo / todo es mentira" (That's life / that's how the world is / don't put too much thought into it / it's all a lie).

In the mid-1950s, as Fidel Castro's revolution against Fulgencio Batista's dictatorship intensified, Arsenio composed and recorded the bolero "Adórenla como Martí" (Adore Her as Martí Did), which is his most well-known patriotic song. In it, he appeals to all Cubans to resolve their differences in peace and love and to unite the country so that the sacrifices of the Cuban independence patriots would not have been in vain. As stated in the refrain, Arsenio implores his fellow Cubans to "Amenla como Bermúdez / cuídenla como Agramonte / defiendala como Banderas / y como Carlos Manuel / amenla como Aguilera / cuidenla como Moncada / defiendala como Maceo / adórenla como Martí" (Love her [Cuba] as Bermúdez did / care for her as Agramonte did / defend her as [Quintín] Banderas did / and as Carlos Manuel [de Céspedes] did too / love her as

Aguilera did / care for her as [Guillermón] Moncada did / defend her as [Antonio] Maceo did / adore her as [José] Martí did). It is important to note that Arsenio was fascinated by and had a deep knowledge of black *mambises* (Cuban independence fighters), especially black generals Quintín Banderas, Guillermón Moncada, and Antonio Maceo.[30] He premiered "Adórenla como Martí" in 1957 for the Club Cubano Inter-Americano, a social club of primarily Cubans and Puerto Ricans of color, in the South Bronx. Soon after, he recorded it with his conjunto for the LP *Sabroso y caliente con Arsenio Rodríguez y Su Conjunto* (Puchito 586) (see chapter 3).

He once again pleaded for peace in "Cuba llora" (Cuba Is Crying), which he composed in 1958 and recorded for his conjunto's LP *Arsenio Rodríguez y Su Conjunto Vol. 2* (Ansonia 1418). The lyrics characterize the burning of sugarcane, tobacco, and coffee fields—a tactic that was carried out by Castro's rebels in Oriente and the Sierra Maestra to destabilize Cuba's economy and, hence, Batista's power—as well as war in general as acts of "capricious vanity." As evidenced in the words of these and other patriotic songs, Arsenio's sole concern with respect to politics was for peace. He did not affiliate himself with any one political party or orientation, as was also evidenced in his refusal to join the Cuban Communist Party, which owned Havana's Radio Mil Diez, in the mid-1940s. As his brother Raúl recounted, Arsenio's conjunto was performing daily on Radio Mil Diez, the directors of which eventually approached Arsenio with respect to his political affiliation:

> Arsenio told them, "No, no, no. I don't belong to any party. I play for both the conservatives and the liberals. And if they'd pay me I'd play in a cemetery. My [politics] is music." . . . Joaquín Ordoqui [Communist Party leader and representative from the province of Las Villas] asked him, "Arsenio, why don't you play ball?" Arsenio answered, "I don't believe you've ever heard of a blind ball player. Talk to the members of the conjunto, and whoever wants to join the party, fine. That's their business. But me, Arsenio, no." . . . And since Arsenio was very popular, and his conjunto was heard throughout Cuba, they let Arsenio work for the station without belonging to the party. (Raúl Travieso interview, August 3, 1998)

In his response (as recollected by Raúl) to their demands, Arsenio poignantly stated his contempt for political parties, even to the party that had given his conjunto access to its radio station and had fought for the protection against discrimination. On the other hand, he remained artistically and professionally dedicated to the working class of Havana (see chapter 2).

In two other songs, however, he did make unambiguous statements against the colonial and imperialist relationships that Puerto Rico and Cuba had with the United States. In the bolero "A Puerto Rico" (To

Puerto Rico) he expressed his empathy with the island's colonial status, blaming its unhappiness on "a foreign reason." He composed this song on returning to Havana from New York City in 1947 and recorded it in Havana in the following year. On March 12, 1949, three drunken American sailors urinated on the statue of the nation's father, José Martí, located in Havana's Parque Central. An angry crowd threatened to lynch them, but the Cuban police intervened and arrested the sailors. The next day, however, they were effectively released when they were turned over to officials of the U.S. Navy. Cubans were disgusted not only by the sailors' desecration of the statue but also by their government's submissive attitude toward the U.S. Navy and government (Phillips 1959, p. 251). Arsenio expressed his own condemnation of this incident in the bolero "Amor a mi patria" (Love for My Country), which the conjunto later recorded in Havana in 1951.[31]

Although Arsenio condemned violence in some of his patriotic songs, he was known on occasion to lash out against figures of authority when he felt that an injustice was being committed. For instance, in 1953 the internationally famous Cuban group Conjunto Casino performed its first show of a two-week stint at the Tropicana Club, which was located in the South Bronx. Frank Ugarte, a delegate of New York's Musician's Union Local 802, was also in attendance to enforce the union's strict regulations, allowing Conjunto Casino to perform only as a show attraction and not for dancing. The union also stipulated that if the club's management allowed the audience members to dance, they would be fined and Local 802 musicians would not be allowed to perform. Audience members, however, did dance, and after Conjunto Casino's set was finished Arsenio's musicians began to take the stage when Ugarte ordered all union members back off the stage. Arsenio told his musicians that whoever did not want to play did not have to. Then, he, his brothers Kiki and Raúl, and his vocalist Candido Antomattei proceeded to take the stage. According to Raúl, Arsenio went to the microphone and addressed the audience, asking, "Why is this, for they [Conjunto Casino] are our fellow countrymen? Why shouldn't we play?" (Raúl Travieso interview, July 31, 1996). Babby Quintero, a columnist for the Spanish-language newspaper *La Prensa*, quoted Arsenio, saying that "He, as a Cuban, will play even if the union terminated his membership" (*La Prensa*, October 14, 1953). Arsenio and his other bandmates were eventually fined by the union.

Besides showing contempt for the union's stringent regulations, Arsenio expressed in no uncertain terms his solidarity with his fellow Cuban nationals, despite the fact that Conjunto Casino, an all-white group with the exception of percussionist Carlos "Patato" Valdés, performed almost exclusively for white social clubs in Havana throughout the 1940s. Hence, as can be readily seen in his patriotic songs as well as in his defense of the musicians of Conjunto Casino, Arsenio was not antiwhite. He was, however, very critical of the legacy of colonialism and white racial supremacy as manifested in the degradation of African culture and the discrimination against black people throughout the African diaspora. This represents an opportunity to compare Arsenio's transnational sensibility of the black experience and his Cuban national identity with those espoused by other black thinkers from Cuba and the United States.

Like Arsenio, Nicolás Guillén, Gustavo Urrutia, and other black Cuban intellectuals were pro-Cuban and anti-imperialist. They also condemned racism as experienced among blacks everywhere (see White 1993; Schwartz 1998). Although Guillén in particular became an ardent communist, ultimately attributing the suffering of blacks to capitalism (Ellis 1998, p. 135), Arsenio remained nonpartisan in Cuban politics before and after Castro's revolution. In addition, Urrutia and Alberto Arredondo, drawing in part on the notion of the "New Negro" as devised by their African American contemporary Alain Locke, viewed Afro-Cuban culture as having evolved over time, constituting an indivisible part of Cuban national culture (Schwartz 1998, p. 116). In discussing the music of Gilberto Valdés, a white composer of the afrocubanismo movement, Arredondo stated, "The rhythms that Valdés revives were from a bygone era of our musical development. Those rhythms integrated with others [i.e., Spanish rhythms] in a process of *superación* and synthesis what today is called Cuban music" (Arredondo 1938, p. 5).

By eschewing the black vernacular traditions of their respective nations, Locke, Urrutia, Arredondo, and many others conceded to some of the tenets of white supremacy (see Ramsey 2003, p. 114). As Lisa Brock points out, the ideas of "superación" and "racial uplift" significantly shaped the discourse on race and national identity among the black middle class of both Cuba and the United States (Brock 1998, p. 18). For those blacks throughout the Americas who espoused the prevailing social Darwinist ideology of the day, claiming Africanness would have bound "them to a continent cast as primitive and backward while separating them from the dominant notions of civilization and progress" (ibid.).

Arsenio, on the other hand, always affirmed his blackness and African heritage. He was never influenced artistically or philosophically by the high modernisms of Europe, nor was he preoccupied with how he appeared to whites, as seemed to be the case with Locke and other black American and Cuban intellectuals of the 1920s and 1930s (see West 1999, pp. 453–54). And though he never promoted Marcus Garvey's back to Africa movement, he did advocate and celebrate African independence from political and ideological colonial rule, as Frantz Fanon did in his *The Wretched of the Earth* (see Fanon 1968, pp. 41–46). Ultimately, in accordance with the African diasporic condition of double consciousness, Arsenio always felt and affirmed his "double-ness"—*cubano* and *negro*—not as contradictory halves of an ambiguous whole but as a subversive act against Cuba's dominant notions of race and national identity.[32] He continued to affect the revaluation of Cuba's African heritage, thereby exposing mestizaje and superación as ideological acquiescence to the racial logic that produced and sustained slavery and colonialism in the first place, through the development of his conjunto and son montuno style.

2 *Negro y Macho*: Arsenio Rodríguez's Conjunto and Son Montuno Style

THE CUBAN SON is a vocal, instrumental, and dance genre that is as stylistically varied as blues and jazz.[1] By the early twentieth century son had proliferated into numerous regional styles that were performed by a wide range of mostly string and percussion instruments. Son music's commercialization through sheet music, recordings, and film, beginning in the 1910s, contributed to its stylistic diversity as well as its geographic and social dissemination. By the 1920s Cuban writers, artists, and others embraced son music, primarily in its commercialized form, and claimed it as a symbol of national identity (see Moore 1997). Since then, the dominant rhetorical representation of the son has centered on the discourse of mestizaje and national identity, whereby its Cubanness is said to have developed from the "mixture" or "blending" of its original African and Spanish elements (e.g., Orovio 2004, p. 203).

Son montuno (literally, "son from the mountains") was one of a variety of older styles of son music associated with the mountainous interior and eastern half of the island. By the early 1940s Arsenio had adapted structural aspects of this rural son montuno style as well as principles and procedures common to other Afro-Cuban musical traditions to his new conjunto ensemble, calling his new way of performing son music son montuno. As Cuban musicologist Argeliers León stated, son music has been in constant development, and therefore its meanings are dependent on the particular historical and social contexts in which it has developed (León 1984, p. 125). Indeed, Arsenio's innovations marked a significant watershed in the development of son music nationally as well as internationally in the form of the mambo. It is important, however, not to conceive of the son montuno's and mambo's developments in a teleological framework, representing, for example, the mambo as popularized internationally by Dámaso Pérez Prado and others as the ultimate or ideal stage of the son montuno's stylistic evolution. Rather, I treat Arsenio's son montuno style as always contemporary with the transnational mambo of which Arsenio claimed to be the creator throughout his career. In this chapter I focus on the initial development of Arsenio's conjunto and son montuno style, its relationship to the mambo as developed in Havana, and the social impact Arsenio and his music had locally among primarily the black working class.

Throughout the 1940s Arsenio's son montuno style was never referred to as mambo, even though central principles and procedures of his style, such as playing in *contratiempo* (against the beat), also defined the mambo as performed by charangas and Cuban big bands. Instead, Cuban musicians and dancers of all colors distinguished his style for its "blackness" and "masculinity," differentiating his *estilo negro y macho* or black and masculine style from the *estilo blanco y hembra* or "white" and "feminine" styles of other Cuban groups, such as Conjunto Casino and La Sonora Matancera. The fact that La Sonora Matancera's members were black and mulatto shows us that the terms "negro" and "blanco" were deployed to identify not the musicians' actual color but in part the racial and class background of the group's primary audience in Havana. In addition these racialized and gendered characterizations were deployed because of the meanings they carried in the context of traditional Afro-Cuban sacred and secular musical performance. Arsenio's son montuno style not only contributed to the flowering of Cuban popular music beginning in the early 1940s but also affected the racialization of son styles that ultimately contradicted the son's status as a symbol of Cuban mestizaje and national identity.

The Early Septetos and Conjunto, 1926–44

Not long after he arrived in Havana from Güines in 1926, Arsenio began to perform with small groups around Marianao. By 1928, at the age of seventeen, he had formed Septeto Bóston, which at various times included relatives, friends from the same and nearby *repartos* (wards), as well as childhood friends from Güines.[2] From the late 1920s to the early 1930s, Septeto Bóston performed regularly in the rough, working-class *cabarets de tercera* or third-tiered cabarets, especially La Verbena, in Playa, Marianao. Other notorious third-tiered cabarets included El Niche, La Choricera, La Playa, Las Fritas, and El Pompilio, which were also located along the beaches of Marianao, in barrio Playa. These cabarets were patronized primarily by black working-class Cubans and occasionally individuals with criminal records, bad repute, and predilection for violence. The entertainment, although sometimes having the reputation for being vulgar, included son groups and dance routines featuring female solo dancers (see Acosta et al. 1999, p. 19; Martínez 1993, p. 219; Moore 1997, pp. 184–85; Valdés Cantero 1988, p. 43).

In stark contrast to the third-tiered cabarets, *cabarets de primera* and *segunda* were patronized by tourists as well as the white Cuban middle and upper classes. First-tiered cabarets such as La Tropicana, Sans Souci, and Casino Nacional, in particular, offered tourists and the elite elaborate shows. These acts were accompanied by tuxedo-clad all-white Cuban big bands, some of which were popular nationally and internationally. These big bands also performed dance music for the audience, usually U.S. popular music by Cole Porter, George Gershwin, Benny Goodman, Tommy Dorsey, and others (Touzet interview 2000; Padilla 1983; Valdés Cantero 1988, p. 43). Septetos, which played Cuban popular dance music, especially son, were also included in the night's entertainment.

By 1934 Arsenio had dissolved the failing Bóston to join Septeto Bellamar,[3] whose director and trumpet player was his uncle-in-law José Interián and whose first vocalist was his cousin Elizardo Scull. On September 7, 1936, the members of Bellamar officially registered the group as a Musical Association with the Governor's Office of the Province of La Habana.[4] Septeto Bellamar had a steady gig throughout the 1930s at Sport Antillano, an *academia de baile* or dance academy, which was located on the border of the working-class barrios of Cayo Hueso and Pueblo Nuevo, west of downtown Havana. Like the third-tiered cabarets, the working conditions at dance academies were excessive. Big bands, charangas, and son groups were expected to perform one-minute fragments of songs with no breaks to increase turnover for the female dancers who were paid by male dancers per song. Unlike cabarets and sociedades, however, dance academies were not overtly categorized by class, race, or ethnicity, but they were exclusive locations in that they were patronized by men, usually middle and upper class, who sought dance partners with women who often doubled as prostitutes. On the other hand, the strict working conditions brought forth cohesion among musicians and served as a testing ground for many charangas and son groups that would later become nationally and internationally popular (Valdés Cantero 1988, pp. 43–45). Despite the dance academy's significance in the development of son music and performers, it was stigmatized for its association with prostitution.

There were other significant advantages for Arsenio in performing with Bellamar at the Sport Antillano. First, Interían, the group's first director, had recorded with the famous Septeto Habanero in 1930 and probably had connections to important people in the recording industry. Second, compared to performing at La Verbena, which was in the periphery of Marianao and Havana, Arsenio was able to gain much more attention and recognition in Sport Antillano, especially among important musicians such as Miguelito Valdés and Antonio Arcaño, who were regularly passing by the Musician's Union office (about three blocks away), and who would meet at the popular musician's hang-out Café El OK, next door to the office. Third, playing with Bellamar also brought some economic stability for the now twenty-four-year-old Arsenio, who was supporting his first wife, Manuela Montecino Herrera, and their daughter, Regla María (b. September 8, 1935) in an apartment in the barrio of

Peñalver, about ten blocks from the Sport Antillano (Montecino Herrera interview 1999).

In addition to the exposure in downtown Havana, playing with Septeto Bellamar had its musical advantages. By 1938 Arsenio had taken control over the musical direction of the septeto (even though Reguira was still the official president and director of the group) and began to establish the foundations for what would soon become his conjunto (Ruíz et al. 1995, pp. 335–36). Meanwhile, his song "Bruca maniguá," which was recorded by Orquesta Casino de la Playa in 1937, had become internationally popular.

The Formation and Early History of Arsenio's Conjunto, 1940–43

Between 1934 and 1941, tourism accounted for 13 percent of Cuba's gross national product (third to the sugar and tobacco industries). This fueled the prosperity of cabarets, nightclubs, hotel ballrooms, and, in conjunction, performance opportunities for musicians. The years 1940 and 1941 were particularly fruitful for Arsenio, both professionally and artistically. On September 12, 1940, he made his first two recordings for RCA Victor with the newly formed group he called Arsenio Rodríguez y Su Conjunto. The generic meaning of the word *conjunto* is "group" or "ensemble." After the popularization of Arsenio's conjunto, however, the name *conjunto* became associated with a specific ensemble type, which between 1940 and 1946 consisted of two first voices (with one doubling on clave and the other on maracas), two trumpets, piano, tres, guitar (doubling on second voice), bass, bongó, and tumbadora (conga drum).[5] This format was an extension of the septeto's instrumentation, with the addition of a second trumpet, piano, and tumbadora. Although it is unclear which group first incorporated these instruments, Arsenio is often credited with this achievement because his group became the most popular and, hence, quintessential conjunto beginning in the early 1940s (see Figure 2.1).

Arsenio continued to use the smaller septeto format, however, after the 1940 recording session when his group Conjunto de Arsenio Rodríguez performed at Sans Souci, a first-tiered cabaret, from December 28, 1940, to February 1, 1941.[6] Evidently, Arsenio transformed this septeto into a conjunto by adding a second trumpet, piano, and tumbadora for his first recording session. He used the same conjunto format again for his second recording session on March 31, 1941.[7]

The fact that Arsenio succeeded in getting contracts with RCA Victor and Sans Souci suggests that by 1940 he had established himself as a successful composer and bandleader. As in dance academies, septetos

FIGURE 2.1. Arsenio Rodríguez y Su Conjunto, Havana, c. 1943. *Center:* Arsenio Rodríguez, tres. *Clockwise from top center:* Benetín Bustillo, trumpet; Rubén Calzado, trumpet; Pedro Luís Sarracent, first voice and clave; Marcelino Guerra, guitar and second voice; Adolfo "Panasea" O'Reily, piano; Nilo Alfonso, bass; Kiki Rodríguez, tumbadora; Miguelito Cuní, first voice and maracas; Antolín "Papa Kila" Suárez, bongó. *Source:* Photographer unknown; photograph courtesy of Raúl Travieso.

formed part of the regular entertainment in cabarets. But unlike the Sport Antillano, where Arsenio performed through most of the 1930s, Sans Souci was an aristocratic and exclusive first-class cabaret, whose guests typically included tourists and, as Havana's *Diario de la Marina* put it, "distinguished families" of Havana's "elegant society." It was located in reparto La Coronela, in barrio Lisa, on the outskirts of Marianao, and it was usually open two nights a week, Thursdays and Saturdays (*Diario de la Marina*, December 5, 28, 1940). From December 1940 to February 1941 the show included four dance acts: the Stadlers (who were billed as a dance couple from Hollywood), Hugo y Tyra (a Mexican dance couple famous for their dance number "Baile de la serpiente"), Phyllis Addison (classical ballet dancer), and Elpidio y Margot (the obligatory rumba dance act).[8] Australian singer Monica Moore, who debuted on January 16, 1941, sang U.S. popular songs. The big band Orquesta Bellamar, directed by Armando Romeu Jr., provided the musical accompaniment for the dance and singing acts, which, based on the descriptions of their routines, required a diverse repertory of international genres and styles. And Arsenio's septeto was "contracted to perform vernacular [dance] pieces," the genres of which would have included son, afrocubano, bolero, *guaracha*, *pregón*, and conga (*Diario de la Marina*, December 28, 1940).

According to Raúl Travieso, Arsenio was performing only with his septeto at Sans Souci at this time, and he did not begin to use his conjunto format for public performances until after the contract at Sans Souci ended in February 1941. However, he may not have made this transition for at least another year. In February 1942, for example, Social Club Buena Vista, a sociedad *de color* (black social club), printed an advertisement announcing its dances for the carnival season, the music of which was to be performed by "el septeto de Arsenio Rodríguez" (*Hoy*, February 24, 26, 1942). Finally, in May 1942, his group had started to be referred to in Havana's newspapers as "el conjunto de Arsenio Rodríguez" (*Hoy*, May 22, 24, 1942).

During World War II, Cuba's tourist industry experienced a significant lull, resulting in a pronounced decline in the patronage of first-class cabarets, which were crucial for the steady employment of many musicians (Otero et al. 1954, p. 710; República de Cuba 1943, pp. 696–97; Touzet interview 2000). In fact, 1941 was the last tourist season for several years; street *comparsas* (carnival street groups) were suspended, although sociedades continued to celebrate carnival in their private dance halls (see Ortero González 1953, p. 54; Phillips 1959, p. 208; Fernández 1997, p. 106).[9] As a result, Arsenio and many other musicians became more reliant on Havana's dozens of sociedades for work. To facilitate the transition from performing at cabarets and dance academies to social clubs, Arsenio established a partnership with Antonio Arcaño. Arcaño's charanga, the musicians of which were mulattoes, performed regularly for exclusive and elite sociedades *españolas* (Spanish regional social clubs) and black middle-class social clubs.[10] By 1942, however, Arcaño began to have difficulty finding work due to a group of vocalists who had presumably convinced dance impresarios not to hire his charanga because he did not employ vocalists (Arcaño interview1988). To gain advantage over his detractors, Arcaño's strategy was to ally his charanga with two other bands and perform for the many black working-class social clubs, worker's unions, and other groups in the working class, largely black barrios of Havana. The directors of these groups regularly organized dances in their homes, club houses, and at *cervecerías* or beer gardens. Arcaño eventually chose to book gigs with Arsenio's conjunto because he believed that it was "the best conjunto" in Havana at the time (ibid.).

Mil Diez and Los Tres Grandes

On April 10, 1943, nine days after going on the air, the directors of Radio Mil Diez organized their first public event in celebration of the station's inauguration. The musical acts, which were also Mil Diez's first regular artists, included Trío Matamoros, Conjunto Camacho, Julio Cueva y Su Orquesta with Orlando "Cascarita" Guerra, Las Maravillas de Arcaño, and Arsenio Rodríguez y Su Conjunto (*Hoy*, March 21, 1943, and April 4, 1943). From the beginning, Mil Diez's artistic orientation was proletarian and nationalist, and their political and social orientations were pronouncedly procommunist and prounion. For example, the station's slogans were "Todo lo bueno al servicio del pueblo" (All the best in the service of the [common] people) and "La emisora del pueblo" (The radio station of the people) (*Nuevos Rumbos* 1/7, 1946). More important, the station played virtually no prerecorded music, and their proletarian and noncommercial orientation gave musical groups a mass medium to perform live on the air and thus disseminate their original and progressive music throughout the Caribbean (*New York Times*, April 28, 1946).

This was especially significant for Arsenio, who had crystallized his new style only a year before his conjunto began to perform live on Mil Diez in April 1943. As Arcaño noted "Mil Diez . . . gave us the facilities that no other radio station could have given us. We played music that was more technical, and there was an incredible [artistic] frankness and freedom" (Boudet 1974, p. 35). Moreover, Mil Diez's hiring of Arsenio's conjunto reflected their commitment to include black groups whose primary audience, especially in 1943, was the black working class. Nevertheless, Mil Diez's programming was largely in the control of the Communist Party and the Confederación de Trabajadores de Cuba

(Confederation of Cuban Workers) (García Montes and Alonso Avila 1970, pp. 304–5). Accordingly, some of Mil Diez's musicians, actors, and technicians were members of the Communist Party. Despite their "tolerance," however, the directors of Mil Diez did try to convince, sometimes even intimidate their employees into joining the party. As I discussed in chapter 1, Arsenio threatened to stop performing for the radio station rather than join the Communist Party, a move that was consistent with his overall suspicion of Cuban politics, which he held throughout his life.

By 1944 Arcaño y Sus Maravillas, Orquesta Melodias del 40, and Arsenio Rodríguez y Su Conjunto, best known as Los Tres Grandes (The Three Giants), had become very popular performing on Radio Mil Diez as well as for black working-class social clubs, including Social Club Buena Vista (in Almendares, Marianao, now immortalized in Ry Cooder's CD and Wim Wenders's film), El Bouquet Cubano (in Cerro, Havana), Club de las Aguilas de Luz 56 (in Víbora, Havana), Club Artístico Cultural (in Redención, Marianao), Marianao Social (in Marianao), Deportivo de la Fé (in Cerro, Havana), and Jóvenes del Vals (in Luyanó, Havana). They also played for workers' unions, such as Los Yesistas (plaster workers) and Sociedad Tropicalina (La Tropical workers) as well as the butchers, bakers, and trash collectors unions. In addition to their own locations, these social clubs and workers unions as well as dance impresarios organized *giras*, verbenas, and *merenderos* at the beer gardens of La Tropical and La Polar.[11] Generally, giras took place on Sundays, lasting anywhere from 1 p.m. to 4 a.m. Verbenas also took place on weekends all day and evening long, but it was a larger affair, often featuring more than ten musical groups who would perform in adjacent dance floors two or three at a time. Merenderos took place on weekdays, lasting from about one to six in the afternoon. Entrance fees for these dances averaged $1 for men, while women were often given free entrance.

By 1946 the directors of Mil Diez had eased their position on pressuring their artists to become members of the Communist Party and had begun to contract other popular artists, including Miguelito Valdés and Celia Cruz, to attract more listeners and thus compete with CMQ and RHC-Cadena Azul, Havana's most popular radio stations (García Montes and Alonso Avila 1970, p. 305). They also continued to hire black groups such as Las Melodias del 40 and René Álvarez y Su Conjunto "Astro," who also performed regularly for the black working class. However, Mil Diez's association with the Communist Party and overall leftist and anti-imperialist political tone did not diminish. This drew the concern of not only the Cuban government but also the U.S. government.[12] On May 1, 1948, the Cuban government closed down Mil Diez after the station aired a prerecorded speech given by Jesús Menéndez, a communist member of the House of Representatives and head of the Sugar Workers' Union, who denounced the bourgeois sugar industry and U.S. imperialism (López 1981, pp. 331–33).[13]

The loss of Mil Diez was a severe setback for the Cuban Communist Party as well as an obvious loss for musicians and audiences. Apart from his confrontation with the directors regarding his political nonaffiliation, Arsenio had a favorable relationship with Mil Diez and its personnel. Manolo Ortega, who was an announcer, coined Arsenio's nickname, "El Ciego Maravilloso," which he would affectionately be known as for the rest of his life.[14] More important, Mil Diez gave Arsenio, his conjunto, and other black groups and musicians access to audiences across social, regional, and national boundaries, including Puerto Rico and the Netherlands Antilles (Phillips 1945, p. 675; López 1981, p. 315). Therefore, unless one lived in Havana and was able to go to a social club or beer garden, the only way one had access to the conjunto's live performances was through radio.

After the closure of Mil Diez in May 1948, Radio Salas contracted many of Mil Diez's former artists, including Arsenio's conjunto, Las Melodias del 40, and Arcaño y sus Maravillas (see Figure 2.2). Recognizing their popularity among dancers, the programming directors at

Figure 2.2. Arsenio Rodríguez y Su Conjunto, Radio Salas, Havana, c. 1950. *Top row from left:* Félix Chappottín, trumpet; Oscar "Florecita" Velazco, trumpet; Alfredo "Chocolate" Armenteros. *Middle from left:* Luís Martínez Griñan, piano; Lázaro Prieto, bass; Arsenio Rodríguez, tres; René Scull, first voice and maracas; Miguelito Cuní, first voice and clave; Carlos Ramírez, guitar and second voice. *Bottom from left:* Félix "Chocolate" Alfonso, tumbadora; Antolín "Papa Kila" Suárez, bongó; Kiki Rodríguez, tumbadora. *Source:* Photographer unknown; photograph courtesy of Jordi Pujol.

Radio Salas started a daily show during the week titled "Los Tres Grandes," featuring these three groups. The show began at 4:30 in the afternoon with Las Melodias del 40, followed by Arsenio Rodríguez y Su Conjunto at 5:00, and ending with Arcaño y Sus Maravillas from 5:30 to 6:00 (Béltran interview 1996; Méndez Bravet and Pérez 1991, p. 6). Although the entire show became extremely popular throughout Cuba, Arsenio's conjunto, according to ratings in April 1949, attracted the most listeners (*Carteles*, April 19, 1949).

Although the conjunto's recordings and live radio performances did not grant Arsenio international stardom, his conjunto did gain recognition among aficionados and young musicians of Cuban popular music throughout the Caribbean. In addition the young musicians Dámaso Pérez Prado, Bebo Valdés, and René Hernández, who would become the most important arrangers of mambo music in Cuba and abroad, were known to attend Arsenio's live performances at the studios and wait around after the shows to ask him questions about his new style, son montuno (Cubillas 1952, p. 25).

Contratiempo and the Emergence of the Son Montuno Feel

Arsenio and his conjunto, according to many Cuban musicians, revolutionized the son. In addition he along with Jesús López and Israel "Cachao" López of Arcaño's charanga are popularly credited for inventing the mambo. To be sure, nothing like Arsenio's style had ever been performed or recorded before. Yet what had made the conjunto and son montuno style so innovative was in fact Arsenio's and his musicians' deep knowledge and utilization of aesthetic principles and performance procedures rooted in Afro-Cuban traditional music in which Arsenio had been immersed as a youngster in rural areas of Matanzas and La Habana. Drawing from these principles and procedures, Arsenio and his colleagues formulated new ways of performing Cuban son and danzón music that arrangers for big bands soon after adapted and popularized internationally as mambo.

The Son Montuno Texture

Whether recording a son, guaracha, or *guaguancó*, Arsenio used two basic arrangement schemes: a one-part scheme and a two-part scheme (see Table 2.1).[15] There are five and six distinguishable subsections in the one-part and two-part schemes, respectively. The two-part form includes a *canto* or verse section, which consists of harmonic patterns of various lengths and no vocal call and response. In contrast, the one-part scheme,

TABLE 2.1. Arrangement Schemes: Son Montuno, Danzón-mambo, and Guaracha

Son montuno: one-part arrangement scheme (conjunto)					
Introduction	Montuno	Solo (tres, piano)	Cierre	*Diablo	
Son montuno: two-part arrangement scheme (conjunto)					
Introduction	Verse	Montuno	Solo (tres, piano)	Cierre	*Diablo
Danzón-mambo arrangement scheme (charanga)					
A (flute)	B (flute)	A (flute/piano)	C (violins)	A (flute)	*Mambo
Guaracha arrangement scheme (big band)					
Introduction	Verse	Montuno	Solo (piano)	*Mambo	Montuno/Coda

like older or rural styles of son, consists almost entirely of a two- or four-bar harmonic cycle with various forms of vocal and instrumental call and response, essentially making this scheme a continuous montuno.[16] The montuno section proper in the two-part form follows the verse. The montuno in general is basically call and response, in which the call consists variously of trumpet improvisations, *glosas* (short riffs precomposed for the trumpets), *coplas* (two-line stanzas) and *cuartetas* (quatrains) sung by the first voice, and *guías* (single-line improvisations)[17] also sung by the first voice. The response consists of an *estribillo* or refrain sung by the first and second voices or a *coro* (chorus), which is usually a shorter version of the refrain.[18] Both schemes conclude with a solo section, a *cierre* or short break, and a climactic finale which Arsenio called "diablo" (devil).

In expanding the old septeto format into a conjunto and in developing his son montuno style, Arsenio was guided by the aesthetic principles of timbral heterogeneity, musical fullness, and sonic power. As Arsenio put it, "I organized a new system for the conjunto. I thought that the septeto with the one trumpet, guitar, and tres couldn't produce the necessary harmony. So I added a piano and three trumpets" (Cubillas 1952, p. 25). We should interpret his reference to harmony as meaning something more than just the harmonic potential of a piano and trumpet section. In fact, he integrated the trumpet section (the third trumpet was not added until 1946), piano, and tumbadora into the conjunto to add more contrasting timbres. Furthermore, the "new system" he implemented was, in actuality based on the performative procedures referred to here as (1) contratiempo (offbeat accentuation); (2) the correspondence of sound and dancers' bodily movements; (3) the interweaving of rhythmic, melodic, and dance patterns; and (4) the steady increase in energy toward a climax, all of which were fundamental to the performance of Afro-Cuban music in general (see Ortiz 1993, pp. 97–100, 104).[19] These procedures became central to the crafting of the son montuno's dense texture and thus harmonious musical sound.

To characterize the son montuno style in terms of texture focuses attention on the *feel* of the music as described by those who experienced it as musicians, dancers, and listeners.[20] Bebo Valdés pointed out that to dance to Arsenio's son montuno style involved dancing "in contratiempo" (literally, "against the beat"). "You have to *feel* 'the beat from below' [or downbeats] with your body. And you dance [son montuno] in *contratiempo*... You have to know how to dance it well. You dance it better yet with your body and feet as well" (Valdés interview 2000). Indeed, the son montuno style featured much more contratiempo or offbeat accentuation than earlier styles of commercial son music. Offbeat accenting patterns would also constitute the primary musical index of the mambo as performed by big bands in Cuba, New York City, and elsewhere. What made Arsenio's style unique, however, was its rhythmic texture, which corresponded directly to and accentuated the son's footwork and son dancers' bodily movements. Rubén González (one-time pianist of Arsenio's conjunto) remembered: "Practically all of Arsenio's fans were very good dancers. That's why, although he did not object to his musicians playing something different, he always insisted that they maintain the [rhythmic] structure [or groove] already established by the conjunto" (Méndez Bravet and Pérez 1991, pp. 16–17).

There are three defining characteristics of the son montuno texture or groove that distinguished it from earlier styles of son music. The first is the consistent accentuation of the "and-of-four" on the "two-side" of the clave pattern and the "and-of-two" on the "three-side" (see the examples for transcriptions of the clave pattern). These two offbeats are especially important because they coincide with two syncopated steps in the *son's* basic footwork, the transcription of which is also included in the bottom staff of the following examples.[21] For example, in "No toque el guao" (Don't Touch the *Guao*) the sung refrain and accompanying piano and tres patterns accent these two offbeats and dance steps as the bass consistently marks the final three steps of the son footwork (see Example 2.1). The conjunto's collective and consistent accentuation of these two important offbeats gave the son montuno texture its unique groove and, hence, played a significant part in the dancers *feeling* the music and dancing to it, as Bebo Valdés noted, "in contratiempo."

The second innovative and defining aspect of the son montuno texture is the bass line. Arsenio's bass patterns accented not only the offbeats but also the melodic material of the sung refrain parts. As Raúl Travieso recounted, Arsenio insisted that his bass players make the bass "sing." "[Arsenio] used to [say] 'the bass will sing, because if it doesn't sing this [i.e., the music] will be *cojo*' [lame; crippled; weak]" (Raúl Travieso

Example 2.1. "No toque el guao" (1948), son montuno texture.

interview, February 8, 1997). These patterns were especially distinctive in comparison to the conventional bass patterns that contemporary as well as earlier commercial son groups favored. The bass pattern in Arsenio's "Mi chinita me botó" (My Girl Left Me), recorded in 1944, was particularly extraordinary because it consists almost entirely of attacks on offbeats (see Example 2.2).[22] Although the bass pattern in "Mi chinita me botó" does not appear in any of the other recordings that Arsenio's conjunto made in the 1940s, it does appear more frequently in the recordings that Chappottín y Sus Estrellas and Conjunto Estrellas de Chocolate made in the 1950s and early 1960s.[23] Two variations of it, however, were favored by Lázaro Prieto, Arsenio's steady bassist from 1946 to 1952. Although the variations involve less accentuation of offbeats, they nevertheless accent the melodic content of the sung refrain patterns, many of which are also in contratiempo.

In contrast, the conventional patterns, referred to here as bolero, guaracha, and *tresillo*, accented the downbeat of each bar, although the

EXAMPLE 2.2. "Mi chinita me botó" bass line and two variations in contratiempo.

guaracha and tresillo patterns include one syncopated attack on the "and-of-two" (see Example 2.3). Also, the pitches in these conventional patterns, including the anticipated pattern, almost always accented the root and fifth scale degrees of the corresponding triad, giving these patterns a strictly harmonic function as opposed to the more melodic nature of the bass lines in Arsenio's music.

The third innovative characteristic of the son montuno texture is the actual interweaving of parts. This is particularly relevant to all of the conjunto's parts in the climactic diablo section (discussed shortly). But it was also essential to the incorporation of the tumbadora into the rhythm section. For instance, bongó players in pre-1940 recordings of son music alternated between playing the basic pattern known as *martillo* (see Example 2.3) and playing auxiliary attacks and rolls in freer passages.[24] To avoid clashing with the tumbadora player's slaps and open-toned attacks, Arsenio's bongó player dramatically curtailed freer passages and interwove auxiliary slaps into a question-and-answer relationship with the tumbadora's and bass's attacks. One such sequence of question-and-answer attacks occurs in "No toque el guao" (see Example 2.1), beginning with the bass's first, second, and third notes (bar three) followed by the bongó's response of two slaps on the *hembra* or larger drum (bar four); the bass, in turn, responds with the last three notes of its pattern (bar four). Also notice the bass's staccato notes, which lend its pattern an

EXAMPLE 2.3. Conventional bass and bongó patterns in pre-1940 Cuban son music.

added percussive effect. Meanwhile, the tumbadora adds an opened-tone attack on the first and third bars' "and-of-four." The interweaving of attacks predominated over conspicuous individual playing, and this particular sequence formed one of the most common question-and-answer sequences of the son montuno's rhythmic texture.[25]

Arsenio's bass and tumbadora players also interwove their patterns with the son's basic steps. The relationship between the bass pattern and son footwork in "Soy el terror" is particularly noteworthy. For the first three bars of the four-bar cycle, the bass and footwork interlock, completely avoiding simultaneous attacks and steps. In the fourth bar of the cycle the bass and footwork finally come together. The bass, with the exception of the first downbeat of the four-bar cycle, could not be depended on by the dancer for accenting either the downbeats or their basic footwork. Instead, the "beat from below," as Bebo Valdés described it, is facilitated in the refrain and tres patterns, which accent almost all of the dance steps in the second and third bars of the four-bar cycle.

Once the song was started the conjunto provided dancers a steady and consistent groove or feel for them to lock into. Meanwhile, the music's tempo and energy gradually increased, beginning at a steady pace in the introduction and verse, and then picking up from the call-and-response sequences. Then, commencing with a highly syncopated cierre (break), the climactic diablo section ended the typical son montuno arrangement scheme. As we will see shortly and in later chapters, the interrelated kinesthetic and aural climax that marked the son montuno's diablo would also become a defining aesthetic aspect of mambo and salsa music.

The Mambo and Arsenio's Diablo

In 1948 Cuban musicologist Odilio Urfé wrote one of the earliest published articles on the mambo as performed in Havana. In it he characterized the mambo as *anarquía dentro de un tempo* or "structured anarchy," adding that to "produce a genuine mambo the instrumentalists should employ, only in the 'climax' or 'crux,' rhythmic effects: rhythm against rhythm; no tunes or distinct melodies. . . . Anarchy should rule" (Urfé 1993, pp. 31–34). In 1951 Fernando Ortiz gave his own interpretation of the essence of the mambo (in response to Urfé) in which he underscored the actual rhythmic structure in the form of interwoven patterns.

> It is all nothing more than a link of lines coordinated in a *weave* that is composed of the spontaneity of each rhythm, individually played to each musician's whim, but whose *threads* are *crossed* and *interlaced* into one *warp*. . . . Although arbitrary and capricious, there is no "anarchy" or "lack of order," but rather a wonderful concert of individual freedoms taken to the maximum within a minimal but unshakable structural arrangement. . . . Also, this occurs only . . . in that precise paroxysmal moment characteristic of *música afrocubana*. (Ortiz 1993, p. 100; emphasis added).

Whereas Urfé directed his definition of the mambo to its performance by charangas, Ortiz made no reference to charangas, conjuntos, or big bands in his definition of the mambo. Both, however, portray the mambo not as one rhythm in particular but a confluence of rhythms. Indeed, the rhythm that would become known as the mambo rhythm by the late 1940s and 1950s was one of several rhythms or figures in contratiempo that predominated in Cuban dance music of the early to mid-1940s (see Example 2.4). In addition, although Urfé claimed that charanga musicians were the first to use the word *mambo* to refer specifically to their syncopated patterns and style, other musicians suggested that most groups in the early 1940s were playing "with a mambo flavor" before "mambo" was actually coined as a commercial music genre (Touzet interview 2000).[26] In another early article on mambo published in 1948, writer Manuel Cuéllar Vizcaíno stated that "the term 'diablo' was acquiring strength in the beginnings of the 'mambo'," further suggesting that Arsenio's and Arcaño's styles emerged concurrently (Cuéllar Vizcaíno 1993, p. 97).

All of this along with the recorded evidence shows that by 1943 Arsenio's conjunto and Arcaño's charanga had standardized (1) offbeat accenting musical figures, which lent their music a "mambo flavor" (see

(a) "Mi chinita me botó" figure

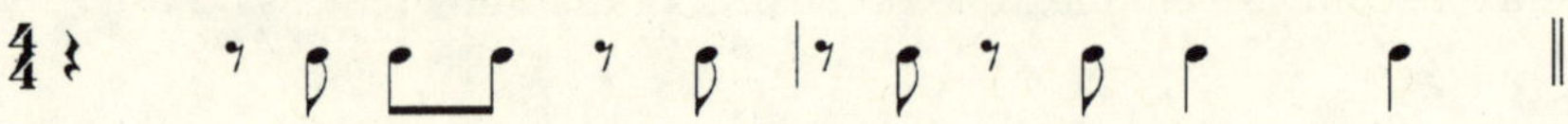

(b) "Oye como va" figure

(c) "Triplet" figure

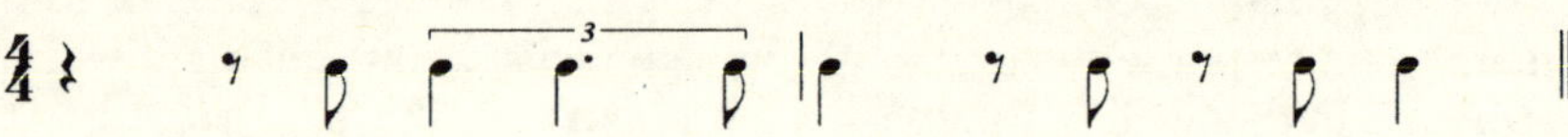

(d) "Mambo rhythm"

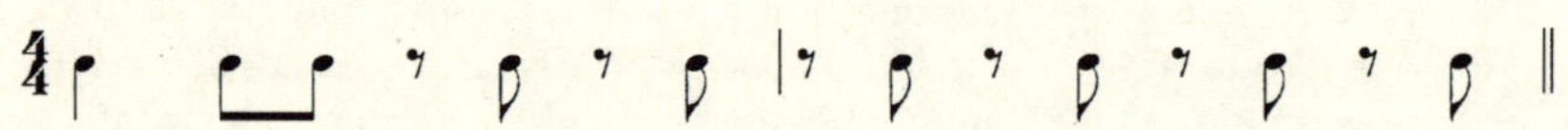

Example 2.4. Common figures in contratiempo in Cuban dance music, 1943–48.

Example 2.4); and (2) the diablo and mambo sections of their respective son montuno and danzón-mambo arrangement schemes in which contratiempo and interweaving patterns were especially predominant (see Table 2.1). Both innovations, the figures and arrangement schemes, transformed the performance and dance styles of son and danzón music. By 1945 René Hernández, Bebo Valdés, and Dámaso Pérez Prado had begun to implement these figures and arrangement schemes in their arrangements for Julio Cueva, Casino de la Playa, and other Cuban big bands.

Figure a in Example 2.4, which first appeared on a recording as the bass line in Arsenio's "Mi chinita me botó," recorded in 1944, was also used by the violins in the mambo section of Arcaño's "Llegaron los millonarios" (The Millionaires Have Arrived; TCD-029) recorded in 1948. Figure b, which is perhaps best recognized as the opening piano figure of Tito Puente's "Oye como va" (Listen to How It Goes), recorded in 1963, can be heard performed on the piano during the diablo section of Arsenio's "Pilla con pilla," recorded in 1943. Immediately preceding the diablo section, Arsenio or someone else in the conjunto is heard calling out "mambo," making this recording one of the earliest recordings, if not the earliest containing the word *mambo* spoken or sung. Figure b is also heard performed by the violins in pizzicato during Arcaño's flute solo in

"Arcaño y Su Nuevo Ritmo" (Arcaño and His New Rhythm; TCD-029), recorded in 1944. In Bebo Valdés's arrangement of "A la United Cafe" (To the United Café; TCD-032), recorded in 1945, the saxophone section and bass execute figure b during the montuno section. Figure c is performed by the trumpets during the diablo section of Arsenio's "El reloj de Pastora" (Pastora's Watch; TCD-031), recorded in 1946, and by the trumpets during the mambo section of Orquesta Casino de la Playa's "La última noche" (The Last Night; TCD-033), recorded in 1947. Finally, figure d, most commonly known as the mambo rhythm, can be heard in various guises, including in the violins during the mambo section of Arcaño's "Rarezas" (Rareties), recorded in 1940; in two trumpet solos in Arsenio's "Yo no como corazón de chivo" (I Don't Eat Goat's Heart) and "Yeye," recorded in 1944 and 1945, respectively; in the lead trumpet during the diablo section of Arsenio's "Cangrejo fue a estudiar" (Cangrejo Went to School; TCD-031), recorded in 1946; and in the saxophone section in Bebo Valdés's arrangement of "La rareza del siglo" (This Century's Rarity; TCD-032) as recorded in 1946 by Julio Cueva's orchestra.

By 1948 the mambo rhythm (Example 2.4.d) had become so ubiquitous that Urfé criticized contemporary danzón musicians for lacking variety in the rhythmic patterns they played in the mambo section of their arrangements (Urfé 1993, pp. 33–34). Arrangers for big bands such as Bebo Valdés, René Hernández, and Dámaso Pérez Prado also increasingly favored the mambo rhythm which they wrote for the saxophones and brass in their arrangements' mambo sections as well. Arsenio, however, continued to favor the crossing and interlacing of various figures or rhythmic threads rather than utilizing any one particular rhythm, including the mambo rhythm. Although Fernando Ortiz did not mention Arsenio's style (or anyone else's), his definition of the essence of the mambo is especially applicable to the musical procedures active in the performance of the diablo section. Before discussing some examples of Arsenio's diablos, it is worth reflecting on the cultural meanings of the words *mambo* and *diablo* to further understand the relationship between Arsenio's diablo and traditional Afro-Cuban aesthetics and sacred mythological beliefs.

The term *mambo* had originally been used in religious practices as well as among creolized Ki-Kongo speakers in Cuba. For instance, mambos, which are also known as *cantos de fundamento* or *cantos de palo*, are chanted by priests of the Palo Monte religion to begin a ceremony and to persuade a spirit or spirits to participate (León 1984, pp. 67, 78–81; Thompson 1984, pp. 110–11; and Cabrera 1992, pp. 127–29). Arsenio himself explained that the word *mambo* was used in *controversias* or sung poetic duals, in which it commonly appeared in the phrase *abre kuto güiri mambo* or "open your ears and listen to what I'm going to tell you" (Rodríguez interview 1964; Cubillas 1952, p. 24). The notion of a diablo (devil) is also steeped in Palo Monte as well as Abakuá cultural traditions. In her dictionary *Vocabulario congo (El Bantú que se habla en Cuba)*, Lydia Cabrera identifies over a dozen equivalences of *diablo* as they are used in mambos by *paleros* or Palo Monte priests (Cabrera 2000). Some of these include *Tata Luibisa*, which appears in the phrase "Tata Luibisa está acabando con el mundo" (The devil is putting an end to the world); and *Kadiampémbe* and *Lukankánsa*, both of which are figures also equated with the devil.

Elsewhere, Cabrera explains that in Palo Monte mythology both evil and good reside in objects in nature and are personified as evil and benevolent figures, the powers of which are invoked by priests to do harm and good (Cabrera 1992, p. 254). Among the Abakuá *diablitos* (little devils) refer to masked dancers who performed in carnival celebrations and in other Abakuá rituals (Ortiz 1993, pp. 333–59). Diablitos personified the living ancestors and functioned to expel evil spirits while also inspiring fear in onlookers, all in a festive context. As others have shown, pan-African cosmologies in the Americas such as those of the Congo, Lucumí, and Abakuá play not on opposites (evil versus good, male versus female, living versus dead) but on doubleness. For instance, rather than closing off unity, evil signifies the passage to good and vice versa as sides of a whole (see Gates 1988, pp. 29–31). Accordingly, Ortiz noted that diablitos symbolically represent "the 'living dead' who fleetingly appear from . . . the invisible side of the world" (Ortiz 1993, pp. 358–59). Cabrera adds that although equated with the devil, the *Lukankánsa* figure and its equivalent *Eshu* in Santería are also tricksters who mediate as interpreters and diviners of an individual's *Ifá* or destiny (Cabrera 1992, pp. 76–94, 485). However, the tricksters' mediations can themselves be tricks (Gates 1988, pp. 5–6).

In using the name *diablo* I believe that Arsenio was signifying on this notion of doubleness or playful deception. Indeed, he materialized its philosophical and aesthetic tenets in the actual musical content of the diablo section. Not unlike the diablito of the Abakuá, the diablo section, including the cierre leading up to it, was intended, as Arsenio himself stated, to give dancers or onlookers, in general, *el cocimiento* or "a kick in the ass" (Cubillas 1952, p. 24).[27] Specifically, before Arsenio cued the diablo section by yelling out "diablo," which he did only in live performances and not in the recordings, the conjunto played a precomposed highly syncopated break, which propelled the music and dancers into the diablo section by way of metric and rhythmic ambiguity. Although many breaks occur within one, two, or four bars and maintain the quadruple meter, other breaks deviate from the meter and as a result, intensify ambiguity and expectation for the diablo section. The break in "Yo no engaño a las nenas" (I Don't Deceive the Girls), recorded in 1948, for example, consists of a harmonic sequence in which the chords move up a fourth and down a third in ternary units, thereby "tricking" the dancers with a triple-meter sequence for four bars. The last two bars of the break reestablish the quadruple meter, yet in a very syncopated manner, leading to the climactic diablo section.[28]

The entire conjunto enters at the start of the diablo, and the first and second voices and trumpet section resume their original alternating scheme usually of four bars from the montuno section. In many diablos after the singers and trumpet players execute one full cycle of the original alternating scheme, they truncate their pattern so that the singers sing only half of their phrase and leave the other half open for the trumpet section. This was the quintessential structural aspect of Arsenio's diablo section. After several cycles, the trumpet section drops out of the alternation and is replaced by the lead trumpet player, who plays short improvisations during his half of the cycle. The diablo concludes with the restatement of the sung refrain in its original form or with the cierre that preceded the diablo.

The climax of the diablo occurs in the first segment when all the parts of the conjunto superpose and interlace their patterns into one "warp." Specifically, the guitar and maraca maintain the eighth-note pulse (not transcribed), and the remaining parts produce interwoven patterns and in some cases cross-rhythms. The conjunto's recording of "Kila, Kiki y Chocolate" (TCD-031)—named after the conjunto's bongó player, Antolín "Papa Kila" Suarez, Arsenio's brother Kiki, and tumbadora player Félix "Chocolate" Alfonso—exhibits, perhaps better than any other, the full effect of the mambo as defined by Fernando Ortiz. In this case, the three trumpets, tres, piano, and bass affect the climactic intensity of the diablo by creating an intricately woven rhythmic texture, within a two-bar cycle, while the bongó and tumbadora execute flams in call-and-response form (bars one through four, Example 2.5). The diablo increases in intensity in the next four bars when the second and third trumpets produce a hocket-like effect while the first trumpet continues to add its one note to the texture, creating "rhythm against rhythm" (as Urfé would have it).

In "No hay yaya sin guayacán" (There's No Yaya without Guayacán; Cubanacán CD 1703), recorded in 1945, the two trumpets create a partially interwoven pattern whose rhythmic effect is reminiscent of the mambo rhythm so common in the recorded repertories of charangas and big bands (see Example 2.6). The interwoven trumpet parts, along with the bass part, also accent melodically the sung chorus in the first bar and

Example 2.5. "Kila, Kike y Chocolate" (1950), diablo section.

form a response in the second bar of each two-bar cycle. In addition, the phrase figuration that the chorus, trumpet, and bass parts collectively create accentuates the dancer's basic footwork. The climactic energy of this sequence is most clearly signaled by one of the vocalists (probably Joseíto Nuñez) who shouts "candela" (candle or fire), encouraging the musicians to "give it all you got!" Arsenio similarly shouts "¡Candela, Rosa Cocimiento!" (Rosa, you're hot! Kick 'em in the ass!) at the beginning of the diablo section in "Mi china me botó."

Besides the music, the title "No hay yaya sin guayacán" and its verses relish in the principle of doubleness, demonstrating a deep resonance with Palo Monte mythology. For example, yaya is a type of tree that in Palo Monte is considered to be female, and whose branches, bark, leaves, and other parts are considered powerful natural objects. Guayacán is another type of tree, which is considered to be male and also very powerful

EXAMPLE 2.5. (Continued.)

(Cabrera 1992, pp. 439–41, 555–56). The power of both yaya and guayacán trees can be used to do well and harm, hence, the principle of doubleness. The first verse, most likely a Congo proverb, states: "Yo vi una piedra de hielo que nunca se derritió. Y el congo que le inventó le había salido hasta el pelo" (I saw a ball of hail that never melted. And the *congo* [i.e., palo priest] who made it, his hair had fallen out).

As an entirely new aspect in Cuban dance music, the diablo affected changes in the typical choreography of son dancing. Cuban music historian Radamás Giro opined that Arsenio's son montuno style engendered a new style of dancing son, differing from the classic son dance style made popular by Cuban septetos of the 1920s (Giro interview 1999). The history of Cuban son dancing remains severely underresearched; hence, the following observations are preliminary. For instance, the older son dance style of the 1920s as presented in the video *Ignacio Piñeiro* was somewhat more stately, stressing the footwork more, whereas

Example 2.6. "No hay yaya sin guayacán" (1945), diablo section.

upper-body movements and gestures were less conspicuous or absent altogether.[29] In contrast, Arsenio's dancers not only emphasized more bodily movement but also coordinated their choreography to the son montuno's arrangement scheme, highlighted by the climactic diablo section. The following ethnographic description is from a rehearsal by Conjunto Arsenio Rodríguez (a local Havana conjunto that specializes in Arsenio's repertory) that I attended at which Mercedes "Cheché" Scull (Arsenio's niece) and a neighbor demonstrated the son montuno dance.

As the conjunto reached the montuno section of Arsenio's "Dame tu yoyo, Ma' Belén" (Let Me Have You, Ma' Belén), Cheché and her partner began to dance, executing the son's basic footwork. As the conjunto went through the montuno's sequence of alternations, Cheché and her partner alternated between dancing embraced and apart, all the while maintaining the basic footwork. Following the piano solo, at the climactic section of the arrangement, Cheché separated herself from her partner and began to use livelier gestures and movements, including hand-clapping, smooth arm thrusts outward from her chest, and shoulder movements. Ending this climactic sequence of body movements, she raised both arms as she circled around her partner, who joined in with his arms raised. The partners embraced once more only to part again as Cheché executed a full turn, at the end of which she was met by her partner in a mini-crouch position on beat four of the clave's three-side. The couple held this position for the next three beats, at which point they took a step on the "and-of-four" of the clave's two-side, thereby recommencing the son's basic footwork in step with the son montuno rhythmic texture. As we will see in later chapters, Cuban immigrants as well as many Puerto Rican dancers in New York City and abroad were very familiar with the son montuno dance style, in contrast to most mainstream mambo and salsa dancers, who were not.

By 1945 Cuban vocalists Orlando "Cascarita" Guerra and Miguelito Valdés, both of whom were already popular throughout Latin America, began to refer to the mambo as *the* new musical and dance style in their songs.[30] As their recordings and those of other Cuban big bands continued to be circulated internationally through the popular music, film, and print media industries, mambo became associated almost exclusively with the big band format by the late 1940s. As a result, these big band recordings became the model for what would become the transnational mambo style of the 1950s. Meanwhile, the styles of Arsenio's and Arcaño's groups continued to gain in popularity nationally and even throughout the Caribbean region through their own recordings as well as their daily live performances on Cuban radio. Ultimately, their groups had less of an impact on transnational Latin styles than Cuban big bands. In Havana, however, their performances and music contributed directly to the flowering of social dances and new dance styles primarily among the black working class for whom Arsenio's style in particular embodied the essence of musical blackness and masculinity.

Placing the Emergence of Son Montuno

In his study of black music in the United States, Ronald Radano emphasizes the importance of accounting for the varieties of lived experience in relation to the historical development of black music (Radano 2003). To do this he proposes drawing on a notion of place that encompasses more than "merely a physical, fixed locale" but also "lives" that are constituted "through the interplay of sensory perception and physical reality" (ibid., p. 94). He goes on to say that "bodily sound provides a means of constituting place that is at once linguistically bound as it is felt and heard" (p. 95). This idea of place is especially useful here because it helps particularize, historicize, and most important, privilege the words and experiences of musicians and dancers who performed with Arsenio's conjunto and other groups. Hence, their descriptions of his son montuno style as negro (black) and macho (masculine) should be read as socially and historically bounded texts that reveal the ways in which his style resonated with perceptions of musical blackness, masculinity, authenticity, and complexity in Havana in the 1940s.

Son Montuno and Afro-Cuban Aesthetics and Performance Practice

Many Cuban musicians and dancers of the 1940s that I interviewed applied the term *negro* to describe the styles of Arcaño's charanga, Melodias del 40, Orquesta Ideal, as well as Arsenio's style. In contrast they used *blanco* to describe the styles of La Sonora Matancera, Conjunto Casino, Orquesta Casino de la Playa, Belisario López y Su Charanga, and others. The application of these terms in part indicated the racial and class background of these groups' local audiences. The following statement given by Raúl Travieso represents a typical example of how and to which musical groups and audiences people attributed the terms *black* and *white*. "Whites had their orchestras, like Casino de la Playa, La Gloria Matancera, La Sonora Matancera, and Belisario López.... The black man didn't buy or very rarely [bought] records by Casino de la Playa. What he bought were the records by people that had the black swing—Arcaño, Arsenio, or Melodias del 40" (Raúl Travieso interview, December 13, 1999). José Carbo Menéndez (white Cuban composer) declared that Arsenio "created the black style of dance music... black Cuban music of the common [working-class] people" (Carbo Menéndez interview, March 6, 1998).

In addition to race and class, negro, as attributed to Arsenio's style, also signified musical authenticity, complexity, and even modernity or progressiveness. As Horatio Riambau (white Cuban professional dancer) stated: "Arsenio played [in an *afro* style] and by 'afro' I mean in a pure style" (Riambau interview 2003). Agustín Caraballoso (Cuban trumpet player of mixed heritage) described the rhythmic patterns played by some groups as "easy" and "more simple" than Arsenio's (Caraballoso interview 1999). Finally, Humberto Cané (Cuban bassist of mixed heritage) gave the following, rather candid assessment of the white style of La Sonora Matancera, which his father (Valentín Cané) founded and with whom Humberto played tres (1937–45): "There were two styles: a simple style and an afro style. Arsenio began to play in an afro style, which was more difficult and had more *sabor* [flavor, feel]. La Sonora [Matancera] had a very simple, passé... style. That was one of the reasons why I left La Sonora Matancera, because they didn't want to improve, modernize more, and play new things" (Cané interview 1999).

TABLE 2.2. Racialized and gendered terms

Estilo Negro	Estilo Blanco
black	white
modern, progressive	passé
masculine	feminine/small sound
difficult	simple
slow	fast
sonero	guarachero

Although these terms signified the racial and class background of groups' audiences as well as notions of musical authenticity, complexity, and progressiveness, actual musical features such as tempo and, most important, sonic power and fullness also indexed musical blackness and masculinity. Carlos "Patato" Valdés (black Cuban percussionist), who became Conjunto Casino's only black member, claimed to have requested that Casino play in slower tempos: "They played too fast, and when I joined I slowed the tempo down. Before I joined the group played like a 'white' conjunto" (Valdés interview 1995). Conjuntos who played in faster tempos were also known as conjuntos guaracheros, particularly because of the dominance of the faster-paced guaracha in their repertoire, whereas Arsenio's and other black style conjuntos, who played in slower tempos, were referred to as conjuntos soneros (Valdés Ginebra interview 1999).[31] With respect to sonic power, Raúl Travieso opined, "The conga player [in La Sonora Matancera] only . . . kept time . . . and [that style] was what they used to call hembra [female], which meant that it had a small sound. . . . [Arsenio's] conjunto was macho, but La Sonora [Matancera] was not" (Raúl Travieso interview, March 15, 1999). See Table 2.2 for a side-by-side comparison of these racialized and gendered terms.

Raúl's explanation of Matancera's "small" sound suggests that the quality of the music's rhythmic texture also determined its femininity or masculinity. Thus, Arsenio's son montuno style was macho because it had a dense texture, whereas the texture of Matancera's style was empty or small because of its lack of interweaving patterns and hence sonic fullness or force. Indeed, a musical comparison of Arsenio's son montuno style and La Sonora Matancera's style demonstrates the stark contrast between these groups' rhythmic textures. In the montuno section of Matancera's "Vive como yo" (Live Like I Do; TCD-045), recorded in 1949, none of the patterns are in contratiempo (see Example 2.7; compare with Example 2.1). Instead, the piano pattern accents every strong beat, as the bass, which plays an abbreviated tresillo pattern, similarly accents the downbeat of each bar. Furthermore, the tumbadora part simply keeps time throughout by accenting beat four, all of which produce a "small" sound. Last, the parts in the montuno section of Matancera's guaracha

EXAMPLE 2.7. "Vive como yo" (1949), La Sonora Matancera, montuno section.

accent mostly strong beats and, most important, correlate little with the steps of the son footwork.

Clearly, for Cuban musicians and dancers of the 1940s, racial and gendered discourse became the predominant rhetorical mode through which they articulated their experience performing and dancing to popular music. It was Arsenio's style that established the musical criteria for a black and masculine style of son music. Again, it is important not to attribute the significance of negro and blanco to the actual skin color of the musicians themselves, for some of the groups to which the category white was applied were in fact all black and mulatto (e.g., La Sonora Matancera) or included black musicians (e.g., Patato Valdés of Conjunto Casino). Nor should we mistake the use of macho and hembra as simply sexist. Afro-Cuban religious traditions, for example, attribute spiritual power to both female (Yemayá and Ochún) and male *santos* (Santería saints). In addition sonic as well as spiritual power is attributed to the *iyá*, the most important and largest drum of the *batá* set, which is also known as the mother drum. On the other hand, performances by batá players that are deemed to be effective (i.e., successfully bringing on spiritual possession) are perceived to be determined by the player's masculinity. Katherine Hagedorn's discussion of "performative intent" and swing in batá performance practice is especially useful in understanding the son montuno's relationship to Afro-Cuban aesthetics because it specifies the value that practitioners of this Afro-Cuban tradition attribute to musical rhythmic force (i.e., swing and rhythmic density) and affective interplay between musicians and dancers (Hagedorn 2001, pp. 130–33; see also Ortiz 1993, pp. 58–65, 104).

Hence, people used *negro* and *macho* to describe Arsenio's son montuno style because of these terms' ability to articulate the deep resonance his conjunto's performances and style had with traditional Afro-Cuban performance practice and aesthetics. For instance, the interplay between Arsenio's musicians and dancers determined in large part the son montuno's rhythmic texture and thus sonic power. Also, their characterization of his style as negro was equally informed by dominant race relations, which in fact determined the social setting in which the son montuno emerged and crystallized. While listening to Arsenio's recording of "No vuelvo a Morón" (I'm Not Going Back to Morón) Cuban pianist and arranger Alfredo Valdés Jr. vividly described this social setting, underscoring the artistic interrelationship that obtained between Arsenio's conjunto and dancers:

> There is a close tie between . . . the things that Arsenio did, and what the dancers required. . . . This was all pure functional music for dancing. All of these things that you hear [on recordings] . . . has to do with what the dancers of Cuban folklore music, the best ones, the ones that went to dance halls, liked to dance. They didn't go there to watch, look at the band or look at the musicians . . . They were just going there to dance. . . . It's a service, music as a service for the dancing public, the dancing class. And the dancer was usually black, the ones that danced this type of thing. (Valdés interview 1999)

Situated in the context of self-segregated social club dances, where black dancers constituted Arsenio's as well as Arcaño's primary audience, dancing and playing son montuno and danzón-mambo became powerful modes of articulating one's racial subjectivity. In Havana in the 1940s, black working-class social clubs met many of the social and cultural needs of their members, including education, athletics, and recreation. These social clubs also imparted an ethos of black pride and unity among all-black working-class social clubs, though they couched it in racially egalitarian terms. The directors of Social Club Buena Vista, for example, outlined nine aims in their official bylaws, which they registered with the provincial government of La Habana in 1945. These included to "fight against theories and false concepts regarding inferiority and superiority of the human races through all mediums of diffusion"; "work to make disappear from our nation all practices of racial prejudice and discrimination"; and "establish cultural, ideological, and patriotic interchange with all those organizations and institutions that sincerely share these aims."[32] In short, the institution of black working-class social clubs as well as the dances these clubs organized afforded black dancers and musicians a crucial artistic autonomy in a larger social milieu in which dancing was one of the most segregated cultural activities in Havana. As Raúl Travieso succinctly stated, "they [whites] didn't dance where we were. They had their places for dancing; *we had to have ours*" (Raúl Travieso interview, April 15, 1998).

Yet the experience of musical and artistic dialogue with Arsenio's conjunto was not exclusive to black dancers. In describing his experience dancing to Arcaño's charanga and Arsenio's conjunto, Horatio Riambau (a white Cuban dancer) stated, "They invited me to create. I felt it because what I gave to them, they gave back to me" (Riambau interview 2003). Riambau added that Arsenio "couldn't play for white people," referring not to the barring of black groups in white social clubs—many black conjuntos and charangas, in fact, regularly performed for white social clubs—but rather to the lack of sonic and bodily dialogue or interplay that apparently characterized the performative relationship between musicians and white dancers in the context of white social clubs.[33] As Arcaño explained,

> I didn't like to play for white social clubs, in spite of the fact that the black social clubs paid less. You'd be playing a *danzón* for the white dancers and they'd ask you for a *pasodoble* [a Spanish dance genre]. Blacks went to dance as if they were going to church . . . [T]hey felt proud. They would dance next to a window so that they might be better seen. They were not like white dancers who would hide in order to hold a woman close. (Méndez Bravet and Pérez 1991, pp. 18–19)

Ultimately, these statements suggest that we understand the racialization and gendering of Arsenio's style and the styles of other Cuban groups as texts of Havana's dominant race and class relations in the 1940s. It also speaks to the specific aesthetic qualities that pertained to Afro-Cuban music and dance. Furthermore, although blackness still signified backwardness in other contexts (see chapter 1), people's praising of Arsenio's style as black also signified a shift in the valuation of blackness, which of course his conjunto and style helped affect in Cuban musical discourse. Arsenio did this not only by drawing on Afro-Cuban aesthetic principles and procedures but also by directly praising, in turn, the people of Havana's black working-class barrios in songs he called guaguancós.

Guaguancó in Havana

By 1946, at the height of Arsenio's popularity in Havana, groups of young adults approached Arsenio with lyrics they had written about their barrio and asked him to adapt them to music that could be performed by his conjunto. One of the first groups to make such a request was from Amalia, a reparto in the barrio of Belén. Arsenio accepted and chose to adapt these lyrics to a musical form based partly on the Afro-Cuban drumming style known as guaguancó.[34] The first guaguancó that Arsenio's conjunto recorded, "Juventud amaliana" (The Youth of Amalia; TCD-031), became so popular locally that groups from other barrios asked him to compose songs that praised their barrios as well. From 1946 to 1952 Arsenio recorded nine guaguancós, which I am calling conjunto-style guaguancós, the texts of which praised the predominately black and working-class barrios of Amalia, El Cerro, Belén, Pueblo Nuevo, Los Sitios, Colón, Luyanó, Cayo Hueso, and Pogolotti.[35] In the 1940s he composed and later recorded one of his most well-known guaguancós, titled "Buena Vista en guaguancó" (Antilla Records CD-586), which he dedicated to the directors of Social Club Buena Vista.

In the conjunto-style guaguancó, only the first three sections are reminiscent of the three parts (i.e., *diana*, *canto*, and *montuno*) of the folkloric guaguancó drumming style.[36] In the introduction the trumpet section plays a relatively long melodic phrase in contratiempo that is reminiscent of the melismatic vocal of the folkloric guaguancó's opening diana section. After the canto (verse) and montuno sections, Arsenio's guaguancós proceed with the solo, cierre, and diablo sections of the conventional son montuno arrangement scheme in which all of its principles and procedures are utilized. The only significant difference between the son montuno and conjunto-style guaguancó is the latter's moderately faster tempo. Apart from this, the arrangement scheme and rhythmic texture proceed from his son montuno style.

Throughout the 1930s and 1940s, Arsenio lived in some of the barrios, including Carraguao (which was a neighborhood in El Cerro) and Los Sitios, to which he dedicated his guaguancós. The residents of these barrios were of a working-class background and a majority of them were black.[37] Cayo Hueso, for example, was a working-class barrio in which many *tabaqueros* (cigar workers) lived and workers' unions were located. Luyanó was probably the poorest and most neglected by city and government officials. An article published in 1948 by the communist newspaper *Hoy*, in addition to describing the poor conditions in Luyanó, criticized the local and federal governments for their negligence and poor management of funds destined for various improvements in the barrio (*Hoy*

October 17, 1948). Even the mainstream magazine *Bohemia* published an article in 1953 that described Luyanó's desperate conditions, including its heavily contaminated river, as well as its poorly funded fire station and clinics (Portell Vila 1953).[38] Pogolotti was yet another working-class reparto in the barrio of Redención, Marianao that suffered official neglect (see Grupo Cubano de Investigaciones Económicas 1963, p. 397, and Inclán Lavastida 1943, pp. 126–27).

Life in these repartos and barrios was undoubtedly difficult. Whether in a union stronghold like Cayo Hueso or a poverty-stricken barrio like Luyanó, the standard of living in these sections of Havana and Marianao was markedly lower than in neighboring wealthier sections. Expectations of improving one's standard of living were continuously thwarted by government neglect and in general an unjust socioeconomic structure. As indicated in Social Club Buena Vista's bylaws, black Cubans also continued to struggle against racial discrimination, segregation, and ideologies of racial supremacy in their everyday lives. Indeed, they waged this fight "through all mediums of diffusion," including by reclaiming the idea of "blackness" from its dominant signification of "debasement" to express admiration for Arsenio's style, for example, and distinguish it from those of other conjuntos who performed primarily for white and black middle-class audiences. The act of dancing and performing music at events that were organized exclusively by and for black working-class Cubans constituted a particularly powerful mode of expressing this empowered sense of blackness.

For his part, Arsenio captured the hearts and affection of the dispossessed and marginalized black barrios of Havana, particularly through his guaguancós. To have Arsenio compose a guaguancó praising the youth and spirit of these barrios and perform it for them at their dances as well as on record and radio must have given these young people a strong sense of pride and identity as well as spiritual fulfillment. As José Frías, a former resident of Marianao and dancer of Arsenio's conjunto, recollected, "That was a *great time*, and the young people were something else. I think that there has been no other group of young people in the world that enjoyed themselves more than the Cuban young people at that *time*, from 1940 to 1960" (Frías interview 2000, emphasis added). "Time" in West African and Caribbean music and dance, as many have noted, is best conceptualized as nondurational and qualitative as opposed to sequential and quantitative (see Austerlitz 2003, p. 106). Here, we might interpret Frías's reference to time as both sequential (1940–1960) and nondurational, whereby dancers were transported from their everyday lives by simultaneously identifying with these lyrics in praise of their respective barrios and embodying the son montuno feel in their footwork and bodily movements.

We might also interpret the racialization and gendering of Arsenio's style as engendered not only by the music's qualities but also through the interplay of sensory perception (listening, playing, and dancing) and physical reality (segregated social clubs, economic and political disenfranchisement), all of which speak to the power that Arsenio's music had in articulating the lived experiences of musicians and dancers of the 1940s. The following remarks by Alfredo "Chocolate" Armenteros sum up what Arsenio, his guaguancós, and in general his son montuno style meant to the black working-class social clubs and barrios of Havana:

> He was the one who took pride in the guaguancó, because the guaguancó was danced in the streets or in private homes. He adapted and introduced it to the social clubs. He was a genius in doing that.... Arsenio composed a guaguancó for each barrio.... That was the greatness that he always had, because he was a musician, from head to toe. God took away his sight, but He gave him talent. (Armenteros interview 1997)

As Arsenio would realize in New York City and elsewhere in the following decades, much of the viability of his son montuno style as performed by his conjuntos would depend on the ability of dancers to feel and experience it as it was originally intended.

3 Who's Who in Mambo?

FROM 1948 TO 1966, the Palladium Ballroom was known among Latin music audiences as the mecca of Latin dance music in New York City. In the early 1950s it became specifically recognized in the American mainstream media as the home of the mambo, which featured amateur and professional mambo dancers as well as the Three Kings of the Mambo in New York City, Machito, Tito Puente, and Tito Rodríguez. Its importance to the popularization of Latin dance music in the United States is undeniable, but the Palladium and the music of its principal protagonists have constituted a dominant place in both the American imaginary of Latin culture and the historical canon of Latin popular music. As a result, the entire landscape of Latin music, dance, and culture in New York City during the 1950s has been largely ignored or overlooked.

For example, various dance halls, cabarets, and social clubs that were located in East Harlem or "El Barrio" and the South Bronx were the sites of a local and vibrant music culture whose importance to resident Cubans and Puerto Ricans equaled or even surpassed that of the Palladium. Arsenio was especially important to this milieu for his Cuban music repertory and unique son montuno style. Many residents of El Barrio and the South Bronx even preferred Arsenio's music over the mambo big bands that were popular at the Palladium and whose music was being disseminated internationally by the American popular music industry. Cuban Melba Alvarado, a longtime member of the Club Cubano Inter-Americano, a social club in the South Bronx, stated: "We always danced a lot of bolero, danzón, and son. These are three *típicas* [traditional Cuban genres]. We didn't care too much for mambo. Mambo was played a lot, orchestras played mambo, but it wasn't something that we did with much gratification" (Alvarado interview 2000). Arsenio himself had become very critical of the mambo, maintaining throughout the 1950s that the final section of his arrangements and in general his son montuno style constituted the "original" and "authentic" model of the mambo. In an interview given to Cuban magazine *Bohemia* in 1952, Arsenio articulated his views with respect to Dámaso Pérez Prado's style of mambo: "What Pérez Prado did was to mix the mambo with American music, copied from Stan Kenton. And he did us irreparable harm with it. I'll never forgive him for that, or myself for creating that damned mambo" (Cubillas 1952).

Arsenio's claim of originating the mambo and characterization of Pérez Prado's mambo style as mixed (read: "diluted" and "Americanized") with jazz music speak not to an empirical distinction between an authentic and inauthentic mambo style. Nor do I suggest that the Puerto Rican and Cuban music and dance scene in El Barrio and the South Bronx, in which Arsenio's conjunto formed a central component throughout the 1950s, developed in isolation from those music and dance styles that were most popular in the Palladium and that were being circulated transnationally. In fact, Arsenio's conjunto performed regularly at the Palladium and continued to record with RCA Victor through 1952 and again in 1955 and 1956. He also made temporary changes to his group's instrumentation, attempting to align his conjunto's sound with that of the mambo big band. Finally, Machito, Tito Puente, and other mambo big band leaders actually added the son montuno genre to their repertories. In the end, his statements as well as those of Melba Alvarado and others I have interviewed suggest that some Cuban and Puerto Rican musicians and dancers were ambivalent toward international trends in Latin popular music and dance, namely, the mambo. This ambivalence could be seen as having emerged from the precarious position that many first-generation Cuban and Puerto Rican immigrants, including Arsenio, bore in relation to the hegemonic North *and* Latin American entertainment industries, whose commodification of mambo music and dance conflicted with their identities and, in Arsenio's case, destabilized his professional career.

This chapter problematizes the conventional historical narrative of the mambo that has treated its development in teleological terms—"born in Cuba but made in the U.S.A.," as Gustavo Pérez Firmat put it (Pérez Firmat 1994, p. 80)—rather than as a transnational phenomenon with complex interrelationships with local contemporary styles, cultures, and identities. For this purpose Arsenio is especially significant because his musical career transversed the national boundaries and historical stages that writers have used to locate and periodize the mambo's "evolution." He had an important impact on the local identities particularly of Cuban and Puerto Rican immigrants in New York City. At the same time Arsenio's conjunto actively performed with popular mambo big bands, especially in the early 1950s; he also gained access to the international print media. By tracing Arsenio's activities throughout the 1950s, we uncover a local music culture in ideological tension with the mambo, symbolized by its home, the Palladium, and thereby establish the contemporaneity of his son montuno style and the so-called modern mambo.

Migrating to New York City

Arsenio's music was first propelled internationally in 1937 by Miguelito Valdés and the Orquesta Casino de la Playa, whose recording of "Bruca maniguá" was soon after recorded in New York City by several popular Latin orchestras, including Xavier Cugat's, the most popular Latin band at the time. In the following decades mambo and salsa groups would record hundreds of Arsenio's compositions, especially his son montunos, making him one of the most prolific and recorded composers of Cuban and Latin music. In the 1940s, Arsenio's own recordings and his conjunto's almost daily live performances on Radio Mil Diez and Radio Salas were very instrumental in establishing his popularity outside of Cuba, especially in Puerto Rico and the Netherlands Antilles.

Though he was popular among Cubans and Puerto Ricans throughout the diaspora, his overall recognition in the United States as well as South America, Central America, and Mexico was limited in scope compared to that of mambo big band leaders whose musical and performance styles attracted the fascination of nationally and ethnically diverse audiences. This disconnect between on one hand the son montuno's importance to mambo music as well as local music cultures and, on the other hand, Arsenio's own relative obscurity in the transnational Latin music industry can be attributed to the political economy of mambo music and dance and in conjunction, Arsenio's own professional missteps.

New York City via Tampa, 1947

Arsenio made his first trip to the United States with his brother Raúl Travieso around June 20, 1947.[1] The purpose of their trip was to visit Dr. Ramón Castroviejo, an eye specialist in New York City, who Arsenio hoped would be able to restore his eyesight. With the help of friends in Havana like Antonio Arcaño, Arsenio raised enough money for his trip and an operation, if one was possible, by performing benefit concerts in Havana and Matanzas. On their flight to New York, the two brothers had a stopover in Tampa, Florida, where they expected to stay only a few hours. They were forced to stay for about a week, however, because according to customs officials there was a problem, as Raúl Travieso recounted, with their visas.[2] While in Tampa, the brothers stayed at a hotel in the segregated black section of the city.[3] In the following evenings, the two brothers were invited to the homes of local Cubans, for whom Arsenio played his tres, including his newest guaracha "Pasó en Tampa" (It Happened in Tampa).[4] Based on its enthusiastic reception, he decided he would record it, having the opportunity to do so after he arrived in New York. They were also given a party by Sociedad La Unión

Martí-Maceo, which was established in Ybor City in 1900 by black Cubans, mostly cigar workers.

The brothers were finally allowed to leave Tampa around June 26, but they were required to deposit $1,000 each with U.S. Customs (presumably to prevent them from overstaying their visas), which they were to reclaim on their way back to Havana. Once in New York, they rented a room in an apartment building on Westchester Avenue in the South Bronx. Many of Arsenio's musician friends, such as Cubans Miguelito Valdés and Luciano "Chano" Pozo and Puerto Ricans Bobby Capó and Daniel Santos, made frequent visits to chat and play music. On June 28 the Club Cubano Inter-Americano held a dinner in honor of their special guests, Miguelito Valdés, Olga Guillot, and Arsenio Rodríguez (*La Prensa*, June 28, 1947). On July 12 his friends Miguelito Valdés, Marcelino Guerra (who sang second voice in Arsenio's conjunto from 1940 to about 1943), and others organized a much larger event in honor of Arsenio at the Diplomat Hotel on 43rd Street in Times Square, Manhattan. The Marcelino Guerra and Machito and His Afro-Cubans orchestras as well as Sexteto Puerto Rico performed and accompanied featured artists including Bobby Capó, Noro Morales, Olga Guillot, Jack Sagué, Juan Boria, Trío Johnny Rodríguez, and the guest of honor Arsenio, who according to reports performed "Bruca maniguá," "Camagüey," "Creo en tí" (I Believe in You), and his newest song, "Pasó en Tampa" (*La Prensa*, July 10, 12, and 17, 1947).

In addition to performing, Arsenio participated in eight recordings, which were led by Chano Pozo, for the recently formed independent record company Coda Records.[5] For these recordings, Arsenio was careful not to have his name appear on the label, because he was still under contract with RCA Victor in Havana. As a result, three group names were used for the three respective sessions: Orquesta Chano Pozo con Tito Rodríguez, Chano Pozo y su Conjunto con el Mago del Tres (or the Magician of the Tres), and Chano Pozo y su Conjunto. The musicians included members of the Machito and Marcelino Guerra orchestras and a young Tito Rodríguez, who formed his own conjunto (the Mambo Devils) later that year.

The brothers flew back to Havana on Arsenio's birthday, August 30, where they were met by waiting admirers at the airport and later at La Tropical beer garden. Apart from the fact that nothing could be done about restoring his eyesight, his 1947 trip was a turning point in his career and in the development of Latin music in New York City. After returning to New York in 1948, Raúl Travieso began to make preparations for Arsenio to move to New York. Because of the American Federation of Musician's nationwide ban on foreign orchestras working in the United States, Arsenio could not have brought his entire conjunto from Havana to start a new career in New York City. Hence, Arsenio's brother began to recruit Cuban and Puerto Rican musicians for the new conjunto months before Arsenio would return in early 1950.

There were at least three reasons why Arsenio chose to start a new career in New York in 1950 and eventually stay beginning in early 1952. First, Kiki, who had been jailed for manslaughter and was released from prison in early 1950, was apparently in danger of reprisals by relatives and friends of his victim, Wilfredo Mayo.[6] For the sake of his safety, Kiki moved to New York and never returned to his native Cuba (Coen interview 2000). Second, the pay for musicians in New York was much greater than in Havana, even for small groups who played for local social clubs. Third, the political situation in Cuba and the general mood of the nation was worsening (see Phillips 1959, pp. 255–56; Pérez. 1995a, p. 287). On March 10, 1952, former President Fulgencio Batista seized power through a military coup, thereby ending constitutional government in Cuba. On March 18, eight days after the coup, Arsenio's conjunto in Havana made its last two recordings for RCA Victor. Before leaving, he handed over the leadership of the conjunto to his lead trumpet player, Félix Chappottín. Just four days later, on March 22, Arsenio was in New York performing with his new Conjunto de Estrellas at the Park Plaza in East Harlem (*La Prensa*, March 22, 1952). He did not return to Havana to perform or record until 1956.

"Just a Soldier of the Mambo"

During Arsenio's first visit to New York in 1947, the name *mambo* had not yet emerged as a broadly recognized category of Latin music and dance. Between 1948 and 1949, however, mambo began to appear in the entertainment pages of *La Prensa*, New York's local Spanish-language newspaper, in which the term formed part of the names of local bands; in advertisements for records that were initially labeled as "mambo-bolero," "mambo-son," and "mambo-guaracha"; as part of musicians' titles, such as Cuban Kiko Mendive or "El Rey Del Mambo," who was accompanied by Dámaso Pérez Prado at the Teatro Puerto Rico in the Bronx in 1948; in advertisements for dance lessons; and in advertisements of Manhattan dance spots, including the Cuban Casino and Palladium, the latter of which became known as the home or cradle of the mambo by late 1949.

On his return in 1950 Arsenio was surprised, as he later recounted to *Bohemia*, to find that "[New York City] was filled with 'mambo kings,' 'emperors of the mambo,' 'rajas of the mambo.' And I said to myself, 'then, I'm just a soldier of the 'mambo'" (Cubillas 1952). With the popularization of mambo not only in New York but throughout Latin

TABLE 3.1. Mambo arrangement schemes

"Ran kan kan" (1949), Tito Puente					
Intro Montuno	Solo (timbales)	Montuno	Solo (timbales)	Montuno	
"Mambo No. 5" (1950), Pérez Prado					
Intro Montuno (A, B)	Montuno (A, C)	Montuno (A, B)	*Mambo		
"Vive como yo" (1950), Machito					
Intro Verse	Montuno	Cierre (break)	*Mambo	Montuno Coda	

America, beginning around 1950, Arsenio apparently felt the urgency in claiming ownership of the mambo, which he expressed in interviews as well as from on stage. But what aspects of the mambo was Arsenio claiming to be the creator of? Clearly, it was not the instrumentation of mambo big bands, although timbral heterogeneity was an aesthetic goal that Arsenio achieved with the expansion of the septeto into a conjunto. Besides, the mambo big band instrumental format had already been established and popularized by Cuban big bands for mostly elite and tourist audiences in the mid-1940s. In addition, the repertories of mambo big bands, not unlike those of salsa bands of the 1970s, encompassed several distinct genres, including son, guaracha, bolero, mambo, and by 1955 cha-cha as well as hybridized forms such as bolero-mambo and guaracha-mambo. Even arrangements that were labeled mambos varied in form (see Table 3.1).

Instead, Arsenio was claiming authorship of the underlying rhythmic approach that linked the otherwise idiomatic styles of Puente, Pérez Prado, Machito, and others. This rhythmic approach was marked by the use of contratiempo (offbeat accentuation), which in fact his conjunto and Arcaño's charanga had standardized in their recordings by 1944 (refer to Example 2.4). This was at least two years before the mambo rhythm became the signature pattern of the typical guaracha arrangement scheme as popularized by Cuban big bands (refer to Table 2.1). In addition, he shared in the creation of the mambo section, which like the diablo and the mambo section of the danzón-mambo was the most exciting and danceable part of the big band mambo arrangement scheme. All three formed that paroxysmal moment that Fernando Ortiz identified as characteristic of all Afro-Cuban music (see Ortiz 1993, p. 100).

Despite these shared musical principles and procedures, however, the rhythmic textures of Arsenio's son montuno style and the styles of his big band contemporaries were distinct, and it was the styles of the latter that most audiences in New York and internationally identified as mambo. Accordingly, when Arsenio first arrived in New York, his son montuno style was unfamiliar and novel, particularly for those who had not emigrated from the Caribbean, where otherwise Arsenio's music was relatively well known. Pianist Ken Rosa, for example, was at first uneasy with Arsenio's conjunto: "It was a combination of instruments that I was really not accustomed to. . . . The rhythm section sounded different from what our New York–Cuban rhythm sections were sounding like. I was not familiar with it. I wasn't really comfortable with it at that time" (Rosa interview, December 1, 1999). Percussionist Joe Torres, on the other hand, welcomed the freshness of his style:

> A lot of people were not exposed to conjunto style of music. So it was really innovative to a lot of people in New York because most of the [Latinos] in New York were Puerto Rican. So we had a different style of playing it [i.e., Latin dance music]. We were more used to the big bands, like [Anselmo] Sacasas, . . . Marcelino Guerra, Machito. . . . So when you heard a conjunto like Arsenio's it was really a novel thing and really exciting. (Torres interview 2000)

Indeed, the son montuno's rhythmic texture was quite distinct from the rhythm section of New York mambo big bands as well as those of the few conjuntos that formed in the late 1940s, such as Tito Puente's and Tito Rodríguez's. For example, Arsenio's "Esas no" (Not Those Women; TCD-022), which his Conjunto de Estrellas recorded in New York around 1951, features a characteristic son montuno bass line in contratiempo that in addition to accenting the melody of the sung chorus interlocks with the last two steps of the son footwork (see Example 3.1). In contrast "Ran kan kan" (BMG Music 3226-2-RL), recorded in 1949 by Tito Puente's conjunto, features a bass line that accents beats three and four of each bar with the fifth and root of the chord (see Example 3.2).[7] Sequences of call-and-response (bracketed) are also embedded in the bass, bongó, and tumbadora patterns in Arsenio's example, whereas the bass, timbales, and tumbadora patterns in Puente's example create a less interwoven polyrhythmic texture. Finally, although Arsenio's conjunto included a piano, in "Esas no" it is mostly inaudible, but his tres is prominently heard. To be sure, Arsenio's was probably the only conjunto in New York to include a tres through at least the mid-1950s.

Perhaps no other mambo big band leader and recording has symbolized the mambo more than Dámaso Pérez Prado and his "Mambo No. 5" (TCD-013), recorded in 1950. Pérez Prado's arrangement scheme of this and most of his mambos of the early 1950s is unconventional in its lack of call-and-response sequences, especially between lead and chorus vocals. Nevertheless, "Mambo No. 5" culminates with a mambo section that is marked by the mambo rhythm played by the saxophone section and the "Oye como va" riff played by the trumpets (see Example 3.3 and refer to Example 2.4). But the most striking difference between Arsenio's "Esas

EXAMPLE 3.1. "Esas no" (c. 1951), son montuno texture.

no" and Pérez Prado's "Mambo No. 5" is the latter's use of the bolero bass line, which while abandoned by Arsenio by 1942 continued to be used by other conjuntos, such as La Sonora Matancera in Havana (refer to Example 2.3) and, as can be observed in "Ran kan kan," New York groups.

In contrast, "Tremendo cumbán" (Great Party; TCD-004), recorded by Machito, is a rare example of a mambo that features two defining aspects of the son montuno texture (see Example 3.4). First, the bongó interweaves auxiliary attacks with notes of the bass pattern and open-tone attacks in the tumbadora pattern in a manner especially characteristic of the son montuno style (compare Example 2.1). Second, the bass line is in contratiempo, accenting rhythmically and melodically the sung chorus, both of which also accentuate the "and-of-four" of the two-side of the clave. As I argued in the previous chapter, the son montuno's emphasis on this beat and the "and-of-two" on the three-side of the clave coincided with the son footwork, which includes a step on each of these syncopated beats. It is likely, however, that when dancing to "Tremendo cumbán" most mambo dancers would have executed the mambo footwork and dance style rather than the son footwork and son montuno dance style.

According to contemporary sources, the basic steps for the mambo were executed on three of the four strong beats of each bar, starting on either the first or second quarter-note beat (Byrnes and Swanson 1951;

EXAMPLE 3.2. "Ran kan kan" (1949), Tito Puente, mambo texture.

Luis 1958; Ohl 1958). As can be observed in "Ran kan kan," most bass patterns in mambos accented the same strong beats. Of course, the mambo dance style, as popularized especially by exhibition dancers at the Palladium, was aesthetically vibrant, which some described as "wild, free and expressive," involving a "hodge-podge" of eccentric steps and intricate routines that dancers borrowed from tap and Lindy.[8] According to Robert Farris Thompson (an avid mambo fan and writer during the 1950s) and other contemporary observers, to dance mambo one must have "great stamina," a "forceful personality," and a "hyperkinetic" feel, while taking a "basic callisthenic approach" (Byrnes and Swanson 1951; Thompson 1959).

The footwork as well as the overall aesthetic of dancing son montuno, however, contrasted significantly with the much faster-paced mambo style. I asked Cuban trumpet player (and former member of Arsenio's conjunto in Havana) Alfredo "Chocolate" Armenteros to compare the mambo as it was danced at the Palladium with the son montuno as it was danced in Havana, to which he emphatically responded: "Completely different! In Cuba the music such as son montuno is slower. The only genre that is more or less fast is guaracha, and maybe guaguancó. . . . In

EXAMPLE 3.3. "Mambo no. 5" (1950), Dámaso Pérez Prado, mambo texture.

New York the music is faster, life is faster. . . . They told Arsenio that he had to play faster" (Armenteros interview February 18, 2000). Indeed, compare Arsenio's "Esas no," whose tempo averages around 145 beats per minute, to Tito Puente's "Ran kan kan," which averages slightly over 200. Mario Bauzá, director of Machito's big band, confirmed that the son montuno's moderate tempo accounted for its obscurity among mainstream mambo dancers. "I warned him: . . . But Arsenio didn't want to pick up the tempo, and that's why he never had the success here [in New York] that he deserved, since his style of music was never fully understood" (Padura Fuentes 1997, p. 41).

Other musicians identified the difficulty many mambo dancers had in feeling the son montuno texture as the reason for Arsenio's lack of commercial success and recognition. As New York–born Puerto Rican pianist Hector Rivera explained:

> Not everybody understands Arsenio's music. You play Arsenio for a lot of people and they think it's too, for a lack of a better word, funky. . . . They

EXAMPLE 3.4. "Tremendo cumbán" (1953), Machito, son montuno features.

> really don't *feel* that drive of that music. See, most people, they need the rhythm accented for them and son montuno is not like that. It's free flow. There's no *one*, *two*, *three*, *four*, *one*, *two*, *three*, *four*. You have to *feel* it and it goes to your body. It's something very deep. (Rivera interview 1993)

Professional mambo dancer Horatio Riambau similarly explained: "With Arsenio you had to dance by *feeling* his music. . . . If the dancers didn't *feel* his music . . . they looked like they were foreign because they didn't interpret the rhythm that they played, they didn't carry it inside them" (Riambau interview 2003). In other words, by applying the mambo footwork to dance to Arsenio's music, mambo dancers would not have felt or embodied the son montuno's rhythmic texture as it was originally intended. Central to feeling the groove of Arsenio's style, or interpreting its rhythmic texture and therefore understanding it, was the embodiment of the music's accentuation of those two syncopated beats that coincided with the son footwork.

Another important aspect of feeling or understanding Arsenio's style was the artistic dialogue that the music engendered between musicians and dancers. Pedro "Cuban Pete" Aguilar, another well-known Palladium dancer, found great enjoyment in negotiating Arsenio's rhythmically intricate breaks or cierres leading up to the diablo section: "Arsenio was out of his mind. I mean that in a positive way. *He was crazy*. He made me do things that I never knew could come out of my mind. The rhythms, and the beats, and the breaks that he used to take, I loved it! *I loved that man*. That man was, like I said, he was crazy, and he made me crazy" (Aguilar interview 2002). Many Cuban and Puerto Rican professional dancers like Horatio Riambau and Cuban Pete were familiar with Afrodiasporic dance traditions and therefore receptive to the son montuno's Afro-Cuban principle of sonic and bodily dialogue. Most mainstream mambo dancers, however, probably were not. Adding to Arsenio's precarious career was his own ambivalence toward international trends in Latin music and dance, as well as toward the performative and musical expectations the record industry fostered among musicians and audiences alike.

"I Sell Rhythm!" The Political Economy of Son Montuno and Mambo

Between 1950 and 1955, the mambo took North America, Latin America, Europe, and even parts of Asia and Africa by storm. More than just a musical and dance style, mambo became a spectacle for audiences and dancers alike. Tito Puente and Miguelito Valdés emphasized the importance of showmanship and the entertainment value of mambo. In a 1954 interview with *Down Beat*'s Nat Hentoff, Puente stated, "The reason the mambo is tremendous is [because] it's a great exhibition dance. Everybody who dances it is a star" (Hentoff 1954). In another interview for *Down Beat*, Valdés admonished other Latin musicians "to be entertainers today or quit music. The public looks for a graphic type of music, they want to be entertained as well as listen . . . they want to *see*" (Gleason 1952; emphasis added). Besides their musical abilities, Tito Puente, Miguelito Valdés, as well as Pérez Prado, Tito Rodríguez, and others, understood the importance of the spectacle in popular entertainment and thus developed and refined idiomatic stage personas.

In contrast, according to many who saw Arsenio's conjunto perform in New York, he and his musicians were not entertainers aiming to capture the fascination of American or Latin American audiences. Rather, they were perceived to be austere purveyors of authentic or *típico* Cuban music whose style was better suited for social and not exhibition dancing. As second-generation Puerto Rican Silvio Alava noted, "his style did not change and remained típico and true to his Cuban roots" (Alava interview 2000).[9] Although he did briefly adopt a big band format by including a saxophone section, his primary selling point was the rhythmic ingenuity of his son montuno style. Abby Liman, who briefly played timbales with his conjunto in the mid-1950s, recalled that Arsenio would always yell "'¡Yo vendo ritmo!' [I sell rhythm!]. That was his motto.... That's what he used to yell all the time" (Liman interview 1999). What follows is a tracing of Arsenio's activities from 1950 to 1955, focusing on his intersections with the transnational mambo in New York City and San Juan.

Arsenio Rodríguez y Su Conjunto de Estrellas performed for the first time in New York City at the Teatro Triboro in East Harlem on February 17, 1950. The conjunto performed two more shows at the Teatro Triboro and one dance at the St. Nicholas Ballroom in March. Its members included Puerto Ricans Héctor Pellot (piano),[10] Edil Rivera, and Luís Berrios Serralta (trumpets); Venezuelan Héctor "Venezuela" Vidal (trumpet); Cubans René Scull (vocals), Marcelino Guerra (vocals), and Lázaro Prieto (bass); and brothers Raúl (bongó) and Kiki (tumbadora). Between August and November 1950, Arsenio retuned to Havana to perform and record with his Havana conjunto.[11] Meanwhile, in September RCA Victor switched Pérez Prado from its international listing, which Arsenio was on, to its pop listing, becoming the only Latin recording artist at the time to have been on the pop listing (*Newsweek*, September 4, 1950; *Down Beat*, September 22, 1950; *Variety*, August 15, 1951). Pérez Prado had already become popular throughout Latin America, mainly through his appearances in Mexican films. Also, Machito's orchestra was performing regularly for diverse audiences throughout Manhattan, including the Palladium in Midtown, the Apollo in Harlem, and the Park Plaza in East Harlem.

By December Arsenio had returned to New York to perform with the Conjunto de Estrellas at the Hunts Point Palace and other locations in the South Bronx and East Harlem that catered to mostly local Puerto Rican and Cuban audiences. On Christmas Day, 1950, Arsenio's Conjunto de Estrellas performed at the Palladium for the first time along with Tito Puente's big band and several other groups. Two days later Cuba's *Diario de la Marina* published an article titled "La virtud del mambo" (The Power of the Mambo), which focused on Pérez Prado and the international popularization of mambo music and dance (Ramos 1950). In it, author Juan Ramos stated that the mambo was not "born" in Cuba although its "author," that is, Pérez Prado, was Cuban, adding that the music's "rhythm" is a "hybrid" mixed between an American "tiempo" (beat) and "rumba cubana" (Cuban rumba). In March 1951 New York's *La Prensa* printed a series of reports on Pérez Prado's activities in Lima, Peru. Archbishop of Lima Juan Gualberto Guevara reacted against Pérez Prado's and the mambo's popularity in Lima by condemning the mambo as an immoral and sensual dance and instructing all priests to deny absolution for anyone who danced mambo. In July Federico Ortiz Jr., writing from Mexico City, published an article titled "El mambo y su influencia malsana" (The Mambo and Its Unhealthy Influence) in Los Angeles's local Spanish-language newspaper *La Opinion* (Ortiz 1951). In it Ortiz criticized mambo music and dance and attributed its "shortcomings" to modernity and U.S. popular culture and imperialism. Clearly, Pérez Prado and mambo in general was creating a significant stir throughout Latin America.

Back in New York, *La Prensa* reported that the major record label Columbia Records was undertaking a vast promotion of Machito and His Afro-Cubans throughout Latin America. Meanwhile, Arsenio continued to perform with his conjunto in New York for mostly Cuban and Puerto Rican audiences. He also returned to Havana to record and perform in late May. In September 1951, Arsenio's Conjunto de Estrellas performed at the Palladium with Miguelito Valdés's, Tito Puente's, and Tito Rodríguez's big bands as part of the Palladium's fifth anniversary. His conjunto performed at the Palladium, St. Nicholas Ballroom, and Manhattan Center several more times before the end of the year. Some of the groups who shared the bill with the conjunto included the big bands of Noro Morales, Marcelino Guerra, Miguelito Valdés, Tito Puente, Tito Rodríguez, and Machito.[12]

Then, in January 1952, Arsenio's conjunto performed two shows that included a big band led by Pérez Prado at the St. Nicholas Ballroom in Manhattan. In the months leading up to this show, Pérez Prado had gained much publicity in the American and African American mainstream print media. His successful performances at Los Angeles's Zenda Ballroom and the Pasadena Civic Center in August 1951 were covered in *Variety*, *Down Beat*, and *Ebony*. Other mainstream American magazines were calling Pérez Prado the "Latin-American Kenton" ("Record Reviews" 1950), "El rey del mambo" ("El Mambo" 1950), and the "originator" of the mambo ("Mambo" 1951). Not coincidentally, in August Pérez Prado had signed a five-year contract with the booking agency Music Corporation of America, who in addition with his record company RCA Victor provided him with effective publicity ("Ban by Church" 1951; Gleason 1951).

The first show on January 19, 1952, was promoted in *La Prensa* with an advertisement in Spanish reading: "You will decide on Saturday who is who in the Mambo. 'The King of the Mambo' for the first time in New York. Pérez Prado and his orchestra of 16 professors battle Arsenio Rodríguez's Conjunto de Estrellas" (see Figure 3.1).[13] At one point during the actual show, promoter Federico Pagani invited Arsenio and Pérez Prado to the stage. In his 1964 radio interview with Radio Caracol Colombia, Arsenio described what happened next: "Federico Pagani, asked [us], 'So, we all want to know who is the owner of the mambo?' [Pérez Prado] answered, 'Well, ladies and gentlemen, the mambo belonged to Arsenio. That's the truth. Arsenio created the mambo. But I am the one

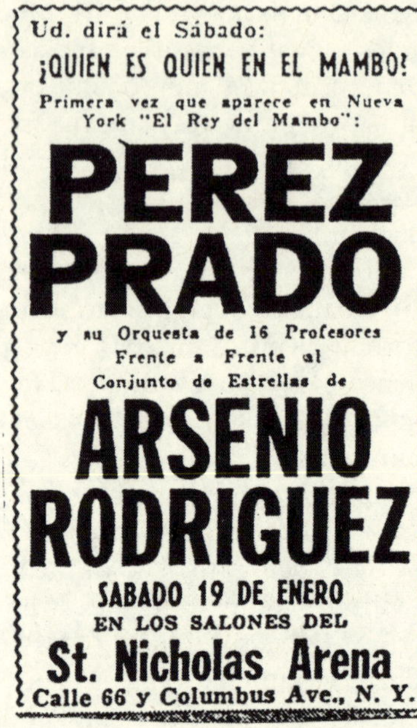

Figure 3.1. *Who Is Who in Mambo?* Advertisement for Pérez Prado's and Arsenio's "face-to-face," New York City, 1952. *Source: El Diario de Nueva York*, January 16, 1952.

who has made all the money' " (Rodríguez interview 1964). Given that this is Arsenio's account, it is difficult to recover what Pérez Prado actually said that night. What is clear is what was at stake for Arsenio: recognition as the originator of the mambo, not to mention financial gain.

But for Arsenio the mambo merely constituted the rhythmic patterns that he and Arcaño's charanga popularized among black Cuban social dancers in the early 1940s (refer to Example 2.4). For most audiences of Latin music in the United States or tropical music in Latin America, however, Pérez Prado *embodied* the mambo. His trademark grunt, zoot suit–like dress, kicks and unconventional dance movements on stage, and blaring big band sound constituted the mambo as much as its musical components. Despite Arsenio's central role in the development of the music, he was virtually unknown among American audiences, whose initial exposure to mambo was Pérez Prado, if not Tito Puente, Joe Loco, Tito Rodríguez, or Machito. His conjunto's name was even left out of the advertisements for the Pérez Prado show that were printed in the *New York Daily News* (January 19, 1952). Nevertheless, he continued to insist in interviews that he was the true creator of the mambo, including in his interview with Vicente Cubillas of *Bohemia* in 1952 (see Figure 3.2).

FIGURE 3.2. Arsenio Rodríguez with Vicente Cubillas Jr. of *Bohemia*, New York, 1952. *Source:* Oswaldo Salas, photographer (from *Bohemia* 44, 49: 1952).

In April 1952, less than a month after making his final recordings with RCA Victor in Havana, Arsenio's Conjunto de Estrellas began a one-year contract in New York with the local independent company Seeco Tropical Records. Of the sixteen recordings his conjunto made with Seeco, five were labeled "son-capetillo." Arsenio explained, "Now, I'm trying to introduce the 'capetillo' in New York. I want to destroy that damned mambo which is putting an end to Cuban composers, since no one wants to buy their boleros and guarachas. We are possessed by mambo mania. I was the Dr. Frankenstein who created the monster, and now that same monster wants to kill me" (Cubillas 1952). The capetillo, however, was not much different than his son montuno in terms of its form, arrangement scheme, and overall style, although the harmonic voicings in some of these recordings suggest influences from the jazz and mambo repertories. Nevertheless, these capetillos failed to gain widespread recognition from audiences in New York City as well as Puerto Rico where the conjunto performed from September to October 1952.

Shortly after his arrival in San Juan, Arsenio appeared on radio station WKAQ's morning program "Caravana Musical," hosted by José Antonio

Figure 3.3. Advertisement for Arsenio Rodríguez y Su Conjunto de Estrellas at the Escambrón Beach Club, San Juan, 1952. *Source: El Imparcial*, September 19, 1952.

Purcell (*El Mundo*, September 19, 1952). In addition the San Juan newspaper *El Imparcial* published an article by Rafael Nieves Rivera titled "A Cuban in Puerto Rico: Arsenio Rodríguez Says He's the Creator of the Mambo" (Nieves Rivera 1952). On September 19, Arsenio's conjunto began a one-month contract at the Escambrón Beach Club, which was located close to Parque Sixto Escobar (see Figure 3.3). The contract had been arranged in advance from New York, probably by Puerto Rican vocalist Candido Antomattei, who had joined the conjunto as its second voice, guitarist, and "contractor."[14] The conjunto performed every Friday, Saturday, and Sunday night for the next four weeks. According to pianist Ray Coen and other members of the conjunto, their performances were well attended by musicians and dancers alike. Raúl remembers that the young Rafael Ithier, Martín Quiñones, Rafael Cortijo, and other future members of Cortijo y Su Combo and El Gran Combo de Puerto Rico attended many of these dances. At least one of their performances, their debut, was transmitted on WKAQ (*El Mundo*, September 22, 1952). Coen remembers that many other performances were not only well attended but also transmitted on radio.

According to other contemporary reports, however, not all of the conjunto's performances were well attended or successful. Germán Negroni, who wrote a daily column for San Juan's *El Mundo*, gave two reports on the conjunto's performances at the Escambrón. For its debut, he wrote:

> The debut of the Cuban conjunto of Arsenio Rodríguez was very pleasing but weak in attendance. And I don't see why, since Arsenio's conjunto, in my opinion, is playing as good as ever and really deserves the backing of the

> public. I think that for those who like to dance to the authentic feel of lively and romantic Cuban music must not miss this fleeting opportunity to dance to Arsenio Rodríguez. (*El Mundo*, September 22, 1952)

Less than two weeks later Negroni criticized Arsenio for "avoiding very politely the request of his admirers to please them with one or more [well-known] songs from his repertory. . . . This reminds me of the old saying of the theater that 'when business is going bad, attract the public more with your affection and graciousness.' Here, regretfully, the Cuban 'Ciego Maravilloso' has failed" (*El Mundo*, October 3, 1952). Evidently, the conjunto had only rehearsed his latest numbers, including his capetillos, which he was attempting to popularize as an alternative to the mambo.

Despite the apparent low turnouts at the Escambrón, however, the conjunto was subsequently contracted to perform at the Guaraquibel nightclub, in the Carolina section of San Juan, and at Cobian's Teatro Puerto Rico, in Santurce, where they played from October 2 to 5. Not surprisingly the advertisements for his Teatro Puerto Rico appearances read: Coming to us from New York's Palladium and from the famous Club Tropicana; creator of the mambo; he's a world-famous composer and promoter of the Afro-Cuban musical movement (*El Mundo*, October 2, 1952). The conjunto's stint in San Juan ended on October 12 with a special event in Arsenio's honor, which took place at the Escambrón. Some of the musicians and groups who attended and performed included César Concepción y Su Orquesta, Myrta Silva, Miguelito Miranda y Su Combo, Trío San Juan, and Cuarteto Marcano (*El Imparcial*, October 8, 1952). This *homenaje* (tribute) as well as others that Arsenio received on arriving in New York attest to the fact that he was recognized as an exceptional composer, musician, and bandleader among Puerto Rican musicians in New York and Puerto Rico. Yet demand for his conjunto and broad international recognition of him as the creator of the mambo remained elusive, despite his repeated claims in advertisements and published interviews.

From 1953 to 1955 the mambo's popularity reached its apex in New York and internationally. Although promotion for bandleaders such as Tito Puente, Tito Rodríguez, Machito, and Joe Loco relentlessly continued in the mainstream print media, visibility of Arsenio's conjunto in the local Spanish-language press diminished. Also, these bandleaders were performing regularly in cities across the United States, including Miami, Pittsburgh, Chicago, Detroit, Boston, San Francisco, and Los Angeles. Meanwhile, Arsenio's conjunto continued to record with local independent record companies, including Tico and SMC (Spanish Music Center). But promotion of these records and of Arsenio's conjunto was nonexistent in the American mainstream press as well as in the Spanish-language press locally and in Cuba and Puerto Rico.

Figure 3.4. Arsenio Rodríguez y Su Nueva Orquesta de 14 Profesores, New York City, 1953. *Standing from left to right:* Pablito Díaz, trumpet; Polito Castillo, baritone saxophone; Ramón Agüguí, alto saxophone; Juan Mora, piano; Edil Rivera, trumpet; Candido Antomattei, second voice; Manolo "El Barroso" Rodríguez, first voice. *Kneeling and seated from left to right:* Héctor "Venezuela" Vidal, trumpet; Pito Álvarez, tenor saxophone; Raúl Travieso, bongó; Arsenio Rodríguez, director and tres; José Valiente, timbales; Kiki Rodríguez, tumbadora; Nilo Sierra, bass. *Source:* Photographer unknown; photograph courtesy of Jaime Jaramillo.

In July 1953 Arsenio attempted to align his music with a mainstream mambo sound, this time by expanding his eleven-piece conjunto into a fourteen-piece big band (see Figure 3.4). In addition to his regular three-trumpet lineup, Arsenio added Ramón "Agüigui" on alto sax, Pito Álvarez on tenor sax, and Polito Castillo on baritone sax as well as José Valiente on timbales.[15] Arsenio Rodríguez y Su Nueva Orquesta de 14 Profesores, as the big band was known, premiered at the Tropicana Club in the South Bronx. In addition to performing regularly at the Tropicana Club through early 1954, the orchestra also performed on several occasions at the Manhattan Center in September 1953 and the Palladium in January 1954. Despite the addition of a saxophone section, the music, according to Edil Rivera (who played trumpet with the orchestra), had *el mismo patrón* (the same beat). Rivera recounted that Arsenio wanted to hear how his son montuno style would sound with the addition of saxophones. Hence, he recruited René Hernández, Machito's pianist and primary arranger, in addition to asking Rivera to arrange for the orchestra. Instead of new material, however, Arsenio asked Hernández and Rivera to rearrange charts such as "Mulence" (guaguancó), "Baila Simón" (son montuno), and "Blanca paloma" (cha-cha), which he had already recorded with the conjunto, for the big band format. Unfortunately, the orchestra did not record, and by May 1954 Arsenio had disbanded it because of the added costs in paying more musicians.

On February 20, 1954, Arsenio, without his conjunto, participated in an event called the Mambo Concert at Carnegie Hall. The concert featured a variety of well-known Latin performers, including Pupi Campo, Justi Barreto, Noro Morales, and Myrta Silva. Although the title of the show suggested a mambo theme, the music that was performed seemed to be more varied, including original compositions by Cuban light-classical and popular composers Gilberto Valdés and René Touzet, Afro-Cuban folkloric numbers, and contemporary popular styles such as Tito Puente's "Mambo la roca" (Mambo the Rock) and Enrique Jorrín's chachá "La engañadora" (The Cheater). Arsenio with pianist José Curbelo performed the first piece of the concert, titled "Mosaico," which presumably consisted of a medley of popular Cuban tunes, perhaps including some of Arsenio's. In any event, his participation was clearly peripheral to the show itself, even though its program suggests that it was a musical journey through the various styles of the mambo.

In May 1954, Tito Puente, Joe Loco, Miguelito Valdés, and Arsenio's conjunto performed at the Apollo as part of a Mambo Festival. *Down Beat* reported that this festival stopped at sixteen cities (through June 16), including New York, Boston, Philadelphia, Washington, DC, Richmond, Baltimore, Detroit, Cleveland, Pittsburgh, and other cities (*Down Beat*, June 16, 1954). It is unclear, however, whether Arsenio participated in all of these dates. Finally, on October 22, 1954, Carnegie Hall again was the site of a mambo concert titled Mambo U.S.A., which was the opening show of a proposed fifty-six-city tour across the United States.[16] This time Arsenio did not participate, even though one of the organizers of the tour, Tico owner George Goldner, had recorded Arsenio's conjunto in 1951 and 1952. The other organizer, Lenny Greene, was a powerful manager and agent for many mambo big bands. At this time, both Goldner and Greene figured prominently in the careers of Tito Puente, Tito Rodríguez, and Machito, who was one of the headlining acts of the tour (David Carp, personal communication; see also *New York Times*, October 23, 1954).

Although Arsenio did try to fashion his group's instrumentation according to the popular big band format, his lack of showmanship contributed significantly to his difficulty in marketing himself and his ensembles. Candido Antomattei, who sang with and helped manage

Figure 3.5. *Authentic Cuban Mambo's: Arsenio Rodriguez and his Orchestra* (Tico LP 135), LP cover, 1955.

Arsenio's conjunto for most of the 1950s, explained: "The only thing that killed him was his indifference toward [developing] an act" (Antomattei interview 1998). In 1955, despite Arsenio's growing obscurity in the mambo scene, Tico released two ten-inch LPs that were named *Authentic Cuban Mambo's: Arsenio Rodriguez and His Orchestra*, volumes 1 and 2 (see Figure 3.5).[17] Presumably, Tico's owners, with perhaps Arsenio's encouragement, attempted to target the conjunto's core audience in El Barrio and the South Bronx, where it had been performing regularly for local Cuban and Puerto Rican residences since 1950. Among these audiences Arsenio's conjunto and son montuno constituted an authentic alternative to Manhattan's mambo scene.

The Pueblo Pueblo of El Barrio and the Bronx

By 1957 the decline in popularity of the mambo and cha-cha accounted for the Palladium's diminishing audiences, thereby creating stiff competition among big bands for fewer jobs at the Palladium and other dance halls in Manhattan.[18] As a result, Arsenio's conjunto had become almost entirely reliant on peripheral locales, particularly the Park Palace/Plaza dance hall in El Barrio and the Tropicana Club and Club Cubano Inter-Americano in the South Bronx.[19] Unlike the majority of mambo dancers, many in the Cuban and Puerto Rican communities of El Barrio and the South Bronx enthusiastically embraced Arsenio's comfortably paced son montuno style and his típico or traditional Cuban-based repertory.

Si Quiere Bailar lo Bueno

In the mid–twentieth century Puerto Ricans accounted for the overwhelming majority of Latinos living in New York City, growing from an estimated 45 percent of Latino in 1940 to 80 percent in 1960 (Haslip-Viera 1993, pp. 8–18). The Puerto Rican population itself grew from an estimated 61,500 in 1940 to 612,574 in 1960, an increase of almost 900 percent. Neighborhoods with an established Puerto Rican population in particular—such as El Barrio as well as the South Bronx, Hunts Point, and Morrisania sections of the Bronx—grew and expanded. The Cuban population of New York City also grew, but in significantly lesser proportions than the Puerto Rican population. From 1940 to 1960 the Cuban population increased by 84 percent, from an estimated 23,124 to 42,694. Cubans in New York did not form any outstanding core of settlement. Instead, they resided primarily in Puerto Rican sections, although class and race often dictated in which neighborhood Cubans settled. For example, concentrations of Cubans and Puerto Ricans of color existed around 167th Street and Stebbins Avenue in the Morrisania district and on Prospect Avenue on the South Bronx and Hunts Point border (Greenbaum 1986, p. 20; Jonnes 1986, p. 329).

Throughout most of the 1950s, Arsenio lived in El Barrio with his wife, Emma Lucía Martínez (who was born in Puerto Rico), at 152 East 116th Street, between Third and Lexington Avenues. He also regularly stayed in the Bronx with Kiki and his family, who lived at 811 Tinton Avenue, between East 160th and East 161st Streets.[20] Raúl also lived in the Bronx, and between 1956 and 1958 he owned the El Dorado restaurant on East 163rd Street and Intervale Avenue (Coén interview 2000; Rodríguez 1998; Travieso 1999; Valdés 1997). The area in and around Westchester Avenue, Southern Boulevard, Prospect Avenue, and East 163rd Street, which adjoined the South Bronx and Hunts Point, was known for its numerous resident Cuban and Puerto Rican musicians, which in addition to Arsenio included Marcelino Guerra, René Hernández, Fernando "Caney" Storch, Alfredo Valdés, Joe Loco, and Tito Rodríguez. Other younger Puerto Rican musicians, who would spearhead the popularization of pachanga, boogaloo, and salsa, beginning in 1960, also lived here, including Charlie and Eddie Palmieri, Manny Oquendo, Ray Barretto, Alfredito Valdés Jr., Hector Rivera, and many more (Boulong interview 2000; Marin interview 2000; Valdés interview 1997).

As he did for many working-class barrios of Havana in the 1940s, Arsenio saluted the music culture of El Barrio and the Bronx in the lyrics to two guaguancós—"Como se goza en El Barrio" (El Barrio Is a Lot of Fun) and "El elemento del Bronx" (The People of the Bronx)—which his conjunto recorded with Tico in 1951 and were later released on the ten-inch LP

Authentic Cuban Mambo's in 1955 (see TCD-022). The lyrics to "Como se goza en El Barrio" describe a lively street scene stretching from 98th to 125th Streets along Lexington Avenue. The song concludes with the following lines: "Si quiere bailar lo bueno, camina y venganse al Barrio. Los que viven en downtown vienen a gozar al Barrio" (If you want to dance to good music, walk to El Barrio. Those who live downtown come to have fun in El Barrio). In these lines, however, Arsenio more than saluted El Barrio's music culture. He was urging dancers from downtown (or the Palladium) to come to El Barrio and dance to good (or authentic) music.

In the 1940s and 1950s, the Park Palace/Plaza, located on the corner of East 110th Street and Fifth Avenue, was the most popular dance hall in El Barrio. In its initial days of operation in the 1930s the Park Palace/Plaza catered to upwardly mobile patrons of diverse ethnic backgrounds.[21] By the early 1950s, however, it had become known for its more Cuban- and Puerto Rican–oriented dance music as well as its predominately local working-class Cuban and Puerto Rican dancing public. Puerto Rican Luís "Máquina" Flores, who is considered to be one of the greatest dancers of the Palladium era, vividly described the social and musical differences between the Palladium and the Park Palace/Plaza in the following manner:

> The Palladium always got the fascination of people because it was situated on 53rd Street and Broadway.... The Plaza never got in the limelight because it was smack in the middle of the ghettos.... But I'll tell you one thing. Machito, Arsenio, all of these bands—you never heard these people swing like they swung when they were playing at the Plaza because the music belonged to the ghettos. And the people that spent the money and went to the dances in droves were the people from the ghettos.... So all these musicians knew that they could not pull the wool over these people's eyes.... The Plaza had the distinction that everybody knew everybody... [It] had a soul of its own. It had the heart of the barrio itself. It had the essence of the poor people.... You could not have the same feeling in the Palladium. When you went to the Palladium, you were more starchy, you know, a little more phony. (Flores interview 1993)

Although some have praised the Palladium for its egalitarian milieu (e.g., Salazar 2002, p. 87; Loza 1999, p. 222), Flores's observations, in conjunction with Arsenio's lyrics in "Como se goza en El Barrio," suggest that from the perspective of many Latinos in El Barrio, class, ethics, community, and musical integrity distinguished the music and dancing of the Park Palace/Plaza from that of the Palladium.

Similar sentiments prevailed among Cuban and Puerto Rican residents of the Bronx. In his "El elemento del Bronx," Arsenio describes a community that knows how to dance contemporary popular styles (mambo and swing) as well as Cuban styles (danzón, guaguancó, and rumba): "El elemento del Bronx, igual bailan swing que guaguancó. Igual bailan mambo que danzón. Igual bailan rumba que danzón" (The people of the Bronx, they dance swing as well as guaguancó. They dance mambo as well as danzón. They dance rumba as well as danzón). Here he recognized both the popularity of mambo and swing and the maintenance of traditional Cuban dance styles (guaguancó and danzón) among "the people" (i.e., Cuban and Puerto Ricans) of the Bronx.

Such was the case among members of the Club Cubano Inter-Americano, which from 1946 to 1960 was located at 914 Prospect Avenue, off Westchester Avenue, on the border of the South Bronx and Hunts Point. Although the majority of its members were Cubans and Puerto Ricans of color, the social club welcomed, as Raúl Travieso emphasized, "whites, blacks, everyone!" This was in contrast to other social clubs, such as the Ateneo Cubano and the Club Caborrojeño, both of which were located in Manhattan and were known to discriminate against Cubans and Puerto Ricans of color in the 1950s (Berrios interview 2002; Carp 1999, p. 29).[22] In addition, although the Club Cubano's cultural leaning was Cuban, Puerto Ricans and Dominicans who regularly attended its functions and who were not already members felt nevertheless accepted as family. For example, Sara Martínez Baro, Arsenio's sister-in-law and the wife of his Cuban bassist, Evaristo "Cuajarón" Baro, remarked that "it was a delightful environment, one that felt as if we were all family. Everyone knew each other" (Martínez Baro interview 2000).

The majority of the Club Cubano's members were skilled workers, including barbers and accountants, from middle- and working-class backgrounds. The purpose of the club was to provide members and their family and friends with social and recreational activities, mostly involving the celebration of Cuban patriotic holidays. The club also hosted birthday parties for members and their families and King's Day and Easter celebrations for their children. In addition, members organized a dance troupe that specialized in Cuban son and danzón dancing. Most of these events were held at the club, whose size could only accommodate about 100 people total. As a result, club officials were unable to hire big bands because of the limited capacity, the funds from which would have been needed to pay for such bands. The club did, however, present solo piano and poetry recitals and, on occasion, small musical groups.

In January 1957, for example, the club celebrated José Martí's birthday. The political situation in Cuba had worsened after Fidel Castro began the second phase of his revolution in the prior month against the Batista dictatorship. Arsenio attended the club's celebration and, together with Puerto Rican singers Luís "Wito" Kortwrite and Candido Antomattei (who were members of his conjunto), debuted "Adórenla Como Martí" (Love Her as Martí Did), one of Arsenio's most well-known political songs (see Figure 3.6). In this song's lyrics Arsenio implores all

FIGURE 3.6. Arsenio Rodríguez, Luís "Wito" Kortwrite, and Candido Antomattei performing at the Acto a Martí gathering at the Club Cubano Inter-Americano, South Bronx, 1957. *Source:* Photographer unknown. Club Cubano Inter-Americano Photograph Collection. Photographs and Prints Division. Schomburg Center for Research in Black Culture. New York Public Library. Astor, Lenox, and Tilden Foundations.

Cubans—namely, the warring factions—to resolve their differences in peace and love and to unite the country so that the sacrifices of the Cuban independence patriots would not have been in vain. The audience was moved emotionally and enthusiastically applauded Arsenio's message of reconciliation (Alvarado interview 2000).

Arsenio regularly performed for the club for a modest fee, as he had done for black social clubs in Havana. He varied the size of the conjunto according to how much the club was able to pay. Sometimes he even performed for no fee at all. The club's officials recognized Arsenio's cooperation by regularly hiring his full conjunto to perform for the club's larger events, which it usually held at the Hotel Diplomat in Times Square. In any case, the Club Cubano's celebrations always involved Cuban music, whether it was played on a record player, by a trio, or in informal jam sessions, such as one that included Machito, Wito Kortwrite, Arsenio, and others in 1959 (see Figure 3.7).

The social club's objective in celebrating important Cuban holidays and with it Cuban music made it one of the very few locales in New York

FIGURE 3.7. Acto a Martí gathering at the Club Cubano Inter-Americano; musicians include Kiki Rodríguez (playing the tumbadora), Arsenio Rodríguez (partially hidden), and Machito (playing the maracas), 1959. *Source:* Photographer unknown. Club Cubano Inter-Americano Photograph Collection. Photographs and Prints Division. Schomburg Center for Research in Black Culture. New York Public Library. Astor, Lenox, and Tilden Foundations.

City during the 1940s and 1950s that featured Cuban son and danzón music and dancing. Puerto Rican pianist Ray Coén pointed out that the Club Cubano "was like an outlet for our type of music" (Coén interview 2000). The fact that the music was invariably Cuban did not prevent non-Cuban members and musicians, such as Ray Coén and others in Arsenio's conjunto, from embracing it as theirs. New York–born Puerto Rican and percussionist Joe Torres remembers participating in a performance of a *comparsa* or conga by Arsenio's conjunto:

> I played with him in the Bronx on Prospect Avenue. And they played a comparsa that I thought would never end. But I didn't care because I was having so much fun. We must have played that comparsa for a half an hour. Oh man, they [audience] were doing the conga line! Oh man, they were having a party! That's why we wouldn't stop. It was just great. That was one of the highlights of my career, playing with Arsenio. I think they were mostly Cubans, but they were mixed with Puerto Ricans because it was a social club and when they threw dances they'd have other people. (Torres interview 2000)

About one block east of the Club Cubano Inter-Americano was the Tropicana Club. It was owned and operated by Cubans Tony and Manolo Alfaro, who were brothers, and Pepe Sánchez, and its core audience as well as the performers consisted of local Cubans and Puerto

Ricans. For example, in the late 1940s and early 1950s the Tropicana regularly presented Puerto Rican performers such as Juanito Sanabria, the Conjunto "Puerto Rico" de Tonito Ferrer, Conjunto Alfarona X, and Luís Cruz y Su Conjunto Marianaxis, as well as Arsenio's conjunto and Cuban Gilberto Valdés's charanga. In November 1952 the Tropicana featured Arsenio's conjunto and Valdés's charanga (under the direction of Cuban Alberto Iznaga) every weekend. Gilberto Valdés y Su Charanga, the first Cuban charanga in New York City, was performing regularly at the Tropicana Club by 1951.[23] In New York during the 1950s, Valdés dedicated himself to the flute and leading his charanga, which consisted of black and white Cubans and other Latinos. Although his charanga never recorded, he participated as the flute player on Arsenio's *Sabroso y caliente* (Puchito 586), which was released in 1957 (Carp 1999b).[24] Arsenio's and Valdés's groups also performed together at least once at the Park Palace/Plaza on January 1, 1955, and regularly for the Club Cubano Inter-Americano through at least 1961.[25]

Placing Arsenio and the Son Montuno Style in New York City, 1950s

Most people who performed with or danced to Arsenio's conjunto in New York characterized its style as típico cubano. In addition, many such as Puerto Rican Israel Berrios claimed that his style never changed (Berrios interview 1998). On the other hand, some Cubans who became fans of Arsenio in Havana and never lived in New York remarked that his style had changed in the 1950s. In Dandy Beltrán's opinion, his arrangements had become more "commercial" and fashioned for the broader Latino audience of New York City (Beltrán interview 1996). These two seemingly contradictory characterizations of Arsenio's style of the 1950s in fact speak of distinct experiences among populations in different social contexts and historical periods. Though Havana's racial and class divisions contributed to the characterization of Arsenio's style in racial terms, the immigrant experience and intersections of the Latin music industry and local music cultures helped determine the reception of his style in New York as típico cubano.

Although Arsenio did indeed make changes to his music for commercial aims, what mattered most for the largely Cuban and Puerto Rican immigrant population of El Barrio and the Bronx was that his conjunto and music offered an alternative to international styles of mambo. His conjunto's repertory and style gave resonance to the national identities and nostalgic feelings for home shared among his mostly Cuban and Puerto Rican audience. The fact that his son montuno style resonated with Puerto Rican musicians and dancers in terms of national identity and nostalgia is particularly significant. Puerto Rican Sara Martínez Baro, who was a regular patron of the Club Cubano's social events in the 1950s, described what Arsenio's style still means to her: "It's a beautiful style, a graceful style, a style that invariably takes a person back home, as do *plena*, *danza*, danzón, *bomba*, and bolero" (Martínez Baro interview 2000). Most Puerto Rican immigrants had probably listened to Arsenio's records and live performances on Cuban radio in Puerto Rico. In fact many of his Puerto Rican musicians, including Israel Berrios, had become fans of Arsenio in Puerto Rico prior to joining his conjunto in New York. But his music could have also transported Puerto Ricans back home through the Afrodiasporic principles it shared with bomba as well as plena. As observed in several statements given throughout this chapter, Puerto Rican musicians and dancers recognized, engaged with, and celebrated such underlying principles of the son montuno style.

What was also significant to the reception of his style as típico was his conjunto's contribution to the local music culture of El Barrio and the Bronx. His music and performances along with those of other local groups engendered a shared identity of community among dancers and musicians as well as a sense of cultural resistance to modern or Americanized mambo styles. As both Luís "Maquina" Flores and Sara Martínez Baro stated everyone knew each other at places like the Park Plaza/Palace and the Club Cubano Inter-Americano. This deep sense of community, rooted in their shared immigration experience and racial and class marginalization, differed from the culture of the Palladium, whose "spatial logic," according to Robert Farris Thompson, consisted of "an outer circle of rich visitors and celebrities seated at tables . . . an inner circle of Latino and black dancing connoisseurs seated on the floor communally, and, in the sovereign center, the star dancers themselves" (Thompson 2002, p. 341). This setting was distinct from not only the locations where Arsenio performed in El Barrio and the Bronx but also from those social clubs in which he and Arcaño developed their respective styles in the first place.

For Arsenio as well as his audience, his son montuno style and the "modern" mambo represented not the same musical repertory at different stages of its development but related musical repertories facing each other at the same time. Only by focusing on the intersection of his style and the "modern" mambo, symbolized best by his face-to-face encounter with Pérez Prado, can we see the destabilizing force that the mambo and in general the Latin music industry had on some Cuban and Puerto Rican musicians and dancers. This was made especially clear in Arsenio's many claims of having originated the mambo. For Arsenio the real mambo sound did not emerge in contact with North American music (see

Pérez Firmat 1994, pp. 80–81). It had already crystallized among black working-class Cuban musicians and dancers, and, more important, it remained vibrant as ever in El Barrio, the Bronx, and the barrios of Havana as well as among other populations in the Caribbean and the diaspora. For most Latin music audiences, however, these music cultures remained largely inaccessible or peripheral in the workings of the transnational popular culture industry.

4 Remembering the Past with *El Ciego Maravilloso*

THE FINAL DECADE of Arsenio's career and life has been the subject of much speculation. As can be observed on many Web sites and in liner notes to CDs, Arsenio, it is widely believed, died "in poverty" and an "almost forgotten figure."[1] To be sure, by 1960 the forty-nine-year-old bandleader and his conjunto of mostly middle-aged Cuban and Puerto Rican musicians were struggling to capture the attention of young Latin music dancers whose tastes in music spanned doo-wop, rock and roll, and Motown as well as the newest Latin dance craze, pachanga. By the end of the 1960s this repertory would include boogaloo and salsa. Nevertheless, for many first-generation Cuban and Puerto Rican immigrants in New York City, Chicago, and Los Angeles as well as for Curaçaoans, Arsenio was never forgotten, and his music and performances continued to have an important impact on their local music cultures.

In researching the last decade of Arsenio's career, three anomalous aspects emerge that raise broader questions concerning the role of nostalgia in Latin popular music of the 1960s. First, in Chicago, Los Angeles, and New York, Arsenio's primary audience continued to be first-generation Cuban and Puerto Rican immigrants. These musicians and dancers, in addition to those from Curaçao, had first become enthusiasts of his son montuno style in the 1940s by attending his performances at black social clubs in Havana or by listening to his conjunto's records and live performances on Cuban radio. Practically every individual that I interviewed fondly recounted their memories of this period (1940s) of Arsenio's career. As Reginald Villareal of Curaçao stated, "We had the good fortune to have a neighbor who played records of Arsenio and Chappottín every day... from morning until night. And that has stayed in our heads since childhood" (Villareal inteview 2003). For many, attending Arsenio's performances in the 1960s represented an opportunity to relive this past through dance and music. Yet Arsenio, unlike some of his contemporaries such as Celia Cruz, did not capitalize on the influx of Cuban political and economic exiles into south Florida and New York beginning in 1960; this was a population that especially thrived politically on idyllic memories of prerevolutionary Cuba (see Guevara 2003).

Figure 4.1. *Cumbanchando con Arsenio (Fiesta en Harlem)* (SMC-1074), LP cover, 1960.

Second, despite his difficulties in sustaining a lucrative performance career, Arsenio's conjunto recorded eight LPs between 1958 and 1968. SMC label owner Gabriel Oller, for whom Arsenio recorded *Cumbanchando con Arsenio (Fiesta en Harlem)* (Partying with Arsenio [Party in Harlem]) (SMC-1074) in 1960 (see Figure 4.1), stated that El Barrio was "the only place he felt comfortable in," suggesting that Arsenio and his audiences continued to favor his conjunto ensemble and son montuno style despite the new vogues (pachanga, boogaloo, and eventually salsa) in Latin popular music (Salazar 2002, p. 25). Unfortunately, there are no data on the numbers and demographics of his LP sales. What is clear is that Arsenio maintained an active recording career through 1968, even though his records were poorly marketed (if at all) by record executives.

The third and most striking anomaly involves the noticeable presence of Arsenio's music in the recorded repertories of early salsa musicians and his own professional demise in the presalsa performance landscape in New York. Clearly, his aging conjunto did not resonate with young salsa musicians and dancers as well as the burgeoning salsa recording industry. For instance, he was overlooked by the upstart salsa record label Fania and powerful musician's agent José Curbelo. Yet several of Fania's artists, like Johnny Pacheco and Larry Harlow, rerecorded many of Arsenio's songs of the 1940s and 1950s. Moreover, the central principles of his son montuno style directly shaped the musical styles of some of the most critically acclaimed salsa musicians of the 1960s and 1970s (see chapter 5).

To be sure, the Latin popular music industry was going through a period of transformation, marked by the decline of mambo big bands, the closing of the Palladium, and the international popularity of the Beatles and rock music (Rondón 1980, pp. 19–20). "Confusion," opines César Miguel Rondón, "was the dominant characteristic [of Latin popular music in the mid-1960s] and not even nostalgia could save it" (ibid., p. 20). In fact, nostalgia played important and distinct roles in shaping and giving meaning to the local and transnational landscapes of Latin popular music throughout the 1960s. Only by bringing local music histories into the historiographical narrative can we bring much-needed specification of Latin popular music of the 1960s and of the distinct roles nostalgia played in its local and transnational trajectories. As was the case in the mambo period of the 1950s, focusing on Arsenio's presence in New York in the 1960s forces us to treat early salsa music and his son montuno style not as musical repertories at different stages of development (i.e., modern versus traditional) but different musical repertories facing each other at the same time.

Arsenio Rodríguez in Chicago, Curaçao, and Los Angeles

Soon after arriving in Los Angeles around October 1964, Arsenio was interviewed by Colombian radio personality José Luís Logradia. In addition to discussing his long career as a composer and bandleader, Logradia asked Arsenio if he was working with any new rhythms, to which Arsenio replied:

> I'm struggling to introduce a new rhythm that I call "quindembo." But I've been unable to because here [the United States] one can't give it exposure by playing it live on radio like it was done in Cuba, like it's done in Colombia, like it's done in our countries. Here, almost everything that is played on radio is from a record. I haven't been able to give it much exposure. (Rodríguez interview 1964)

Arsenio had recorded *Quindembo* (CLT 7049) for Columbia Records in New York in 1963. Pedro Rosaly, A&R for Epic Records (a subsidiary of Columbia), contracted Arsenio to record his new style of music, which he called "quindembo."[2] In fact, the LP consists of nine arrangements of various Afro-Cuban folkloric chants and rhythms and three swing-son and swing-bolero hybrids. What was undoubtedly unprecedented for Arsenio, however, was the instrumentation that he used for this LP, which included tres (Arsenio), tumbadora (Kiki), bass (Evaristo Baro), flute and tenor saxophone (Mauricio Smith), alto saxophone (Walter Gene Jefferson), trap set (Evelio Quintero), percussion (José Valiente), and vocals (Raffi Martínez and Israel Berrios). Panamanian Mauricio Smith transcribed and helped arrange the music for the woodwinds. He recounted what his initial reaction was to the music: "When I heard it the first time it was kind of funny to me. But it was swinging. It was really swinging. . . . He didn't say anything about trying to crossover. He was just going for something totally different" (Smith interview 1999).

Despite its musical ingenuity, *Quindembo* does reflect a certain sense of indirection that as Rondón states characterized Latin popular music in general in the 1960s. Moreover, without the promotional backing from radio and Columbia Records, the LP failed commercially. Indeed, his conjunto's almost daily performances on Cuban radio during the 1940s had played a central role in the popularization of his music in the Caribbean. Although Arsenio's conjunto struggled to remain marketable stylistically in a Latin music industry already in flux, it continued to have an important impact on some local audiences who, no matter how small or peripheral to the dominant market, drew much pleasure and nostalgia from his conjunto's performances.

Chicago, 1958 and 1962

In early 1958 Arsenio recorded *Primitivo* (RST 2261) for the jazz label Roost. Teddy Reig, who owned Roost, had an interest in recording Afro-Cuban folkloric music. He developed a particular interest in Arsenio after having listened to his 1948 and 1950 recordings with SMC (SMC Pro Arte C-508). Reig made it a point to "get to know Arsenio" and eventually, in 1958, he contracted him to record an LP consisting of Cuban son music in its most basic or "primitive" style (Reig with Berger 1990, p. 65).[3] In fact, Arsenio prepared twelve new songs (six son montunos, four guaguancós, and one bolero) for a group consisting of two trumpets (Arsenio had not used the two-trumpet format to record since 1944), three vocalists, guitar, bass, tumbadora, timbales, and himself on tres. He did not use a piano or bongó.

In spring 1958 Arsenio, along with a similar version of the group on the *Primitivo* LP, went to Chicago, where they performed at the Teatro América, Teatro El Senate, El Capri, and other venues (Caraballoso interview 1999). The group included Arsenio (tres), Agustin Caraballoso (trumpet), Casamor (guitarist), Raúl Díaz (bass), Raúl Travieso (bongó), and Kiki (tumbadora). Local musicians from Chicago, including Puerto Rican percussionist Rafael "Congo" Castro, also performed with the group. The Teatro América put Arsenio's group on the same bill with famous Puerto Rican vocalist Daniel Santos, Los Codos (a Mexican duo comedian act), and Julio "Tito" Díaz, a Cuban folkloric dancer who danced Abakuá and other Afro-Cuban folkloric dance traditions. In addition to performing, Arsenio's group also accompanied Daniel Santos as well as Tito Díaz.

On his return to New York, Arsenio reconstituted his conjunto for performances and recording sessions. Between 1959 and 1960 his conjunto made a number of recordings, twelve of which Gabriel Oller released on *Cumbanchando con Arsenio: Fiesta en Harlem* (SMC-1074) (see Figure 4.1). Between 1960 and 1962 he recorded two additional LPs with the more reputable company Ansonia, which had a much broader catalog of internationally known artists.[4] Although many of these recordings feature aspects that are uncharacteristic to Arsenio's style (e.g., faster tempos, the absence of the bongó, and abbreviated diablo sections), some retain the central aspects of the son montuno style. "Hachero pa' un palo," for example, features the conventional schematic for the diablo section as well as bass patterns in contratiempo and a relatively slow or moderate tempo.

Arsenio returned to Chicago in 1962, performing again for the Puerto Rican and Cuban community in north Chicago. In addition to appearing in local nightclubs, like the Capri, he performed for local Puerto Rican civic and cultural events. Cuban folkloric dancer Tito Díaz had particularly fond memories of Arsenio, who offered to perform at his daughter's baptism, which was celebrated in the basement of Díaz's apartment house (see Figure 4.2). Arsenio had been close friends with Díaz's sister Eva Díaz back in Havana in the 1940s. And Díaz himself remembered regularly attending Arsenio's dances at black social clubs in Havana. He excitedly described what dancing to Arsenio's conjunto meant to him. "Son montuno allowed one to . . . execute steps from rumba. It had a much more solid [macho?] sound with the tumbadora, with the bongós. . . . He geared his music to the *clase típica cubana, al negro, típico cubano* [traditional Cuban class, the black, traditional Cuban]!" (Díaz interview, September 27, 2004). Because of the immense popularity of the youth-oriented pachanga music and dance style, it was particularly important for Díaz that Arsenio's group still performed son montuno. He affirmed that at this time Arsenio appealed to *contemporáneos* (contemporaries) and not to *la juventud* (the youth).

Arsenio i su conhunto in Curaçao, 1960

Prior to arriving in Willemstad, Curaçao, Arsenio's conjunto performed in San Juan and other cities in Puerto Rico from about March through May 1960. In San Juan the group performed at the Teatro Cobian and Tres Palmas as well as many private dances. The members of the conjunto included Frank Sufrón (vocals), Macucho (piano), Luís Berrios Seralta (trumpet), Raúl Travieso (bongó and timbales), and Kiki (tumbadora). By

FIGURE 4.2. Baptismal celebration at the residence of Julio "Tito" Díaz, Chicago, c. 1962. Raúl Díaz (playing bass) and Arsenio Rodríguez. *Source:* Photographer unknown; Tito Díaz, personal collection. Used by permission.

the end of May the conjunto had arrived in Willemstad, where they first performed in Cinelandia, a theater in the downtown section of the city, on May 31 and June 1 (see Figure 4.3). The conjunto then performed at the Roxy, another theater also located downtown, on June 2, returning to perform several more shows at Cinelandia on June 5 and 6 (see *Amigoe de Curaçao*, May 30 through June 4, 1960). In addition, the conjunto performed at several *hòfis* or outdoor gardens, which, like the cervecerías (outdoor beer gardens) in Havana, featured regular dances for all social classes.[5] Arsenio's conjunto performed at various hòfis including Chobolobo, Popo Rojer, and Kas di Pueblo. Although these performances were not advertised in local newspapers, they were publicized on radio and as a result well attended (Bernadina and Statie interview 2003).

As early as the mid-1940s, Cuban conjunto music and in particular Arsenio's son montuno style became extremely popular throughout the Netherlands Antilles. Curaçaoans credit sugarcane workers who migrated

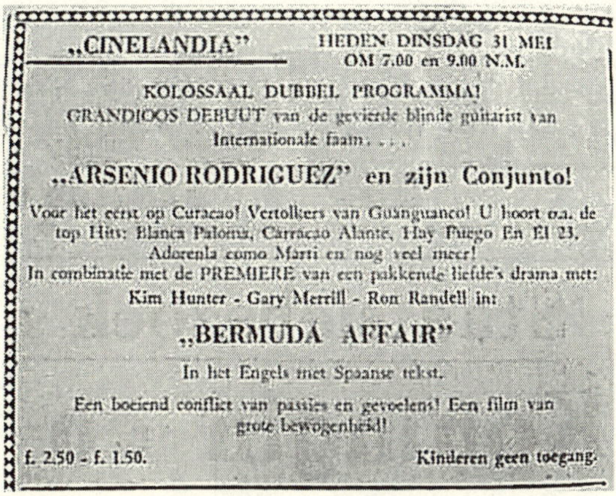

FIGURE 4.3. Advertisement for Arsenio Rodríguez y Su Conjunto at Cinelandia, Willemstad, Curaçao, 1960. *Source: Amigoe di Curaçao*, May 31, 1960.

to Cuba in the late 1910s and early 1920s for first bringing Cuban son music to Curaçao (Villareal interview 2003; Jansen interview 2003; Bernadina and Statie interview 2003; see also Benjamin 2002, pp. 58, 78).[6] In the 1940s, Curaçaoans enthusiastically tuned in to the performances of La Sonora Matancera, Conjunto Casino, and Arsenio's conjunto that were broadcasted live by Cuban radio stations Radio Progreso and Radio Salas (Suarez interview 2003). Local "conhuntos" also formed, playing both original son montunos (sung in Papiamento) as well as Cuban conjunto arrangements. Conhunto Típico Moderno, established in 1940, was by the late 1940s known for specializing in Arsenio's music (Jansen interview 2003; see also Martijn 1991, p. 145). Around the same time local DJs with early portable sound systems played almost exclusively Cuban conjunto recordings on 78 rpm discs for private parties.

By 1960, radio stations in the Netherlands Antilles continued to play these recordings on a regular basis. For example, in the months leading to Arsenio's arrival, Radio Kelkboom aired daily programs showcasing the recordings of Conjunto Casino, Chappottín y Sus Estrellas, Estrellas de Chocolate, and Arsenio Rodríguez y su Conjunto (see *Amigoe di Curacao*, January through May 1960). Curaçaoans were also listening to Arsenio's most recent recordings; "Hay fuego en el 23," "Blanca paloma," and "Adorenla como Martí" from his 1957 LP *Sabroso y caliente* (Puchito 586) were particularly popular at the time (Suarez interview 2003; Jansen interview 2003).

Arsenio's conjunto was invited to perform in Curaçao by Angel Job, also known as "El Gordito de Oro" (The Fat Golden Boy). Throughout the 1950s Job was a well-known dance promoter as well as a record store and dance club owner in Curaçao (Martijn 1991, pp. 162–65). By the late 1950s, Job began to contract Cuban conjuntos to perform in Curaçao, Bonaire, and Aruba. He usually contracted those conjuntos that were already on their way to neighboring Venezuela to perform (Villareal interview 2003). In April, one month before Arsenio's arrival, Job contracted Chappottín y Sus Estrellas to perform at the West End Theater, located in downtown Willemstad (*Amigoe di Curaçao*, April 27–29, 1960). In July he contracted Estrellas de Chocolate to perform at Cinelandia and the Roxy Theater (*Beurs en Nieuwsberichten*, July 11, 1960). For Arsenio's visit, he booked the conjunto to perform with three of the most popular Curaçaoan conhuntos at the time, Conhunto Melodia '57 at Popo Rojer and Conhunto San Jose and Estrellas de Caribe at Chobolobo (Villareal interview 2003; Jansen interview 2003).

In addition to performing, Job had Arsenio's conjunto record two sides of a 45 rpm record on his label, Grabaciones Angel Job. For the recording session Arsenio composed "Curazao" and "Son montuno en Curazao." In "Curazao," a bolero-cha, Arsenio praises Curaçao's natural tranquility and beauty, writing: "Parece que la naturaleza / ha dejado aquí su bendición / no conocen los quebrantos ni tormentos / vive todo el mundo de ilusión / Curazao eres un ejemplo" (it looks like nature / has left its blessing here / where misfortunes and storms are unknown / everyone lives in a dreamy state / Curaçao you are exemplary). "Son montuno en Curazao" further demonstrates his poetic flair for capturing the local *ambiente* (atmosphere), this time referencing the regular opening and closing of the Queen Emma Bridge, which connects the Punda and Otrabanda sections of Willemstad, to shipping: "Curazao jamas de olvidare, Curazao / se escucha perenemente / otra frase de protesta / 'ahora hay que dar la vuelta / porque ya abrieron el puente' " (Curaçao I'll never forget you / you always hear / another complaint / "now you have to go back / because they've opened the bridge").

Arsenio further charmed Curaçaoans by inviting the very popular conhunto singer Jose Casseres to sing lead on "Curazao."[7] Although this record was probably never heard outside of the Netherlands Antilles, it became very popular in Curaçao and was played regularly on the radio (Suárez interview 2003). Moreover, Arsenio's conjunto and son montuno style have had an exceptionally strong impact on popular music of the Netherlands Antilles. When I asked Richard Jansen, former manager of Conhunto San Jose, which was more popular in Curaçao, mambo or son montuno, he emphatically answered "son montuno, even now!... There's not much mambo here" (Jansen interview 2003). Its proximity to the Cuban national music industry (i.e., radio) and historical links with Cuba through migration certainly facilitated the extraordinary appeal to Cuban popular music and specifically son montuno that is still strong among Antillanos. But it is Arsenio who retains a unique place in the development of and historical discourse on popular music in the Netherlands Antilles. Only by tracing his performances, no matter how marginal or peripheral to New York or even Havana and San Juan do we learn of the extent to which his music continued to have significance for local audiences.

Starting over in Los Angeles, 1964–66

By October 1960, Arsenio's conjunto had returned to New York and resumed its intermittent performances at the Tropicana Club and the Club Cubano Inter-Americano in the South Bronx as well as in other locales throughout the city. His stagnant performances continued until 1964, when his conjunto was playing less than ever before. Alfredito Valdés Jr., who was Arsenio's regular pianist in the early 1960s, described his bleak situation:

> Arsenio's gigs didn't pay that much. He was struggling, trying to make ends meet and trying to keep the band together. And I helped. I was all over with the band, always with the band. We were doing the New York scene and we were getting the crumbs. We were getting something like $15 a gig, $10 a gig, you know, like shit! So to me it was a disappointment, which led to my disenchantment with New York and my decision to leave New York altogether. (Valdés 1999)

By fall 1964 Arsenio, too, had decided to move with Kiki to Los Angeles and join their brother Raúl, who had arrived the year before.

Arsenio and Kiki moved into an apartment in the Exposition area of South Los Angeles. In 1965 African Americans totaled about 81 percent of the population in South Los Angeles, whereas Latinos totaled only 10 percent (Fair Employment Practice Commission 1966). Los Angeles was a sprawling metropolis with no significant concentrations of Cubans and Puerto Ricans in any one neighborhood in the city. In addition, the Cuban and Puerto Rican population in Los Angeles paled in comparison to the city's dominant Mexican and Mexican American population (see Abler and Adams 1976; Boswell and Curtis 1984, p. 62; U.S. Commission on Civil Rights 1980, p. 19; Modarcs 1994, p. 49).[8] Nevertheless, Cuban dance music had been popular among Mexican and Mexican American audiences in Los Angeles since at least the 1930s (see Loza 1993, pp. 83–84). In the 1960s, Cuban music continued to be popular among Latinos in general, as seen in the number of local groups, headed by both Cuban and Mexican American bandleaders, who specialized in Cuban music as well as mambo and other Cuban-derived styles.[9]

Arsenio formed his new conjunto in Los Angeles soon after he arrived in fall 1964. There are some indications, however, that his conjunto did

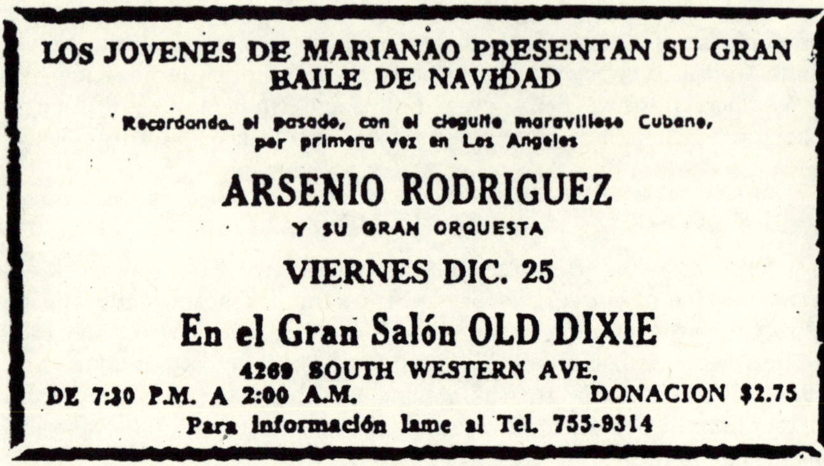

Figure 4.4. Advertisement for Arsenio Rodríguez y Su "Gran Orquesta" at the Old Dixie, Los Angeles, 1964. *Source: La Opinión*, December 23, 1964.

not include a trumpet section. According to Mexican bandleader Rudy Macías, for example, Arsenio's group did not have any trumpet players for one dance that both groups performed at in May 1965. In fact, for seven out of the ten dance numbers in his LP *Viva Arsenio!* (BLPS-216), which his conjunto recorded in New York in April 1966, Arsenio did not use any trumpets or even a piano. Apart from Arsenio and Kiki, Raúl could not remember the names of the other musicians who played with Arsenio in Los Angles, suggesting that the group was unstable in its personnel.

The conjunto's first performance in Los Angeles was on Christmas night 1964 at the unknown Old Dixie dance hall, which was located in Exposition, South Los Angeles. The advertisement (see Figure 4.4) announcing the dance in the local Spanish-language newspaper *La Opinión* included the heading "Los Jóvenes de Marianao Presentan Su Gran Baile de Navidad, Recordando el Pasado con el Cieguito Maravilloso Cubano, Por Primera Vez en Los Angeles" (The Youngsters of Marianao, Remembering the Past with the Marvelous Blind Cuban, for the First Time in Los Angeles) (*La Opinion*, December 23, 1964). Another advertisement, published a few days prior, stated that Arsenio was going to play "authentic music from the Caribbean as well as many of his newer songs," which probably included some from his recently released Ansonia LPs (*La Opinion*, December 20, 1964). Apparently, the promoters of the dance—probably Arsenio himself—wanted to evoke Havana of the 1940s when his conjunto was at its height in popularity performing for mostly black social clubs. Of course, most non-Cuban Latinos would have been unaware of this milieu and its importance to Arsenio's music. As a result, the advertisements and Arsenio's name only attracted a small, mostly Cuban audience. Several of those Cubans who attended his performance notified Pedro Ferro, a black Cuban leader of the local Cuban exile community, of Arsenio's modest debut and encouraged him to help the elder composer and musician market himself to a broader audience (Ferro interview, September 2, 1997). Ferro, who indeed was an admirer of Arsenio and whose cousin, Papa Kila, was Arsenio's bongó player in the 1940s, sympathized with his difficult situation and agreed to be his manager.

Despite the fact that he had never managed a musical group, Ferro succeeded in getting contracts for Arsenio's conjunto in prominent locales by drawing on contacts he had made as a political leader in the local Cuban and Latino community. Evidently, these included dance promoters and club owners and not other local Cuban social and cultural leaders. The conjunto's first two performances under Ferro's management took place in February 1965 at the Paramount Ballroom, in East Los Angeles, and the little-known Blarney's Castle Ballroom, just north of Koreatown. This latter show included Cuban Mariano Mercerón's band, Mexican crooner Alberto Vázquez, and cumbia bandleader Tony Camargo. Later that month Arsenio's conjunto performed at the popular Hollywood Palladium. The bill included the headliner Alberto Vázquez and four local Cuban music groups, led by René Touzet, René Bloch, Albertico Pérez, and Rudy Macías. The promoters and MCs of this dance, Antonio de Marco and his wife, Rita, were Ferro's friends and apparently agreed to add Arsenio's conjunto to the program. Ferro also convinced another acquaintance of his, Frank Fauce, to include the conjunto as part of the week's entertainment at the popular Million Dollar Theater in downtown (*La Opinion*, March 21, 1965). Others in the variety show included Hermanos Martínez Gil and Lilia Guizar (Tito Guizar's daughter). According to one reviewer, Arsenio's conjunto "performs Afro-Cuban music excellently. The audience enjoys itself and applauds after every one of his numbers" (*La Opinion*, March 24, 1965). At the same time, the conjunto also performed nightly for two weeks at Jackie Thorne's Virginia's nightclub, just west of the Million Dollar in the Westlake area of downtown (Ferro interviews 1997 and October 2000).

Ferro also succeeded in engaging Arsenio's group in the most popular hotel dance halls in downtown. On April 17, 1965, the group performed for promoter Gabby Cancel's Spring Dance at the Statler Hotel, the entertainment of which included two other dance bands along with Puerto Rican singer Hilda Morales (*La Opinion*, April 15, 16, 1965). Then, on May 7 and 8, Arsenio's group participated in a show that was promoted as a battle between La Sonora Santanera from Mexico City, Arsenio

Rodríguez from Cuba, and Rudy Macías from Los Angeles, at the Hotel Alexandria (*La Opinion*, May 6, 1965; Macías interview 1999; Ferro interviews, September 2, 1997 and October 20, 2000). Established in 1956 in Mexico City, La Sonora Santanera was a Cuban-type conjunto that derived its name and style from La Sonora Matancera's.[10] In the months prior to and following its battle with Arsenio's group, Santanera performed in Los Angeles, San Francisco, Chicago, and throughout the Southwest United States as well as in Mexico and Central and South America (*La Opinion*, June 7, 1964, and June 13, 1965).

Arsenio's recognition (much less popularity) among the largely Mexican audience paled in comparison with Santanera's. In addition, because the bands were scheduled to perform practically simultaneously in adjacent ballrooms inside the hotel, Arsenio's performance was not well attended. He thus decided to take things into his own hands, attempting to draw people from Santanera's audience into his ballroom. Macías, who had just finished his set and entered the ballroom where Santanera was playing, described what happened next:

> We were there for about five minutes. All of a sudden, I [heard] another rhythm from the [back] of the ballroom.... Little by little, the music was getting closer and closer, and... here comes Arsenio, his brother, and the rest of the musicians [playing a conga]. Everybody stopped and looked at them. Then, the director of Santanera just stopped the music completely. And then when [Arsenio] came to the bandstand he said, "Now that the three of us are playing here, La Sonora Santanera, Rudy Macías, and I, we want to welcome you to Los Angeles. An applause for La Santanera!" Everybody [applauded] *y empezó a tocar* [and he began to play] [on his way] back to his ballroom. Some of the people followed him to the ballroom. But I think he used a little gimmick, [thinking], "I'm gonna bring some of their people over here." And he did. It was funny. (Macías interview 1999)

The fact that through Pedro Ferro's work Arsenio was contracted to perform at the Million Dollar and with La Sonora Santanera in the first place suggests that awareness of him and his music did extend, however tenuously, into the Mexican population of Los Angeles.

Following the Santanera dance, Arsenio began an eight-month contract, performing every weekend through December 1965 at the Paramount Ballroom in East Los Angeles (Ferro interviews 1997; see *La Opinion*, May through December 1965). Audiences from other parts of the city avoided the Paramount because of the area's notoriety. Nevertheless, both Arsenio and Albertico Pérez's groups performed Cuban music for a local audience made up of mostly Mexican Americans but that included Puerto Ricans, Cubans, and some South Americans. Arsenio's group managed to impress Ray Rodríguez, whose brother Mitch owned the Paramount Ballroom. Ray was a local dance promoter who engaged mostly Mexican and Mexican American rock and pop bands for the Mexican and Mexican American populations in East Los Angeles and downtown. Ray contracted Arsenio for two events. The first, which took place on June 13, 1965, was promoted as another "mano a mano," this time, however, between Arsenio and Tito Puente at the Hollywood Palladium (*La Opinion*, June 11, 12, 1965). The bill included Mexican crooner Rubén Reyes and the East Los Angeles rock band Thee Midniters, both of whom were extremely popular among local Mexicans and Mexican Americans (see Loza 1993, pp. 78–79, 99–102).

Tito Puente had developed a strong following among Mexican Americans. According to Rudy Macías, for example, although Mexicans tended to favor the mambo style of Pérez Prado, Mexican Americans favored the "more jazzy, more Americanized" style of Tito Puente and Tito Rodríguez (Macías interview 1999; see also Loza 1993, p. 83). Evidently, Arsenio's style did not resonate as much with either group. Ray engaged Arsenio once more for a dance on New Year's Eve 1965 at the Rodger Young Ballroom in downtown (*La Opinion*, December 31, 1965). Again, Arsenio's group was billed with a Mexican group, Los Moonlights, and a Mexican American rock band, Los Románticos. This performance was probably his last before leaving for New York in early 1966.

Through his contacts and diligence, Ferro succeeded in getting Arsenio's group to perform in Los Angeles's most prominent locations, namely, the Hollywood Palladium and the Million Dollar Theater. As one musician noted, "In order to get into the Million Dollar, you needed connections" (Moran interview 1997). Soon, though, Arsenio's performances were relegated to the Paramount Ballroom, a local and peripheral location compared to places in downtown and Hollywood. Ultimately, his style and repertory did not permit him to successfully maintain a performance career among Los Angeles's mostly Mexican and Mexican American Latin dance music audience or in its nationally diverse Latin social club milieu.

For example, Cuban singer and bandleader Dandy Beltrán explained: "[In Los Angeles] not everyone is Cuban and 90 percent of the people who like Arsenio's music are Cubans, Puerto Ricans, but not South Americans. They listen to that music and they don't understand exactly what it is. And, as it is here, the Latino is so divided" (Beltrán interview 1996). Mexican bandleader Rudy Macías also noted that Arsenio's style was "entirely different; it was more like real Cuban style, old Cuban style" (Macías interview 1999). When I asked him if he thought Arsenio was "out of place" in Los Angeles, Macías responded: "I don't think the Mexican-American people went for his style because it wasn't too popular here. See, it all depends what they play over the radio. . . . Arsenio had his own crowd, let's put it that way, like any other band. . . . So, here in L.A. there's a crowd for everybody and I'm sure that there were people that went for his style" (ibid.). In René Touzet's opinion, however, Arsenio "did not make a big hit in Los Angeles," stressing, for example, that the audience that Arsenio evidently had at the Paramount Ballroom represented a distinct and marginal section of the broader Latin dance music audience (Touzet interview 2000). When asked about the difficulties that Arsenio encountered in Los Angeles, his manager Pedro Ferro answered: "Logically, for example, [Los Angeles] was a large Mexican market, a large market for René Touzet—he had a great orchestra—and, more than anything else, [a large market for] Mexican music. And all of the nightclubs were Mexican. Cubans didn't have popular nightclubs" (Ferro interview, September 4, 1997). Hence, although there was a market for "Cuban dance music" among, in particular, Mexicans and Mexican Americans, it was the more Americanized, commercialized, or jazz-oriented styles that Touzet and Latin bands from New York, like Tito Puente's, performed that appealed to the broader Latino population of Los Angeles (Boulong interview 2000; Macías interview 1999; Torres interview 2000).

Repertory, in addition to style, was another important factor in Arsenio's modest performance career in Los Angeles. Latin American social clubs constituted an important market for local Latin dance bands. The addition of songs from respective regional repertories, in addition to Cuban and Cuban-derived dance music, however, was obligatory. Although Arsenio probably performed versions of the Mexican standards "La bamba" and "Cielito lindo" (he adapted these two songs into his son montuno style and recorded them for his 1966 LP *Viva Arsenio!*) in Los Angeles, there is no evidence that he added other transnational Latin styles, such as cumbia, to his repertory. Neither is there evidence that he performed for any Latin American social clubs in Los Angeles, including the few Cuban ones. In contrast, those bands that reached out to the Latin American population, even in their lyrics, increased their marketability. Examples include Dandy Beltrán's "La cumbia de Ecuador" and La Típica Tropical's "Guatemala," both of which were tremendously popular among Ecuadorians and Guatemalans, respectively (Moran interview 1997). Nicaraguan pianist Rocky Moran, who played piano for Arsenio briefly in 1969, commented: "I'm sure if Arsenio would have come up with something like that, but he refused. He wanted to stay with his same thing [son montuno]. Can't blame [him], but it's a gimmick" (Moran interview 1997).

Arsenio's activities in the late 1950s and early 1960s provide important insight into the complex nature of the Latin or presalsa music industry and the diverse Cuban music landscapes across the Caribbean and the United States. Clearly, his conjunto continued to record and perform, whether for local civic and baptismal celebrations in north Chicago, outdoor social dances in Curaçao, or weekend dances in East Los Angeles. Because these locations were located outside of the dominant center of the presalsa music industry (i.e., New York), they have been overlooked by salsa music historians and scholars. Even now, scholarly attention on salsa continues to be focused on the local centers (Cali, San Juan, New York, Caracas) of the transnational salsa recording industry, whereas a critical history of salsa's emergence in New York in the 1960s has yet to be undertaken.[11] Like Arsenio's own relationship with the Latin or presalsa music industry in New York, these cities and the audiences that went to his performances were marginal in terms of the industry's initial regional reach and targeted age.

Nostalgia, Exile Politics, and the Presalsa Milieu in New York City

From 1959 to 1972, close to 500,000 Cubans fled Fidel Castro's communist Cuba and migrated to the United States. Although the overwhelming majority of these migrants settled in south Florida, roughly 9 percent migrated to New York City, nearly doubling the Cuban population there from 42,694 in 1960 to 84,179 in 1970 (Aguire 1976, p. 103; Boswell and Curtis 1983, p. 63; Haslip-Viera 1993, pp. 14–20). Nevertheless, despite the notable increase in the Cuban population in the greater New York City area (including northern New Jersey), the number and quality of performances of Arsenio's conjunto, as has been already established, continued to decrease through the 1960s. This anomaly might be explained by his relationship to the majority of Cuban exiles in terms of race, political ideology, and his own migration experience.

Although the migrant population became more representative of Cuba's occupational distribution with every yearly influx, it became increasingly white. Benigno Aguire explains that the early overrepresentation of white middle- and upper-class migrants from 1959 to 1965 facilitated a subsequent chain migration through extended family networks after the issuance of the 1965 Memorandum of Understanding, which gave priority to potential migrants with relatives in the United States (see Aguire 1976; Boswell and Curtis 1984, p. 103). As a result, potential black Cuban migrants, lacking the required sponsorship of close relatives living in the United States, were systematically excluded. Those black Cubans who were able to migrate tended to reside in the Northeast United States, whereas a majority of white Cubans settled in the Southern states. As Aguire shows, despite the idyllic perception of pre-1959 race relations in Cuba that white migrants tended to have, black Cubans were nevertheless discriminated against by and largely isolated from the larger white Cuban community. For example, one study concluded that "Within the Cuban community [in Miami], black Cubans seem to be a highly at-risk group. Housing and housing discrimination appear to be unsolved problems for this group even in areas which are predominantly Cuban" (Cortes 1980, p. viii).[12]

Such studies suggest that the dominant attitudes that shaped race relations in Cuba were transplanted and magnified in the United States. In addition, because smaller numbers of the black working-class population, which had constituted Arsenio's primary audience in Havana in the 1940s, participated less in the migration through the 1960s, it follows then that Arsenio's audience remained largely limited to pre-1959 Cuban immigrants and hence virtually nonexistent in Miami. Yet Cuban musicians of color such as Celia Cruz, Olga Guillot, and Rolando La Serie not only performed frequently in Miami, Los Angeles, and New York but also remained viable recording artists. Celia Cruz's career in the United States is especially extraordinary. Although she reached the apex of her popularity after the 1960s, Cruz's continued international success in the late 1960s was facilitated by her recordings with Tito Puente in New York and Memo Salamanca in Mexico City. In addition, her agent, José Curbelo, was instrumental in booking Cruz in the most prestigious venues in the country, including the Million Dollar Theater and Hollywood Palladium in Los Angeles and the Montmartre in Miami. In June 1965 the Teatro Radiocentro of Miami presented a concert titled Artistas cubanos en el exilio (Cuban Artists in Exile) featuring Rolando La Serie, Celia Cruz, Orlando Vallejo, Olga Guillot, Rosendo Rosell, and others (Ramírez Bedoya 1998, p. 163). At the same time, Arsenio's conjunto was performing at the Paramount Ballroom in East Los Angeles.

In Raúl's opinion, Arsenio's commitment to remain nonaffiliated politically, as he had been in Havana during the 1940s, contributed to his isolation from the post-1959 Cuban migration population in New York, Los Angeles, as well as in Miami (Raúl Travieso interview, June 19, 1996). Furthermore, because Arsenio and his brothers Kiki and Raúl had immigrated to New York in 1950, perhaps they could not fully empathize with the post-1959 Cuban migration experience, which was instigated under tragic and bitter circumstances. In contrast, Celia Cruz had experienced that migration process firsthand, having defected from Cuba while touring with La Sonora Matancera in Mexico in 1960. Cruz was an outspoken critic of Fidel Castro and often expressed this and her nostalgia for the idyllic Cuba of the past in her music, all of which made her a beloved spokesperson for the Cuban exile population. In contrast Arsenio continued to speak out in his songs against racism as experienced by all populations of African descent (see chapter 1). Although he did compose songs about the political situation in Cuba (e.g., "Cuba llora"), he never expressed his support for any one political ideology or party, nor did he ever entertain a nostalgic yearning for an imagined romanticized past that in fact was significantly defined by racial discrimination for Arsenio and many other black Cubans (see chapter 2).

The Emergence of the Presalsa Music Industry

When Arsenio returned to New York from Los Angeles in spring 1966, the Latin dance music milieu must have seemed very promising to him. For one, Cuban conjunto-based groups were now replacing mambo big bands and charangas of the pachanga craze of the early 1960s. Eddie Palmieri's La Perfecta was one of the first conjunto-based groups to form in the 1960s. After some variation in its instrumentation, La Perfecta eventually settled as a conjunto-style ensemble with two trombones and one flute in place of the conventional three or four trumpets. This group was followed by Johnny Pacheco's and Larry Harlow's conjuntos, the latter of which also included trombones. These and other early salsa groups were performing regularly at cabarets and hotels in Manhattan and dance halls in the South Bronx and Brooklyn. The Club Caborrojeño in Manhattan and the Bronx Casino in the South Bronx were two particularly prominent locales that offered live music on a weekly basis.

Originally a Puerto Rican regional social club established in the 1920s, the Club Caborrojeño by the 1960s had become a dance hall that presented dances every weekend, including Sunday matinees, for a primarily older Puerto Rican audience (David Carp, personal communication). In 1968 and early 1969, the Club Caborrojeño featured regular performances by veteran artists Yayo el Indio, Daniel Santos, and Tito Puente as well as popular boogaloo performers Richie Ray, Joe Cuba, and Pete Rodríguez. Meanwhile, the Bronx Casino also presented dances every weekend, catering to a primarily younger audience, however. Regular performers at the Bronx Casino included Puerto Rican stars Ismael Rivera and Cortijo, boogaloo stars Pete Rodríguez and Richie Ray, and future salsa stars Johnny Pacheco, Eddie Palmieri, Ray Barretto, Larry Harlow, and El Gran Combo de Puerto Rico.

Many of these newly formed and future salsa groups included in their repertories a significant number of tunes that were originally recorded by La Sonora Matancera, Conjunto Casino, as well as Arsenio's conjunto in the 1940s and 1950s. Despite this renaissance of Cuban conjunto music, however, Arsenio's reorganized conjunto performed sparingly at the Bronx Casino and the Club Caborrojeño. He did, however, participate in the Tico-Alegre Anniversary Dance on May 4, 1968, at the Manhattan

Center in Manhattan. The show, which featured Tito Puente, Eddie Palmieri, Machito, Ray Barretto, Joe Cuba, Pete Rodríguez, Celia Cruz, Johnny Pacheco, Charlie Palmieri, and Cachao, was broadcasted live by Symphony Sid on WEVD (*Latin New York* 1/4 March 1968, pp. 10–13; *El Diario-La Prensa*, May 5, 1968). A contemporary of Arsenio's, Graciela Pérez (Machito's sister and covocalist), articulated the seemingly conflicting nature of the significance of his music in and his relative exclusion from the emerging salsa milieu: "Larry Harlow copied him. Pacheco copied him too, in the beginning. So, if they played like Arsenio Rodríguez, why then wasn't Arsenio Rodríguez able to play here [in New York City]? ... In Cuba he was very good. So, then, why would other musicians copy and play his style if he wasn't good?" (Pérez interview 1998).

There are several interrelated reasons why Arsenio, unlike some of his contemporaries, did not become a more active participant in the emergence of the salsa industry in New York. Foremost was his lack of a support system. In 1968 José Curbelo, cofounder of the booking agency Alpha Artists of America, printed advertisements listing the artists and groups that were signed with his agency (*Latin New York*, January and March 1968). His top three artists, whose names appear in bold type, were Tito Puente, Eddie Palmieri, and Ricardo Ray. Other artists, listed below, from the top down include Machito, Celia Cruz, Cortijo, Larry Harlow, Joe Bataan, Miguelito Valdés, Orlando Marin, Willie Rosario, La Sonora Matancera, and Arsenio Rodríguez. Despite signing Arsenio to his agency, Curbelo did little to support his conjunto's performance career and hence increase his visibility among audiences, record buyers, and the press. Israel Berrios, who was Arsenio's second voice and guitarist from 1955 to 1968, recounted, "The impresarios of the day had a select group [of bandleaders]. ... There was one impresario named José Curbelo. That man always had an excuse so that Arsenio wouldn't play" (Berrios interview, October 11, 1998).

From the late 1950s through the 1960s, José Curbelo had a near monopoly on the top veteran and new Latin acts in New York and exercised almost complete control over each artist's prospects for work. Puchi Boulong, who started playing trumpet professionally with Arsenio's conjunto around 1954 and later played in Tito Puente's band from 1959 to 1970, compared Curbelo's power at that time with that of the late salsa mogul Ralph Mercado, saying that Curbelo "had some places so sewed up, he almost dictated who played where. And [he controlled] the better places because he had the better bands" (Boulong interview 2000). He was a shrewd businessman, a tough negotiator, and very powerful in the Latin music industry, and these qualities were responsible for the success that some of his veteran acts continued to have through the 1960s (David Carp, personal communication).

For example, Miguelito Valdés toured Panama with Machito's big band in 1966, hosted his own Thursday night variety show on television in the New York area in 1968, and continued to perform regularly in nightclubs and dance halls in New York and Los Angeles (*El Diario-La Prensa*, March 11, 1966, January 5, 19, 1968, and February 22, 1968). In addition to performing regularly at the Club Caborrojeño, Tito Puente hosted his own biweekly Sunday night variety show, called *El Mundo Latino de Tito Puente* (Tito Puente's Latin World), on television in early 1968 (*El Diario-La Prensa*, December 22, 1967). The show, which was produced by Curbelo, featured a wide variety of entertainers and musicians, such as Xavier Cugat and Alpha Artist Richie Ray (*El Diario-La Prensa*, January 5, 1968, and February 11, 1968). Finally, Celia Cruz, known as the queen of the guaracha, successfully toured throughout Mexico in 1967 (*El Diario-La Prensa*, January 22, 1968).[13]

In contrast, Curbelo apparently set out to impede Arsenio's performance career as Berrios suggested.[14] Curbelo may have had personal reasons for his contempt for Arsenio; as Berrios and others insinuated, racism may have been one factor. For example, some musicians felt that Puente and Tito Rodríguez received preferential treatment by Curbelo because of the bandleaders' lighter skin color. As flautist Mauricio Smith explained: "Machito only got token gigs from José Curbelo. He was pushing Tito Puente and Tito Rodríguez, the lighter bands. But the black artists? Forget it. Black musicians? Very, very little. He had the power, he had the connections" (Smith interview 1999).[15] Puchi Boulong, who played with both Machito and Puente's bands, added: "From what I felt, [Machito] couldn't have gotten some of the gigs [that Puente got] even though it was a great band ... When I played with Tito, there was a difference. We played some of the same places with Machito, but I felt in traveling especially, when we went out of town, we went to places where I never saw Machito" (Boulong interview 2000). Finally, Graciela Pérez, Machito's sister and vocalist, remembered: "The only thing I can tell you is many people tried to do him [Arsenio] harm, a lot of jealousy.... After he started to have difficulty he did anything to work; this is after he had a lot of success when he first arrived" (Pérez interview 1998). Cuban vocalist Julián Cabrera, who left Havana and moved to New York City in 1959, stated: "Well, they [i.e., impresarios] closed him out.... He played, but he didn't have recognition like he once had. He played mostly in the Bronx, because there was a lot of racism here," presumably referring to Manhattan (Cabrera interview 1998).

Age and image were also important factors. When Johnny Pacheco, for example, formed his conjunto in 1964 he had in mind "a younger looking group [that was] thin." Also, he was attracted to his lead vocalist Pete "El Conde" Rodríguez's ability to sing and dance (Pacheco interview 1997).

Accordingly, the earliest recording artists on Massucci and Pacheco's Fania label—Larry Harlow, Ray Barretto, and Willie Colón—in fact led young groups with dynamic, thin, and talented front men—Ismael Miranda, Adalberto Santiago, and Hector Lavóe. In contrast, Arsenio had kept the same core of now middle-aged musicians—Julián Llanos, Israel Berrios, Marcelino Guerra, Agustin Caraballoso, and Kiki—that had been members of his conjuntos in the 1940s in Havana or since the 1950s in New York. Despite its indebtedness to Cuban conjunto music of the 1940s and 1950s, the early salsa music scene in New York was indeed a youth music culture. Even the Club Cubano Inter-Americano, whose directors provided regular employment for Arsenio's conjunto through the 1950s and early 1960s, started to hire younger groups, such as Johnny Pacheco's, Larry Harlow's, Ray Barretto's, Willie Rosario's, Orquesta Típica Novel, and Orquesta Broadway more regularly than Arsenio's in the late 1960s.[16] Evidently, the social club's directors, who were Arsenio's contemporaries in age, began to hire groups who would attract younger dancers to its dances and social functions.

Such power networks, coupled with racism, age, and image contributed to the decline in his performance career at a time when younger musicians were noticeably drawing from his recorded repertory. Some musicians, however, did try to make a difference. Phil Newsum, who was a member of Larry Harlow's group, approached Johnny Pacheco with an idea to record an LP with Arsenio for Fania:

> I went to Johnny Pacheco one night and I said, "Gees, Johnny, you know what you ought to do? You got to get the money together, get all of Arsenio's old charts, hire a bunch of guys, bring Arsenio and his brother . . . in the studio and rerecord all of his best tunes with a good modern band, a collection of all of his music before it's all gone, before everybody dies." [Johnny] didn't seem to be particularly interested in it. I thought as an archive it would've been an enormously valuable piece of work. (Newsum interview 2001)

But to no avail. Soon after Arsenio's death in 1970, however, Newsum participated in Larry Harlow's *Tribute to Arsenio* (SLP 00404), recorded with Fania. In the end Israel "Cachao" López, who left Cuba and moved to New York in 1962, offered the following concise explanation:

> Although much of his music has been recorded and some have rendered him tributes, he was never recognized in the United States nor did he have the success he had in Cuba, because in order for a musician to distinguish himself in New York in that era he had to polish the music and have someone to support him. Arsenio's image didn't sell. He was like a museum piece and it was more profitable to loot his music than to support him. That's the truth. (Padura Fuentes 1997, pp. 138–39)

Arsenio's experience in the final years of his life in New York contradicts certain representations of salsa history that have been taken for granted and hence become canonic in much of the salsa literature. For example, in his seminal history of salsa, César Miguel Rondón situates the "definitive" and "authentic" formation of salsa's musical style, values, and social significance in the context of the "barrio Latino de Nueva York," stating that salsa is a reflection of the "violence" and "bitterness" of the "barrio" (see Rondón 1980, pp. 26–34). He adds: "All of them [i.e., Latinos of New York] form one single community, a community united by a cultural root [i.e., Caribbean music, most notably Cuban *son*] that is common to and identical in all of these people" (ibid., p. 30). Similarly, other writers have stated that salsa music assumed an identity representing the cultural symbols, beliefs, and values of all New York Latinos and Latin culture, hence adding to the construction of a homogenous Latino barrio unaffected by commercial and social issues such as materialism and intra-Latino racism (e.g., Baron 1977, pp. 216–17; Padilla 1989, pp. 43–44). Issues of race, age, image, and commercial power persisted and in fact contributed to the exclusion of one of salsa's own musical founders.

Final Performances and Death in Los Angeles

Arsenio returned to Los Angeles in 1969 and formed a new conjunto, many of the members of which were Cuban, including vocalists Manolo Suárez and Oscar López (López interview 2000). Suárez first met and occasionally performed with Arsenio in 1940, when both were performing at the cabaret Sans Souci in Havana. López, who started to sing professionally with Cuban groups in Mexico City in the early 1950s, was a young adult in Havana during the 1940s when he regularly attended dances at Social Club Buena Vista, Marianao Social, and other black social clubs where Arsenio's conjunto performed regularly. Arsenio also had two Puerto Rican musicians, guitarist and singer Frank "El Morro" and bassist Gene Morales. Finally, unlike his first conjunto or sexteto in 1965, he had a three-trumpet section, the musicians of which he hired on a regular basis from the musician's union.

As before, Arsenio's conjunto was not working very often. Pedro Ferro, who had been his manager in 1965, was now unable to work for Arsenio full-time because of his other responsibilities, including his role as a leader of the Cuban exile community in Los Angeles (Ferro interview, September 2, 1997). Nevertheless, he did try to find Arsenio work, free of charge, when time allowed. In any event Arsenio, it seemed, had resigned himself to a slower-paced performance schedule. In characterizing this final period of his career, Alfredito Valdés Jr. stated that "he was already in his retirement years, looking to live more peacefully, and he was at an advanced age. He wasn't understood here [New York City] much less over there [Los Angeles]" (Valdés interview 1997). Pianists Mark Levine and Rocky Moran, both of whom also had very brief stints with the conjunto at this time, added that the Latin music establishment as well as dancers and even most musicians in Los Angeles in the late 1960s were indifferent to Arsenio and his music (Levine interview 1997; Moran interview 1997).

Because of Ferro's unavailability, Arsenio worked as his own agent. It is unclear whether the conjunto performed that summer. Finally, it played its first significant dance on October 11, 1969, not in Los Angeles, however, but at the Jacktar Hotel in San Francisco.[17] The next night the conjunto performed in Oakland. According to Oscar López, who was the conjunto's lead singer, these dances were well attended by a diverse audience, including Cubans and Puerto Ricans. The repertory consisted of primarily Arsenio's hits from Cuba, including the boleros "La vida es un sueño" (Life Is a Dream), "La última carta" (The Final Letter), and "Triste lucha" (Sad Battle) and the afrocubano "Bruca maniguá" (López interview 2000). The conjunto's first advertised performance in Los Angeles did not take place until New Year's Eve 1969. According to the advertisement, this performance was the debut of the "new conjunto." It took place at the Embassy Auditorium downtown and was apparently organized and promoted by Arsenio and Kiki themselves.

After its New Year's Eve gig, Arsenio's conjunto did not have any performances that were advertised in *La Opinión* until September 1970, when it performed at Casa Caribe restaurant in south central Los Angeles. From October 23 to November 20 the conjunto performed on Friday nights at La Canasta Restaurant in Silver Lake, north of downtown. Then, on November 27, Arsenio performed for the Club Alianza Hispanoamericana at the Hotel Clark in downtown. This was probably his last public performance.

Despite the lackluster quality of his conjunto's gigs, Arsenio had, according to several informants, secured a contract to record an LP in 1970. Israel Berrios remembers that he began to rehearse the numbers with Arsenio for this new LP in New York, but Arsenio had to return to Los Angeles to meet some contractual responsibilities, perhaps the gigs in San Francisco and Oakland in October 1969 (Berrios interview, October 11, 1998). Arsenio told Berrios that he would return at the end of 1970 to do the recordings. Alfonso "El Panameño" Joseph, who was Arsenio's bassist in New York through most of the 1960s, remembers that Arsenio returned to New York for about one week in early December 1970, during which time he tried to convince El Panameño to return to Los Angeles with him to record an LP there. El Panameño told Arsenio that he would think it over and call him when he returned to Los Angeles (Joseph interview 2001).

Finally, Oscar López also remembers that Arsenio's conjunto was to record an LP in Los Angeles, but on the day of the recording officials from Los Angeles's Musician's Union (Local 47) canceled the session because Arsenio had not paid his union dues (López interview 2000). According to Berrios, the material that Arsenio was rehearsing to record included some songs by Ernesto Lecuona, but El Panameño remembers that they had rehearsed new material that he and Arsenio had composed together. Although the dates and circumstances of these musicians' recollections do not coincide perfectly, it is clear that sometime within the last two years of his life Arsenio was planning to record another LP.

During the week of December 21, 1970, Arsenio was rehearsing with the conjunto to perform on New Year's Eve at Virginia's, close to downtown Los Angeles (Raúl Travieso interview, June 19, 1996). On Monday, December 28, however, Arsenio suffered a fatal stroke and was taken to Queen of Angeles Hospital.[18] The stroke was brought on by Arsenio's diabetes, which he had been suffering from since at least the early 1960s. Less than two days after he suffered the stroke, Arsenio stopped breathing and was pronounced dead at 1:43 a.m., Wednesday, December 30, 1970. Immediately following Arsenio's death, Raúl made arrangements to have Arsenio's body buried at Rosedale Cemetery in Los Angeles (Raúl Travieso interview, April 5, 1997). But Arsenio's estranged wife, Anadina Rodríguez, who flew to Los Angeles from New York on hearing the news of his death, requested that his body be taken to New York to be buried. Angered over her insistence that his body be flown to New York, Raúl let her take Arsenio's body, refusing to pay for the transfer fees. On Sunday, January 3, 1971, Arsenio's body was flown to New York. His wake took place two days later at Manhattan North Chapels on 107th Street and Amsterdam Avenue, where, according to historian Max Salazar, who was present, funds were solicited by Anadina from the mourners to bury his body and presumably to pay for the transfer fees (Salazar 1994, p. 17). Arsenio's body was eventually laid to rest at Ferncliff Cemetery in Hartsdale, Westchester County, New York, on January 6, 1971.

As I mentioned at the beginning of this chapter, Arsenio's financial situation in the final years of his life has been the subject of much speculation, characterized mostly by allegations of poverty. The circumstances surrounding his burial in New York undoubtedly contributed to this perception. In stressing that Anadina's solicitation for money to bury Arsenio's body was unnecessary because he had already paid for his grave in Los Angeles, Raúl, I believe, was trying to correct the impression that Arsenio left no money for his wife to bury him. Clearly, Arsenio was not wealthy, but as Mario Bauzá noted, "the royalties from his compositions was enough for him to live well, and it's a myth that he died poor and forgotten, a total lie" (Padura Fuentes 1997, pp. 41–42). Indeed, dozens of his songs were being recorded by salsa musicians alone in New York. Another popular myth involves Arsenio's grave site. According to many of Arsenio's fans, his grave site has been "abandoned." Although his grave site is unmarked, lacking a headstone, Ferncliff Cemetery is in fact a prestigious and extremely well-kept cemetery where other notables such as Malcolm X, Thelonious Monk, and Paul Robeson are buried.

Some time around 1960, Arsenio and Kiki became Jehovah's Witnesses. Agustin Caraballoso (who was one of Arsenio's trumpet players) and Bobby Rodríguez (who was Tito Puente's bass player), both of whom had become Jehovah's Witnesses around 1959, were the first to give Arsenio and Kiki Bible study. Before Arsenio's and Kiki's conversions, however, they organized Santería ceremonies. For instance, on December 4, 1959, Arsenio and his wife Emma Lucía Martínez hosted a celebration for Changó, his *santo*, in their apartment in East Harlem (*La Prensa*, December 14, 1959). Although he never had Changó "made" (i.e., he never became an official initiate of the religion), Arsenio believed, according to his niece Xiomara (Kiki's daughter), that "he was born [with Changó], so he didn't need to get crowned" and "he had the blessings from the santos" (Xiomara Travieso interview 1999). Arsenio and Kiki also practiced Palo Monte, the Congo-derived religion taught to them by their grandfather (see chapter 1). As Xiomara remembers, "I think he liked that [Palo Monte] more than Santería because I remember as a child when we lived on Tinton Avenue [in the South Bronx] I would see him work *con el caldero* [with the cauldron (where the spirit resides)] that he had here" (ibid.). According to Agustin and Raúl, however, both Arsenio and Kiki gave up Santería and Palo Monte completely to become Jehovah's Witnesses (Caraballoso interview, April 7, 1998; Raúl Travieso interview, April 15, 1998).

Arsenio had found peace of mind through his faith in and study of the Bible. He expressed his renewed and positive outlook on life in "La verdad" (The Truth), a bolero that he recorded for his final LP *Arsenio Dice* (Tico LP 1175) in 1968. He begins the lyrics by quoting a stanza from his "La vida es un sueño," which he composed in New York in 1947 after being told that his blindness was irreversible. The despair that he felt and expressed then had been replaced by spiritual fulfillment and satisfaction, which he found by becoming a Jehovah's Witness. Perhaps his renewed hope in life also overshadowed what were difficult final years of his nevertheless extraordinary musical life.

5 Salsa and Arsenio Rodríguez's Legacy

FROM THE TIME it was coined in the early 1970s by Fania Records, the term *salsa* has been used to market a stylistically diverse and historically broad repertory of music under one name. Although most agree that salsa has since the 1980s developed into a transnational music, incorporating musical genres and styles from various regions of Latin America and beyond, some musicians, dancers, journalists, aficionados, and scholars continue to debate salsa's national provenance and maintain that the music has either a Cuban or Puerto Rican essence. Patria Román-Velázquez has, I believe, justly described this ongoing debate as a "fruitless attempt to prove beyond doubt that salsa is essentially Puerto Rican or Cuban" (Román-Velázquez 2002, p. 214). This chapter asks two different and much-needed focused questions regarding the development of the musical repertory that would become known as salsa by the early 1970s. (1) How do the stylistic differences and social meanings that pertained to Cuban conjuntos in Havana in the 1940s problematize attempts to assign salsa a national origin and essence? And (2) to what extent did Arsenio's music and son montuno style shape the individual repertories and styles of early salsa musicians in New York City?

In 1990 anthropologist Jorge Duany noted that the "historical sources of *salsa* have yet to be tapped in-depth. Future research should assemble written documents such as personal memoirs, original recordings of *salsa* songs, films of live performances, and interviews with key musicians to reconstruct the origins and development of *salsa*" (Duany 1990, p. 295). Unfortunately, Duany's assessment of research on salsa's musical antecedents and early development still pertains to the state of salsa scholarship.[1] This chapter begins to address these problems by comparing rerecordings made by early salsa groups in the 1960s with the originals as recorded by Arsenio's conjunto and other Cuban conjuntos in the 1940s and 1950s. My comparative analysis focuses on identifying the stylistic divergences in the rerecorded interpretations not to posit the originals as models of ultimate perfection. Rather, I want to highlight these divergences, many of which are subtle but nevertheless significant, as a way to lend both repertories (early salsa and Cuban conjunto music) social and historical specification. At the same time, I want to identify how the son montuno's underlying aesthetic principles shaped the category of salsa referred to as salsa dura, or hard salsa. I begin the chapter, however, by tracing the personal and direct impact Arsenio and his music had on the first generation of salsa musicians, which dates back to the 1950s.

"We Were Disciples of Arsenio"

Many of the first generation of salsa musicians in New York began their professional careers in the 1950s. Some spearheaded the development and popularization of pachanga and boogaloo music in the early and mid-1960s, respectively, before the emergence of the salsa industry. Because most of these musicians grew up and lived in the South Bronx, they had become very familiar with Arsenio's music as well as Arsenio himself who not only lived in the same neighborhoods (Longwood and Hunts Point) but also regularly performed with his conjunto at the local popular Tropicana Club and the Club Cubano Inter-Americano (see chapter 3). "I had the opportunity to grow up with Arsenio Rodríguez, Chappottín, and La Sonora Matancera," stated Johnny Pacheco, who in addition to knowing Arsenio personally studied his records and the records of other Cuban conjuntos (Pacheco interview 1997). Members of Ray Barretto's charanga, which scored both pachanga and early boogaloo hits, were not only fans of Arsenio's music but in fact had performed with his conjunto. Pianist and arranger Alfredito Valdés Jr., whose family often attended dances at the Club Cubano, explained that he and bassist Enrique Jackson played simultaneously with Arsenio's conjunto and Ray Barretto's charanga from about 1960 to 1963. Vocalist Wito Kortwrite, who had been Arsenio's lead vocalist since 1955 (refer to Figure 3.6), left the conjunto around 1958 and joined Barretto's charanga around 1960. Furthermore, Alfredito arranged for both groups. "The original [Barretto] band was an offshoot of the Arsenio orchestra, an extension of Arsenio's sound because we were the backbone of Arsenio's band, the piano player, the bass player, and the singer. . . . It was a charanga, but it was very 'Arsenio' in its feel, very son montuno and guaguancó. We [were] actually disciples of Arsenio" (Valdés interview 1999). Though pachanga and boogaloo were unique musical and dance styles, specific to the music culture of mostly second-generation Latinos in New York, the bass structures and arrangement schemes of both were modeled significantly on Arsenio's son montuno style.

In November 1958, José Fajardo y sus Estrellas, one of Cuba's most popular charangas, performed at the Palladium. This performance initiated a widespread euphoria for the charanga ensemble in New York, which lead directly to the popularity of the pachanga, a musical style initially popularized in Cuba by Eduardo Davidson (Rondón 1980, pp. 13, 19).[2] Indeed, many young musicians from the Bronx—for example, Charlie Palmieri, Johnny Pacheco, Ray Barretto, and the Zervigón brothers of Orquesta Broadway—did form charangas in New York in the late 1950s and early 1960s. These musicians, however, had been exposed to charanga music long before Fajardo's 1958 performance. As I discussed in chapter 3, the charanga ensemble and its related musical styles had been an intimate part of the local Cuban and Puerto Rican dance music milieu in the South Bronx since at least the early 1950s.

Johnny Pacheco, for example, attended performances by Gilberto Valdés's charanga and undoubtedly Arsenio's conjunto as well, both of whom performed regularly at the Tropicana Club in the early 1950s. During the mid-1950s he even played timbales temporarily with Valdés's charanga at the Puerto Rico Casino in the South Bronx (Carp 1997, p. 7). In 1960 Pacheco formed his own charanga and quickly became the prime popularizer of the New York–pachanga dance and music style, introducing both at the Tritons social club in the Bronx (Thompson 1983, p. 48; Carp 1997, pp. 10–11). It became extremely popular among the mostly New York–born Puerto Rican teenagers and young adults who attended the Tritons' dances.[3] In addition to their social club, organizers had dances regularly at local dance halls such as the Hunts Point Palace, and hired mostly young local bands, such as Orlando Marin's (Marin interview 2000). According to Ken Rosa, the pachanga was initially a Bronx phenomenon, separate from the nightclub and dance hall scenes in Manhattan (Rosa interview, December 8, 1999). Soon, however, it became particularly associated with the Palladium, where it became popular among Latinos and non-Latinos (see Thompson 1983; Gelb 1961).

For many of the new generation of New York–born Latinos, particularly those from the Bronx, the pachanga music style was a welcomed alternative to the increasingly jazz-oriented sound of the mambo. Orlando Marin observed: "No Latin jazz nonsense. None of this fancy stuff, and the people loved it. Puente, [Tito] Rodriguez, and Machito, in a way, took a back seat to this, and they were forced eventually to record something that said 'pachanga' in it" (Marin interivew 2000).[4] Its musical style, however, variously labeled charanga and pachanga, was not particularly new. These charanga groups were not known for recording danzón music, although it is possible that they performed it in live situations. Rather, the pachanga's harmonic-cyclic form, arrangement scheme, and use of bass lines in contratiempo evoke comparison to Arsenio's son montuno.

In 1960 Johnny Pacheco recorded his first LP, titled *Pacheco y su charanga* (Alegre LPA 801), which immediately became commercially successful, selling over 100,000 copies (Carp 1998, p. 16). A year later Ray Barretto recorded his first LP, titled *Pachanga with Barretto* (Riverside 7506). Both LPs became two of the earliest and most popular pachanga records recorded in New York. Of the twenty-one recordings in both LPs, seventeen are pachangas. First, like many of Arsenio's son montunos dating from the early 1940s, all of these are based on a continuous harmonic cycle of two or four bars. Second, the arrangement schemes are markedly similar, consisting of an introduction, montuno, solo, an optional cierre, and the diablo. In particular, the alternating scheme between a refrain and verse, which follows the introductions in Pacheco and Barretto's pachangas (with the exception of the latter's "Pachanga suavecito" [Soft Pachanga]), is especially reminiscent of Arsenio's customary son montuno arrangement scheme. As arranger Alfredito Valdés Jr. recalled, "The arrangements I wrote for Ray Barretto were very 'Arsenio.' [They] were all 'Arsenio' ideas. Rather, [they] had that approach" (Valdés interview 1999). Another disciple of Arsenio, pianist and arranger Hector Rivera, arranged "Pachanga suavecito" (Soft Pachanga), which incorporates some of the son montuno's core stylistic elements. They include a slow tempo (110s), a melodic bass line in contratiempo, and, most noticeably, the customary piano cue (i.e., an arpeggiated dominant-seventh chord) followed by a four-bar syncopated cierre, which practically breaks all sense of meter or pulse. Instead of following the cierre with the diablo finale, however, a violin solo follows.

Third, although the tempos of Arsenio's son montunos of the 1940s averaged in the 120s and 130s, his son montunos of the 1950s and early 1960s ranged from the 140s to the 200s. Similarly, although the tempos of Pacheco's and Barretto's pachangas characteristically range from the 170s to the 200s, some are played at much slower tempos. Finally and most important, many of these pachangas consist of bass lines (sometimes doubled by the violins and piano) based on variations of the "Mi chinita me botó" figuration (refer to example 2.2). As I discussed in chapter 2, certain attacks in these bass lines as well as in other parts such as in the chorus correspond with steps in the son footwork, including steps 3 and 4, which are syncopated. But the pachanga dance footwork and style was completely different from the son montuno dance style.

From 1960 to about 1963 the pachanga captivated dancers and record buyers alike. According to Orlando Marin, "You had to go with it because this is what everyone wanted. You could go and play [something else] but no one would pay attention" (Marin interview 2000). Although pachanga was stylistically similar to son montuno, the dance style was extremely energetic, not unlike the mambo dance style. "Killer Joe" Piro, who gave dance lessons at the Palladium on Wednesday nights, described the dance in the following manner: "It was all jumping at first. . . . The flow went up and down. The floors shook, because everyone was hitting the same step, on 2 and 4" (Thompson 1983, p. 48). According to another observer: "The man pirouettes around the woman, waving a handkerchief. In any case, it's done mainly by young people; it's much too strenuous for anyone else" (Gelb 1961). Despite the pachanga's musical borrowings from the son montuno, its dance style hardly resembled the free flow of the son montuno dance style.

Nevertheless, Arsenio remarked on the pachanga's stylistic similarities to son montuno and the pachanga's popularity among the younger generation in his "Sabor de pachanga" (The Flavor of Pachanga) and "¿Qué te parece, Juana?" (What Do You Think about That, Juana?), which were released on the LPs *Arsenio Rodríguez y Su Conjunto* (Ansonia 1337) and *La Pachanga* (Tico TRSLP-1092) in 1960 and 1963, respectively. In fact, most of the recordings in these LPs are son montunos. Nevertheless, the music in *La Pachanga* in particular is noticeably faster than his typical moderately paced son montuno. Because of the faster tempos the music in general lacks the degree of rhythmic density and interplay that had always distinguished his style in the 1940s and 1950s. As Alfredito Valdés Jr. pointed out, Tico's executives urged Arsenio to play faster:

> Remember that this [*La Pachanga*] was probably something to do with the producers. They wanted to make Arsenio more up-to-date with the [times]. Pachanga was hot, everybody was dancing pachanga.... Again, [the music in *La Pachanga*] is not traditionally "Arsenio." This is Arsenio trying to catch up with what everybody else was doing.... Arsenio was gradually pushed into playing faster in an attempt to make his music more appealing to a wider audience, not because it was better. It was just commerce, just business. This [*La Pachanga*] is business. *Le decían* [They'd tell him], "You got to pick up the tempo because the *bailarines* [dancers] are falling like flies." (Valdés interview 1999)

Despite the musical concessions that he made in *La Pachanga*, the LP did not lead to more work or recognition. Nevertheless, Arsenio did take the opportunity to contest the pachanga's originality and complain of his marginal position in the Latin music industry, as Valdés noted: "What Arsenio is saying [in "¿Qué te parece, Juana?"] is that there's nothing new about pachanga, really. What ever you're doing now I've been doing for forty years, and I don't know why I'm not busy" (Valdés interview 1999).

Like pachanga, boogaloo music shared some important stylistic features with the son montuno, but its historical significance was also specific to the social setting in New York of the mid-1960s. As Juan Flores points out Latin boogaloo was the latest musical development emerging from a multicultural context of which African Americans had been a part of since at least the mambo period (Flores 2000).[5] Unlike the mambo and Afro-Cuban jazz, however, boogaloo was distinguished by its overt incorporation of stylistic elements from R&B and soul. In addition to its propensity for English-language lyrics, its divergent aspects included African American stylistic trappings, such as group handclapping on the backbeat (i.e., beats two and four), shouting, and chanting. Montuno figurations played by the piano as well as tumbadora, bongó, and timbales constituted its Latin trappings. What was left was its basic bass figuration, which, like those used in many pachangas, was modeled on the "Me chinita me botó" bass pattern.

Arsenio undoubtedly noticed, yet again the prevalence of this bass figuration in the latest Latin recordings that were hitting the national *Billboard* charts. It is logical, then, that the majority of his son montunos in *Viva Arsenio!* (BLPS-216) would be entirely or partly based on it. On April 18, 1966, Arsenio conducted the first of three recording sessions at Mira Sound Studios in Manhattan for an LP that was to be released by the pop label Bang Records.[6] Bert Berns started the label in New York in 1965 with the backing of Ahmet Ertegun, Neshui Ertegun, and Gerry Wexler of Atlantic Records, which was Bang Records' distributor. According to Berns's son Brett Berns, his father had a passion for Cuban music and specifically Arsenio's music (Brett Berns, personal communication). Bert had visited Cuba shortly before 1959 and, since then, wanted to record an album with Arsenio. With the success of the McCoys's R&B or boogaloo hit "Hang on Sloopy," the label's first number one hit, Berns evidently wanted to record a Latin boogaloo version.[7] As it turned out, he had Arsenio record a Latin boogaloo rendition of "Hang on Sloopy," sung in English by Arsenio himself. It was released as a single, but apparently it went nowhere. The LP, which was eventually released as *Viva Arsenio!* in 1967, contained an eclectic collection of newly composed son montunos, son montuno versions of the Mexican standards "La Bamba" and "Cielito lindo," and rerecordings of his own standards "La yuka (de Catalina)," "Tres Marías," and "El elemento del Bronx."

At the same time, seven out of the ten son montunos in *Viva Arsenio!* do not include a horn section, and none appear to include a piano. This instrumentation amounts to a sexteto (not unlike the Joe Cuba Sextet, a very popular boogaloo group at the time)—that is, vocals, guitar, tres, bass, bongó, and tumbadora—which he apparently used in Los Angeles on at least one occasion (see chapter 4). For those son montunos with no trumpet section, the arrangements and rhythmic textures take on a different character, most notably in the absence of the diablo section. Even in the three son montunos that do include horns—"Hang on Sloopy," "La yuka" (The Yuka), and "Baila conmigo" (Dance with Me)—they are not used in the typical alternation sequence that defined the conventional son montuno arrangement scheme. In addition, though "La yuka" and "Baila conmigo" feature two trumpets and one baritone saxophone (he had used saxophones before, beginning in his *Quindembo* LP in 1963 and Ansonia recordings the following year), "Hang on Sloopy" includes one trombone. Mon Rivera and Eddie Palmieri had already standardized the trombone section in Latin dance music; this, however, was Arsenio's first recorded use of a trombone.

Arsenio had been altering his ensemble as well as the typical son montuno arrangement scheme since the mid-1950s in an attempt to meet mainstream popular tastes. His will, however reluctant, to alter this scheme is evident in his rerecordings of his own music. Earlier examples of this include "El reloj de Pastora" (late 1950s) and "Lo dicen todas" (All the Women Say It, rec. 1960). For *Viva Arsenio!* he rerecorded the son montunos "Como traigo la yuka" (originally recorded in 1942 in Havana) and "Las tres Marías" (The Three Marias, originally recorded around 1950 in New York) as well as the conjunto-style guaguancó "La gente del Bronx" (The People of the Bronx, originally recorded around 1951). "Como traigo la yuka" and "La gente del Bronx," which he retitled "La yuka" and "El elemento del Bronx," respectively, consist of the same basic structures as the original versions, but the arrangement schemes differ, particularly in the use (or lack thereof, in the case of "El elemento del Bronx", of the horn section. In "La yuka" the horns are arranged to provide a background to the alternations between the chorus and lead vocalist, and not to constitute an alternating entity in itself, as is the case in the original. The foremost difference in "La yuka," compared to the original, is the fluid nature of the bass patterns (played by Cachao), the figurations of which are nevertheless consistent with Arsenio's use of contratiempo. Notwithstanding such variations, namely in the arrangement schemes, Arsenio always tried to maintain the core texture of his son montuno style.

There are two other basic similarities between the boogaloo and son montuno. First, boogaloo was played at moderate tempos, noticeably slower than most pachangas of the early 1960s. Many son montunos in *Arsenio Viva!*, too, are played at moderate to slow tempos, ranging from 110 to 148, although two, "Randy" and "La Bamba," are played at 175 and 200, respectively. Second, the boogaloo's basic arrangement scheme is based on a repeating two-bar cycle over which call-and-response (between coros and soneos or improvised vocalizations), group sung and chanted refrains, and ensemble breaks and build-ups occur in regularly repeated sequences; there is little or no use of verses, like Arsenio's one-part son montunos. Despite these similarities, however, Arsenio's son montunos in *Arsenio Viva!* retain that rhythmically dense quality that he had introduced in the early 1940s and that ultimately distinguished his style from boogaloo. For example, the interwoven and percussive patterns of the baritone, two trumpets, and trombone in Arsenio's "Hang on Sloopy" contrast sharply with the unison and legato trumpet lines in Pete Rodríguez's hugely popular "I Like It Like That."

Johnny Pacheco, Ray Barretto, and their arrangers actively drew from Arsenio's son montuno style to develop many of their pachanga and boogaloo hits. As such we might see Arsenio's son montuno style forming what Raymond Williams defined as a "residual cultural practice," that is, a musical style "effectively formed in the past, but . . . still active in the cultural process, not only and often not at all as an element of the past, but as an effective element of the present" (Williams 1977, p. 122). Despite the significance of Arsenio's son montuno style to the development of pachanga and boogaloo, these genres remained unique musical and cultural phenomena if not for their distinctive musical features then for their original dance styles.[8] These musicians and others continued to draw from Arsenio's son montuno style as well as from his recorded repertory through the 1960s and early 1970s, again not through a sense of musical nostalgia but rather as an active process contributing to the development of a new musical repertory.

Son Montuno and Salsa Aesthetics

There are four reasons why Arsenio's music is important to salsa music history. First, his compositions occupy a noticeable space in the recorded repertories of contemporary as well as early salsa groups. The list of his songs and the groups that have recorded them include the afrocubano "Bruca maniguá" (recorded in 1972 by Ray Barretto and in 1990 by NG La Banda), the son montuno "Suéltala" (Let Her Go; recorded in 1970 by Tony Pabon y Sus Estrellas and in 2004 by Conjunto Imagen), the conjunto-style guaguancó "Fuego en el 23" (Fire on 23rd; recorded in 1970 by La Sonora Ponceña and in 2001 by Sonsublime), and the son montuno "El reloj de Pastora" (Pastora's Watch; recorded in 1983 by Pete "El Conde" Rodríguez with Johnny Pacheco). Larry Harlow alone re-recorded at least ten of Arsenio's son montunos and guaguancós between the years 1967 and 1976.[9] Second, many salsa musicians have composed and recorded original son montunos and conjunto-style guaguancós, making both of these conventional genres of the salsa repertory particularly of the 1960s and 1970s. Well-known examples include Johnny Pacheco and Bobby Valentín's son montuno "Quitate tú" (Make Way; recorded live by the Fania All-Stars for the historic salsa LP *Live at the Cheetah*), Rubén Blades and Willie Colón's son montuno "Buscando guayaba" (Looking for a Guayaba; released on the equally historic salsa LP *Siembra*), Johnny Pacheco's guaguancó "La esencia del guaguancó" (The Essence of the Guaguancó, released on *La Perfecta Combinación*), and Eddie Palmieri's "Café" (Coffee; released on *Echando Pa'lante*). Third, the son montuno's defining features of contratiempo, sonic power and density, and climactic energy, as well as its allotment for solos in its arrangement scheme endure as core aesthetic values especially of salsa dura. Today, salsa dura is said to be more authentic than the more commercial salsa romántica because of the stylistic affinity of the former with early salsa music of New York. Hence, the fourth reason why Arsenio's music is important to salsa is the authentication many salsa musicians and aficionados lend to it, no matter that the son montuno dance style, which originally shaped the son montuno texture, has fallen into obscurity among mainstream salsa dancers.

It is important to reiterate here that my goal is not to argue for a national essence or provenance of salsa music but to provide a comparative analysis emphasizing social and historical specification and, most important, the role that dancing and performance in general plays in lending music meaning. According to contemporary reports the footwork to dance salsa was (and continues to be) similar to the mambo's basic footwork, both the "on one" and "on two" versions (e.g., see Roberts 1976, p. 93).[10] Yet the overall dance styles differ significantly (see Hutchinson 2004). Nevertheless, by using other footwork patterns and dance styles, young salsa dancers could not experience the son montuno feel as it was originally intended to be felt. This is particularly important in regard to the rerecordings of son montunos that early salsa musicians made in the 1960s. Because younger salsa dancers did not dance son montuno and because the original dance had a defining impact on the genre itself, these rerecordings were not merely duplications of Cuban music but as much a product *of* their social and historical context as was originally composed early salsa music (see Acosta 1983, p. 33 n18; Rondón 1980).

The Son Montuno and Guaguancó Genres in Early Salsa Music

In his book *El libro de la salsa*, César Miguel Rondón characterized the commercialization of salsa music in the 1970s, represented by Johnny Pacheco and Celia Cruz's popular rerecordings of La Sonora Matancera's hits from the 1950s, as the *matancerizacion* of salsa music. In actuality Pacheco began rerecording Cuban conjunto music in the mid-1960s with his conjunto "Nuevo Tumbao" (New Beat). Much of the material from this earlier period consisted of rerecordings of Chappottín's and Chocolate's son montunos and guaguancós of the 1950s and early 1960s. These two Cuban conjuntos modeled their styles entirely on Arsenio's style. Yet Pacheco chose to reinterpret this material in the style of La Sonora Matancera of which Cuban musicians I interviewed described as lacking in the sonic power and density that distinguished Arsenio's style in the 1940s (see chapter 2). In addition to Pacheco, other early salsa musicians made similar changes not only through their stylistic interpretation but also to the original son montuno arrangement scheme itself.

Subtle yet significant differences can be observed when comparing Chappottín's recording of the son montuno "Me voy contigo" (c. 1955) with Pacheco's rerecorded version (c. 1968). First, the montuno section of the original recording features interweaving sequences created by the bongó, tumbadora, and bass parts. The bongó player (Papa Kila), in particular, executes the most common sequence of slaps that defines the son montuno style (e.g., refer to Example 2.1). Such sequences are largely absent in Pacheco's version. Instead, these parts proceed relatively independent of each other, particularly the bongó, which executes rather nervous and anxious sequences of slaps and flams (or double-stroke rolls). Second, the piano and bass parts in Pacheco's version are rhythmically in unison, creating a somewhat transparent texture compared to the partially interwoven piano and bass parts in the original recording. Last, the overall rhythmic texture or feel created by Pacheco's conjunto seems to better match the basic mambo footwork given the emphasis in the piano, bass, and tumbadora patterns on steps two, three, four, and six, as opposed to steps three and four of the son footwork, both of which are syncopated.

Pacheco's conjunto also reinterpreted Arsenio's own "No vuelvo a Morón" (I'm Not Going Back to Morón; SLP 300) in the style of La Sonora Matancera. In Arsenio's 1950 version (his conjunto had recorded it first in 1948) the interweaving sequences take place between the bass, bongó, tumbadora, and the tres, while the bass and refrain clearly accent the syncopated steps of the son's footwork (see Example 5.1). In Pacheco's version (c. 1966), however, the bongó and tumbadora merely keep time by executing their basic tumbaos or "martillo" in the case of the bongó (see Example 5.2). As Raúl Travieso noted, La Sonora Matancera's tumbadora player was known for this style of playing, which he criticized because it created a small or weak sound (refer to Table 2.2 and Example 2.7). It is important to emphasize that these changes were made deliberately and not out of ignorance of the subtleties of Arsenio's son montuno style. As percussionist Phil Newsum noted "Pacheco understood him [i.e., Arsenio's style] but he had to carve out his own niche for himself" (Newsum interview 2001). Additional changes in the original bass lines and arrangement schemes were made in accordance to personal preference as well as other stylistic conventions.

For instance, Arsenio and his Cuban successors favored two bass patterns that were modeled on the "Mi chinita me botó" bass line (refer to Example 2.2). The main characteristics of this pattern and its two variants involve the simultaneous melodic and rhythmic accentuation of the sung refrain parts and the son's footwork. Besides these melodic and

EXAMPLE 5.1. "No vuelvo a Morón" (c. 1950), Arsenio Rodríguez y Su Conjunto.

rhythmic qualities, particular notes of the bass lines, especially the note coinciding with step five of the son footwork, were attacked in a staccato manner, lending the bass lines an added percussive effect. According to Alfonso "El Panameño" Joseph (Arsenio's bassist in New York throughout much of the 1960s), Arsenio continued to favor these bass patterns and required that they be executed correctly: "He taught me how to play the Cuban [i.e., son montuno] tumbao. It's different from the tumbao that we used playing with Puerto Rican groups. It was more complicated . . . more syncopated. . . . He made me shorten the attack of each note" (Joseph interview 2001).

As can be observed in the original recording of "No vuelvo a Morón" the shortened or staccato attacks in the bass part coincide with steps two and five, respectively. The bassist in Pacheco's version, however, not only uses a different pattern but more notably favors connecting its attacks and playing them legato, lending the bass line a smoother feel instead of the more percussive quality engendered by the staccato attacks of the original bass line. In some cases, the original bass lines in Arsenio's recordings were replaced altogether with the anticipated bass pattern (refer to Example 2.3). For example, in Arsenio's "Hachero pa' un palo" (recorded in New York, c. 1960), the bassist (probably Raúl Díaz) uses the "Mi chinita me botó" figuration. Melodically, the bass line accents

EXAMPLE 5.2. "No vuelvo a Morón" (c. 1966), Johnny Pacheco y Su Nuevo Tumbao.

the first half of the chorus. In La Sonora Ponceña's rerecording of "Hachero pa' un palo," however, the anticipated bass pattern, characterized by its tied notes, is substituted for the original pattern in the montuno and diablo sections. As a result both the piano montuno and anticipated bass pattern in Ponceña's version create a schism against the original chorus figure, which together with the bass and tres patterns accentuated the son footwork.[11]

Despite the fact that the diablo section constituted the culmination of the son montuno arrangement scheme, its import to salsa arrangers was ambiguous at best. In fact, salsa arrangers favored the mambo section over the diablo in their originally composed son montunos as well as in their rerecordings of Cuban conjunto material. Pacheco's reinterpretations tend to stay closest to the original schemes with only some variation in the alternating sequences and substitutions of a mambo section for the original diablo section (e.g., "Campeón" [Champion], "Fania," "Prefiero el son" [I Prefer the Son], and "Me voy contigo"). In contrast, Larry

EXAMPLE 5.3. "Tumba y bongó" (1972), Orchestra Harlow, mambo section.

Harlow included a mambo section in most of his rearrangements of Arsenio's son montunos. The diablo sections that he did keep were nevertheless altered in its typical sequence of events (e.g., "El terror" and "No me llores").

In "Tumba y bongó" (SLP 00404; originally "Kila, Kike y Chocolate") Harlow omitted the diablo section altogether, adding mambo and coda sections to the arrangement (see Table 5.1). Hence, in terms of the arrangement's energy dynamics, the mambo section replaces the diablo as the climactic section. What's more, in comparing the diablo in Arsenio's original recording (refer to Example 2.5) with Harlow's mambo section (refer to Example 5.3) we see that the defining rhythmic and procedural aspects of the original diablo and with it Arsenio's son montuno feel are consequently erased altogether. Specifically, the original bass line is set in variation 2 of the "Mi chinita me botó" figuration (refer to Examples 2.2 and 2.5), while Harlow's bassist uses the notably less syncopated guaracha tumbao (refer to Example 2.3). Second, the question and answer sequence between the bongó and tumbadora in the original diablo is absent in Harlow's mambo. Third, the strict interwoven patterns created by the tres and piano parts in the original contrast with the rhythmically

Table 5.1. Son montuno arrangement schemes in the salsa repertory

"Kila, Kiki y Chocolate" (1950), Arsenio Rodríguez y Su Conjunto								
Intro	Verse	Montuno	*Diablo					
"Tumba y bongó" (1972), Orchestra Harlow								
Intro	Verse	Montuno	Cierre	Solo	*Mambo	Cierre	Montuno	Coda
"Te traigo mi son" (1972), Ray Barretto								
Intro	Montuno	Solos	*Mambo	Montuno	*Diablo	Montuno	Coda	
"Quitate tú" (1971), Fania All-Stars								
Intro	Montuno	Solo	*Diablo	Montuno				
"Buscando guayaba" (1978), Rubén Blades and Willie Colón								
Intro.	Verse	Cierre	Montuno	Solo	*Mambo	Montuno	Coda	

unison patterns of the cuatro and piano in Harlow's version. Finally, the hocket-like effect created by Arsenio's three trumpets differs dramatically from the smooth and orchestrated parts performed by Harlow's trumpets and trombones. In addition, while the tempo progressively increases in the original performance, Harlow's performance begins at about 147 beats per minute, and from there on slowly decelerates to about 134 in the coda, thereby counteracting any sense of climax. By Arsenio's standards, Harlow's rerecordings of "El terror" and "No me llores," too, drag on because the tempo either decelerates or remains static.

Other examples, however, including originally composed son montunos, do include signature features of Arsenio's style, including the diablo section. The rhythmic texture or feel of Ray Barretto's "Te traigo mi son" (I Bring You My Son; SLP 00403), marked by the emphasis on the "and-of-four" of the clave's two-side as well as the familiar sequence of auxiliary bongó attacks, which are interwoven with the tumbadora and bass patterns, is especially akin to the feel of Arsenio's son montuno texture (see Example 5.4). Phil Newsum and some of his contemporaries, including undoubtedly Johnny Rodríguez, the bongó player in "Te traigo mi son," carefully studied Arsenio's recordings from the 1940s, especially Papa Kila's bongó style. According to Newsum,

> That's a style that was followed by almost everybody that came after [Papa Kila]. Manny [Oquendo] does it, I did it. It's directly descended from him. The stuff that he's doing is very simple. We used to call that *golpe seco* [dry hit]. There were no double stroke rolls [i.e., flams]. . . . It was more than martillo, but you had a vocabulary of licks. . . . That's what these guys [Arsenio's percussionists] did with the rhythm. They threw away all the bullshit and just kept the essential lick itself. You're using time and space to make the statements. A lot of nervous guys, neurotic guys, they feel like they

EXAMPLE 5.4. "Te traigo mi son" (1972), Ray Barretto, son montuno texture.

got to fill up every measure with licks. There's no space. Part of the fun of it is in the anticipation, leaving the holes. (Newsum interview 2001)

Clearly, the son montuno and guaguancó genres were important additions to the performance and recorded repertories of early salsa musicians. But whether originally composed or rerecorded, these genres often underwent significant changes especially to their arrangement schemes. The most significant of these changes was in the displacement or omission of the diablo section. Rather than follow Arsenio's arrangement format, salsa arrangers adopted the conventional scheme that mambo big bands instituted, which includes a mambo section that is placed about two-thirds of the way through the arrangement (e.g., "Buscando guayaba" and "Tumba y bongó"; see Table 5.1 and refer to Table 3.1). In other cases, arrangers did use the diablo format, marked by the alternation between sung choruses and brass phrases in a short cycle (two or four bars), but often times not as the finale of the arrangement itself (e.g., "Quitate tú" and "Te traigo mi son").

Regardless of these son montunos' fidelity (or lack thereof) to Arsenio's music and style, the fact is it mattered little if at all to salsa dancers, most of whom did not know the original son montuno footwork let alone Arsenio's music. Furthermore, to dance son montuno involved much more than just the basic footwork. It comprised a certain choreography in which the anticipation and climactic arrival of the diablo section was marked and celebrated with increased upper-body, leg, and hand gestures by dancers (see chapter 2). Hence, with the omission or displacement of the diablo section, in addition to other changes in the original son montuno arrangement scheme, the *performance* of son montuno by musicians but especially salsa dancers engendered experiences that resonated little if at all with its "past" performances, namely in Havana in the 1940s or perhaps even in El Barrio and the Bronx in the early 1950s.

This seems like an obvious point; nevertheless it is intended to problematize the notion of a national provenance of and essence in early salsa music in New York as well as the idea of típico salsa music as recycled Cuban or, for that matter, Puerto Rican music. Arsenio's son montuno style was crafted not by him or his conjunto alone but literally in dialogue with dancers. The culmination of this dialogue bore fruit to the diablo section, whose original intention was to bring the dancers and musicians to an artistic and even spiritual climax. Finally, this dialogue among Arsenio, his musicians, and dancers took effect not in a social vacuum but in a racially charged context in which their racialization and gendering of his style were the logical modes through which his music was given meaning.

In contrast, son montuno and guaguancó in New York of the 1960s and 1970s constituted two of several genres including guaracha-, bomba-, and plena-based music that represented for most musicians and dancers forms of cultural resistance and Latino identity put in action through performance. Even so, son montuno in particular was not as popular among early salsa dancers as were faster genres. After saying that Arsenio's music constituted no more than 20 percent of Harlow's repertory during the 1960s, Phil Newsum explained that young salsa dancers "couldn't relate to that *feeling*, that slow stuff, because Arsenio's stuff was relatively slow. It didn't appeal to the neuroticism of the city. It was more country, roots-oriented stuff" (Newsum interview 2001). Latin music historian and producer René López added that the guaguancós that Arsenio composed and recorded for the barrios of Havana were "irrelevant here in New York. They would like tunes like 'Kila, Kiki y Chocolate' which they [i.e., Larry Harlow] called 'Tumba y bongó' and stuff like that which was not so specific. Rather, if you're singing to Cayo Hueso nobody would know where the hell Cayo Hueso is" (López interview 2004). Indeed, the original feel and meanings that Arsenio's music engendered in the 1940s were irreproducible. But nor were early salsa musicians attempting to reproduce them. Rather, as Johnny Pacheco's pastiche-like treatment of Cuban conjunto music shows, these musicians were actively experimenting with these genres and not trying to revitalize them in their original forms. On the other hand, though early salsa musicians frequently altered the material aspects of Arsenio's son montuno style (e.g., bass lines, interweaving patterns, and the diablo scheme), many noted its aesthetic principles of sonic power and fullness as well as climactic energy and adopted these as underlying principles of their own styles, which are collectively represented in the category salsa dura.

Salsa Dura and the Son Montuno's Aesthetic Principles

In an article titled "The Death of Salsa" (posted online at descarga.com), writer Abel Delgado laments the apparent demise in contemporary salsa music of what he and many other salsa aficionados and musicians consider to be the defining aesthetic qualities of salsa dura. In Delgado's words these three qualities are: (1) polyrhythms that are "strong and syncopated, tailor made for dancing" and "interlocking"; (2) "improvisation"; and (3) "storytelling." The first and second qualities are especially relevant to the son montuno style's direct legacy in salsa music. As I argued before, the son montuno and guaguancó are two of many genres that constitute the salsa repertory. Even then, salsa musicians have often made changes to the original son montuno texture and arrangement scheme to better suit individual preferences and other stylistic conventions. Many salsa musicians, however, have also taken note of the aesthetic principles of sonic fullness, power, and climax in Arsenio's music.

Percussionist Gene Golden described the density and power of Arsenio's style in the following manner: "He was playing *son* with so much bottom . . . He had less guys, but his sound was always fatter then the rest of the guys, you know, like a fat sound. It wasn't because he had his amps loud" (Golden interview 2001). For Eddie Palmieri, the interweaving of patterns in Chappottín's son montuno "Me voy contigo" became his "direction and dedication" from the moment he first heard the record in the 1950s. "I couldn't believe what I was hearing: the question and answers between instruments, conga and bongo" (Roberts 1976, p. 42). Observations like these speak to the consistent sonic and textural effect that Arsenio's son montuno style had on many musicians across generations and nationalities. Recall that Arsenio's Cuban contemporaries of the 1940s similarly distinguished his style for its sonic fullness and rhythmic complexity, culminating in the climactic diablo finale. What is especially important here is that observers, whether referring to Cuban conjunto music of the 1940s or salsa music, have emphasized these principles to distinguish in the case of the former repertory "black" style conjuntos from "white" style conjuntos and, in the case of the latter, salsa dura from contemporary salsa or salsa romántica.

Because many regard Eddie Palmieri's music as the quintessential example of salsa dura, it is appropriate to focus on how Arsenio's music imparted these principles to the development of Palmieri's group La Perfecta and its style in the 1960s and early 1970s. Since at least the mid-1950s, both Eddie Palmieri and his primary arranger and stylistic architect, Barry Rogers, had been astute students of Cuban conjunto records, from which they learned the importance of the dynamics of energy and climax in an arrangement. As Palmieri noted, "That's when I really started to learn my structures—how to present a composition, how to build it up to the exciter, to the high climax" (Roberts 1976, p. 21). Rogers took note of the same structures or principles. David Carp, who has done extensive research on Rogers's life and career, states, "Barry's understanding of Cuban musical structures was further deepened through the intense listening to the music of Arsenio Rodríguez" (Carp 1999a, p. 13). But as Palmieri stressed, trying to copy Arsenio's music would only result in a "terrible mimicry because you can't even imitate it" (Palmieri interview 2002). Carp corroborates: "As much as Barry Rogers respected and loved the Cuban models he studied so assiduously, copying them was not enough" (Carp 1999a, p. 13).

Rather than merely reinterpret Cuban conjunto music, Palmieri and Rogers set out to create their own new music marked nevertheless by the principles of musical fullness, power, and climax. No other feature of their music represented these principles more than that which has become known as *moña*. Moña refers to both spontaneously improvised riffs that are performed on the trumpets and trombones as well as the section of a salsa arrangement in which moñas are executed. In either case, moñas serve to heighten the level of energy of the music especially for dancers; consequently, they contribute to the climax of the typical salsa arrangement scheme. Use of the moña became an integral technique with which Palmieri and Rogers facilitated the climactic energy of La Perfecta's arrangements. In 1967 Robert Farris Thompson described this technique in the following manner: "Rogers has elaborated a splendid usage involving two trombones—one to chant, the other (Rogers) to invent" (Thompson 1967, p. 54). Trombonist and arranger Mark Weinstein also recounted: "When Barry would start to move through a sequence of improvisations [i.e., moñas] there was nothing in the world that was more exciting and the dancers loved Barry Rogers" (Carp 1999a, 11). Recall that in some of Arsenio's recordings of the 1940s, two trumpets at the first alternating sequence of the diablo similarly chant a repeated phrase while the lead trumpet, in call-and-response form, invents figures, parts of which are interwoven with the phrase of the other trumpets (refer to Example 2.5).

Furthermore, Arsenio created and incorporated the diablo into his arrangement scheme to give the dancers, in his own words, el cocimiento (a kick in the ass).

In addition, Robert Ferris Thompson described La Perfecta's new sound as "a new form of New York Latin music, founded on fresh drumming, an astringent bass, a piano mixing fixity of form with counterpoint, and a trombone extracting a maximum of emotion from a minimum of notes" (Thompson 1967, p. 68). This statement should similarly remind us of Odilio Urfé's and Fernando Ortiz's descriptions of the mambo as performed in Havana in the 1940s (see chapter 2). They identified the importance of playing spontaneously within a minimal structural arrangement, creating contrapuntal and interwoven textures, and most important, producing a maximum of energy with a minimum of notes, thereby affecting a climactic and paroxysmal moment that Ortiz identified as characteristic of all "música afrocubana." As I argued, no other group in Havana in the 1940s embraced these features more than Arsenio's conjunto, and it was these same principles that Rogers and Palmieri adopted in their music. As Weinstein explained: "If you know enough about Cuban 78s from the '40s and early '50s you hear a lot of Eddie's arrangements. . . . But it wasn't really a matter of stealing. Because Eddie's band, bizarrely, was Cuban revivalist, and the model of the trombone improvisation came from the way Chappottín, the soloist, would play against the trumpets [i.e., during the diablo section] (Carp 1999a, p. 10).[12] Thus, although the schematic of the diablo did not remain a vital aspect of salsa arrangements, the function it ultimately served endured in the moña, which crystallized in La Perfecta's music and became a standard part of salsa arrangements by the early 1970s.[13]

With La Perfecta, Rogers executed moñas on the trombone typically during flute solos, either by himself (e.g., "Ritmo caliente" [Hot Rhythm], rec. 1962) or in combination with a second trombonist (e.g., "Sin sabor, nada" [Without Feel It's Nothing], rec. 1964), as well as just with a second trombonist, that is, in the moña section proper (e.g., "Los cueros me llaman" [The Drums Are Calling Me], rec. 1965). Although Rogers departed from La Perfecta around 1968, Palmieri's groups continued to feature moñas in originally composed material (e.g., "Se acabo la malanga" [There's No More Malanga], "Revolt/La libertad, lógico," and "Vámanos pa'l monte") as well as in the few rerecordings of Arsenio's music.

Like Harlow and Pacheco, Palmieri omitted the original diablo sections in his rerecordings of Arsenio's "Con un amor se borra otro amor" and "Si las nenas me dejan que." In "Pa' huele" (originally recorded as "Un cachito pa' huele" by Arsenio's conjunto in 1946), however, he remains largely faithful to the original arrangement scheme, although

TABLE 5.2. Diablo in the salsa arrangement

"Dame un cachito pa' huele" (1946), Arsenio Rodríguez y Su Conjunto					
Intro	Montuno	Solo	Cierre	*Diablo	
"Pa' huele" (1970), Eddie Palmieri and His Orchestra					
Intro	Montuno	Solo	Cierre	*Diablo	Coda

the diablo section is noticeably expanded, including an alternating sequence between the coro and guía, which is atypical of Arsenio's diablos (see Table 5.2). Nevertheless, its harmonic cycle remains truncated to half (i.e., two bars) its original length from the montuno section, and every alternating sequence involves a response from the coro. Furthermore, the entire diablo section, which lasts for about two minutes and ten seconds, constitutes a continuous climax that peaks at several points, particularly when the trombones, not unlike the trumpets in Arsenio's "Kila, Kike y Chocolate" (refer to Example 2.5), spontaneously create interlocking patterns, otherwise known as moñas. Specifically, in the second sequence between the coro, trumpet, and two trombones (halfway through the diablo or moña section), the two trombones play interlocking moñas (the lowest pattern of which doubles the bass) for six bars while the trumpet adds ternary-phrased figures for four bars (see Example 5.5). In Arsenio's original recorded version, the two lowest trumpets play a two-bar phrase while the lead trumpet punches in single-note attacks, creating partially interwoven patterns.

On August 26, 1971, at the Cheetah in Manhattan, the Fania All Stars performed what was to be one of the defining concerts in salsa's history. The core members of the group consisted of the leaders of Fania's best-selling salsa groups, Johnny Pacheco (musical director and flute), Ray Barretto (congas), Larry Harlow (piano), and Willie Colón (trombone), in addition to other musicians including Barry Rogers (trombone). According to César Miguel Rondón, the music performed at the concert marked the culmination of the salsa sound of New York (or salsa dura), and via the film and four-LP album of this concert, titled *Our Latin Thing (Nuestra cosa latina)* and *Fania All Stars: Recorded Live at Cheetah* (Fania 748), respectively, this sound was disseminated and popularized throughout the Caribbean region of Latin America. The commercial and artistic success of the music was due to the shrewd marketing of the film and album by Jerry Masucci (Fania's co-owner) and the "freshness," "spontaneity," and "accessibility" of the actual performances (see Rondón 1980, pp. 51–52).

Considering the LP's and film's artistic and commercial success, it is important to note that of the ten tracks released on the LP, seven are son

EXAMPLE 5.5. "Pa' huele" (1970), Eddie Palmieri and His Orchestra, diablo with moñas *(continued).*

montunos, four of which ("Ahora vengo yo," "Estrellas de Fania," "Ponte duro," and "Macho cimarrón") feature bass lines in contratiempo. The bass pattern in "Estrellas de Fania," in particular, approximates Arsenio's "Mi chinita me botó" bass figuration. Expectedly, however, the diablo is largely absent, appearing only in its defining truncated cycle and sequences of alternation in "Quítate tú" (see Table 5.1). After the two initial alternating sequences of the diablo of "Quitate tú," the trombones, initiated most likely by Barry Rogers, execute moñas, creating partially interwoven patterns with the trumpets. This brings the climax of the diablo section as well as the entire arrangement to its highest point. The heightened level of energy is simultaneously indicated by the audience's explosive and sustained applause and most graphically, in the fast sequential cutaways between the band and dancers in the film.[14]

It is not enough to identify Arsenio's compositions and the son montuno and guaguancó genres as his legacy in salsa. The underlying aesthetic

EXAMPLE 5.5. (Continued.)

principles of his son montuno style directly shaped the musical styles of some of the most critically acclaimed salsa musicians. Nor is it enough to limit our understanding of his legacy to only the music. Arsenio and his music are symbols of authenticity for Eddie Palmieri and many others who are critical of contemporary salsa music.

> What we have right now is a tragedy, a rhythmical, lyrical, compositional tragedy. They removed the tension and resistance from the arrangements. So you have a minimum climax or no climax at all, which is a rhythmical, sacred sin in our music.... It's been a total dishonor to the great percussionists that crystallized and did the evolution of these rhythmical patterns to be put into a structure like Arsenio did. We totally have destroyed that. (Palmieri interview 2002)

Although musicians and scholars alike continue to debate salsa's Cuban and Puerto Rican origins, they ignore or are unaware of the musical and social aspects that clearly distinguished the styles of antecedent groups such as La Sonora Matancera and Arsenio's conjunto. What the literature on salsa needs more of is historical documentation and comparative analysis of salsa and its Cuban and Puerto Rican antecedents, with a special focus on the social meanings that obtained in these earlier repertories. It has been the aim of this book to document these significant historical distinctions and relationships to provide some specification and qualification as to which style of Cuban music influenced which style of salsa music and how. Whereas La Sonora Matancera, Conjunto Casino, and other Cuban groups were important to the early history of salsa music, it was Arsenio who first standardized the principles that many salsa musicians and others continue to treasure to this day.

Conclusion

Remembering Arsenio Rodríguez/ Remembering Son Montuno

ON JULY 9, 2000 I attended Recordando el Mamoncillo, a Cuban festival that takes place annually in Astoria, Queens. This festival, marked by traditional Cuban music, dance, and food, commemorates the dances that used to take place at the salón "Mamoncillo," one of several popular dance floors that were located in the beer gardens of La Tropical in Havana and where Arsenio's conjunto performed regularly throughout the 1940s. It also celebrates the Club Cuban Inter-Americano and its importance to the history of Cuban music in New York. Although people of various ethnic and national backgrounds as well as age groups attend the festival, many of the attendees are elderly and middle-aged Cubans. Cuban music and dance, particularly son montuno and danzón, are the focus of the festival's activities. Musicians and groups that have performed at the festival include Orquesta Libre, Orquesta Broadway, Johnny Pacheco, Chico Álvarez y Su Son Montuno, Son Sublime, and many others. In between sets of live music, DJs play mostly son montuno and danzón as recorded by contemporary groups as well as Cuban conjuntos and charangas of the past.

In addition to Mamoncillo's wonderful music and cultural atmosphere, I especially enjoyed meeting and interviewing elderly individuals who had attended many of Arsenio's performances either in Havana in the 1940s or New York in the 1950s and 1960s. Even more exciting was the display of son montuno and danzón dancing, the styles and choreographies of which have become more obscure than ever before. One particularly revealing instance involved three couples dancing to Chappottín y Sus Estrellas' son montuno "Yo sí como candela" (I'm the Best; Antilla CD 107), which was recorded in the early 1950s. The first couple on the floor was an elderly couple. I took special interest in their style of dancing because they executed the same basic son footwork and similar bodily movements that I had observed Arsenio's niece and daughter execute in Havana the year before (see chapter 2). Soon after the beginning of the montuno section, a second and somewhat younger couple reached the dance floor and began to execute the cha-cha's footwork instead of the son's. At the beginning of the tres solo, a third couple, also middle-aged, reached the dance floor and began to execute what looked like to be a bolero-type dance pattern. I could not help but notice the stark difference between the elderly couple's bodily synchronization with the son montuno's rhythmic texture and the other two couples' relatively unsynchronized relationship with the same music. The elderly couple also distinguished themselves by coordinating their choreography to the sections of the son montuno arrangement scheme.

For example, at the cierre before the diablo section, the elderly male separated from his partner, extended his left foot outward, and then circled around his partner, as she continued to execute the son's footwork. Then, as the music reached the initial alternation in the diablo or that paroxysmal moment of the son montuno, the male executed an animated full turn, followed by a thrust of his torso, legs, and arms toward his partner, a gesture that was very reminiscent of the *vacunao* of the Afro-Cuban folkloric guaguancó dance. After his climactic bodily movements executed in synchrony with the arrangement, the elderly couple rejoined in an embrace and recommenced the son's footwork as the diablo section concluded. Meanwhile, during the same cierre and the climax of the diablo section, the other two couples remained embraced, separating and animating their bodily movements only *after* the climactic sequence had passed, suggesting that they had sensed an increase in the energy, though acting on it after the fact.

In addition to demonstrating the son montuno dance style and performance in comparison to other dance styles, this event gives me some indication as to how mambo and salsa dancers who were unfamiliar with the son montuno style might have dealt with Arsenio's music in the 1950s and 1960s. Although the two middle-aged couples seemed to have enjoyed themselves, they nevertheless lacked full embodiment of the son montuno feel. The elderly couple, however, seemed to find particular enjoyment in anticipating or dialoguing with events in the music. But my learning experience did not stop at the end of this dance sequence. Assuming that the first couple was Cuban, I walked over to them, preparing to ask them about their history dancing son montuno and hoping that they had danced to Arsenio's conjunto in Havana in the 1940s. To my surprise they were American and had learned to dance son montuno from Cuban friends in Miami.

Several of the main points of this book emerge in reflecting on the significance of this event. First, the synchronization of sound and bodily movement is a central aspect of the son montuno style, and it remains important particularly for dancers to the understanding of this style as it was originally intended to be experienced. Second, although the son montuno style or *feel* initially developed from the synergetic relationship that obtained among Arsenio's musicians and mostly black Cuban dancers, understanding Arsenio's style is not limited to any one particular nationality or ethnicity, as attested to by many of the Puerto Rican dancers and musicians I interviewed. In fact, some, mostly middle-aged salsa dancers in Puerto Rico continue to dance son montuno to groups such as La Sonora Ponceña and Willie Rosario, which have recorded Arsenio's music since their formations in the 1960s and 1970s (Laurel Zmolek-Smith, personal communication). Third, despite Arsenio's professional difficulties and relative marginalization in the popular culture industry during his lifetime, his music and son montuno style continue to this day to impact popular musical trends as well as the practice of music and dance locally.

The issue of transnationalism has framed much of the recent research and scholarship on salsa music (see Berríos-Miranda 2002; Román-Velázquez 2002; Waxer 2002a, 2002b). With the transnational circulation of culture and music as its central theoretical orientation, this work has largely focused on both the impact of salsa and its musical antecedents from New York City, Puerto Rico, and Cuba on local music cultures in Venezuela, London, and Cali and these spaces' unique musical negotiations of these transnational musical flows. In doing so, some of this work has done much to move the scholarship on salsa beyond the issue of national or ethnic ownership. On the other hand, by focusing on one geographical space, these authors have presented a unidirectional perspective on such flows that not only are circular and multidirectional but also involve the movement of musicians themselves, many of whom have moved between more than two sites, like Arsenio. In addition, not enough historical documentation and critical focus has been given to salsa's musical antecedents whose transnational flows and impact predated that of salsa's and continue to shape local musical trends to this day.

This book has offered a new perspective on the interrelationship between the transnational popular music industry, a seminal figure in Cuban and Latin popular music, and the local communities for whom he performed. Specifically, by tracing the music and career of Arsenio Rodríguez, the book's perspective has moved from Havana to New York and San Juan, from Chicago back to New York, then from Curaçao to New York and Los Angeles, then back once more to New York before ending in Los Angeles. Through these movements it has focused on the distinct reception histories of his conjunto and son montuno style, from negro and macho in Havana in the 1940s to típico cubano among the Cuban diaspora and others in the 1950s and 1960s. But the transnational movements and local impact of Arsenio, his music, and style did not end with his death. In fact, never during his career was the importance of his music and style so tangible in the performance of and discourse on Cuban and Latin popular music than it has become since the 1990s. In addition to serving as a reference of stylistic authenticity among salsa musicians, aficionados, and writers, Arsenio's music continues to be rerecorded and celebrated by one of the most successful world music endeavors to date, *Buena Vista Social Club* and its ongoing solo projects.

The Afro-Cuban All Stars' CD *A Toda Cuba le Gusta* (World Circuit/Nonesuch 79476), which was released prior to the 1997 Grammy Award–winning *Buena Vista Social Club* (World Circuit/Nonesuch 79478), includes Arsenio's guaguancó "Los Sitios, acere" (Los Sitios, My Friend) and son montuno "Tumba palo cocuyé." Ibrahim Ferrer recorded Arsenio's afrocubano "Bruca maniguá" and son montuno "Mami me gustó" (I Liked That, Honey) for his self-titled solo CD (World Circuit/Nonesuch 79532). Rubén González added the son montuno "De una manera espantosa" (In a Horrific Way) on *Chanchullo* (World Circuit/Nonesuch 79503). Then, in 2004, World Circuit/Nonesuch released *Buena Vista Social Club Presents: Manuel "Guajiro" Mirabal* (79810) which is dedicated entirely to the music of Arsenio Rodríguez. These renditions (unlike those of early salsa musicians that I discussed in chapter 5) are much more faithful to the originals, both in style as well as structure. But as some critics, particularly of the Oscar-nominated film *Buena Vista Social Club*, have noted, the presentation of the music in the film as well as the CDs is marked by a certain imagined nostalgia for prerevolutionary Cuba (see Wyndham and Read 2003; Hassan 2002).

For instance, with the exception of pianist Rubén González, very few of the elder musicians had performed in Havana's working-class sociedades de color, including the real Social Club Buena Vista, after which the original Ry Cooder–led group and film was named. In addition the musical content of the CD *Buena Vista Social Club* hardly reflects the two primary musical and dance genres—son montuno and danzón-mambo—that emerged and thrived in Havana's black social clubs in the 1940s. Instead, the music in both the CD and film constitutes a geographically and historically diverse representation of Cuban music. What is also missing in *Buena Vista Social Club*'s historical and musical narrative is the importance fighting racial discrimination, segregation, and ideologies of racial supremacy had for the directors and members of the black social club, not to mention for Arsenio himself. Like the Cuban exile discourse's imaginations of prerevolutionary Cuba (see Guevara 2003), *Buena Vista Social Club* and its subsequent solo projects have largely erased the inequalities of wealth and racial conflict that determined not only the necessity for black social clubs in the first place but also the reasons why Arsenio's and his colleagues' styles were valued as "black" and "masculine."

Arsenio himself raised the same issues of racial, social, and economic injustice in his afrocubanos and other songs that he composed and recorded throughout his career. These songs and sentiments did not endear Arsenio to the political and cultural leaders of the Cuban exile community, particularly in Miami during the late 1960s, when his performance career was at its bleakest. Interestingly, two of Arsenio's son montunos from this period, "Para bailar el montuno" (To Dance the Montuno; BLPS-216) and "Mi corazón no tiene quien lo llore" (My Heart Has No One for Which to Cry; Tico LP 1175), appear on Manuel "Guajiro" Mirabal's solo CD. Not surprisingly, the liner notes make no mention of this most anomalous period of Arsenio's career, one in which early salsa musicians were performing and rerecording many of his songs, while his middle-aged conjunto was marginalized by the budding salsa music industry in New York.

In an article written for *AfroCubaWeb* (www.afrocubaweb.com) Curaçaoan writer Eugène Godfried persuasively offered an alternative perspective to those who have criticized *Buena Vista Social Club* for its nostalgic treatment of the Cuban musical past (Godfried 2000). Godfried argues that from the early 1960s through the 1980s, son music (particularly son montuno as performed by conjuntos) had declined severely in popularity in Cuba. Contributing to this was the Cuban government's decision to discontinue private black social clubs soon after 1959 and to support *nueva trova*, *songo*, and other modern Cuban styles that complemented the government's ideology of radical social, economic, and political change. The son's state of deprivation in Cuba, Godfried continues, began to change after Grupo Sierra Maestra, whose founder Juan de Marcos González helped produce *Buena Vista Social Club*, toured Curaçao in 1989. Godfried, who had helped organize the tour, remembered one dance at Hofi Bill where Grupo Sierra Maestra performed along with the Curaçaoan group Arnell i Su Orkesta. The following recollection by Godfried is worth quoting at length:

> We [Juan de Marcos and Godfried] were trying to find an answer as to why the public was not dancing with the Cuban group but was dancing with the Curaçao group that was playing Cuban son [montuno] music all the time. Juan de Marcos told me . . . that the reason was that Arnell . . . [was] playing Arsenio Rodríguez's style [whose] compositions were carried out in a more relaxed manner. Besides, they were not playing fast and upbeat guarachas all the time, like Sierra Maestra was doing, but they put more emphasis on son montuno, guajira son, guaguancó son [or conjunto-style guaguancós] and romantic boleros. (Godfried 2000)

After adapting its style and repertory around Arsenio's to better meet the tastes of Curaçaoan dancers, Sierra Maestra, according to Godfried, "became the first successful contemporary *son* musical group from Cuba to play in Curaçao" (ibid.). Five years after, in 1994, Sierra Maestra recorded its first CD, titled *¡Dundunbanza!* (WCD 041) for World Circuit/Nonesuch, the same label that would record and release *Buena Vista Social Club* two years later. It included five son montunos that were originally recorded by Arsenio's conjunto in the 1940s. Some of these, especially "Cangrejo fue a estudiar" (Cangrejo Went to School), according to Godfried, were hits throughout the Netherlands Antilles. It is no exaggeration, therefore, for Godfried to identify Sierra Maestra's 1989 reception in Curaçao and Curaçao's own local history with Arsenio's music and style in particular as a significant turning point in the revitalization and international popularity of son montuno and Cuban son music in general. Indeed, de Marcos González has done much to place Arsenio's music into the transnational circulation of contemporary world music by producing the many *Buena Vista Social Club* solo projects since initially collaborating with Ry Cooder.

With the transnational repertories of salsa and world music ever expanding, it is more important than ever for ethnomusicologists and others to conduct historical research with those who experienced the music of pioneering artists as musicians, dancers, and listeners in their original historical and social settings. Their recollections of their experiences are the closest or perhaps the only thing we have left in learning about how the music felt in performing with and dancing to these historically important groups and musicians. They also represent windows into the history of local race, class, age, and political relations and how these informed the performance and reception of the music. It is also important to trace the careers of these musicians as well as their actual musical repertories to the various geographical settings where they and their music have had an impact on local musical and social histories. Studying the interconnectedness between individual musicians, local communities, and transnational flows of music can give us the kinds of critical perspectives that will help us specify which Cuban, Puerto Rican, or Latin popular culture we are talking about.

Discography

Sources

American Federation of Musicians, Local 802, Recording Department, 322 West 48th Street, New York, New York

American Federation of Musicians, Local 802, *Minutes of the Executive Board, 1922–1985*. Reel Nos. 5257–5335.

American Federation of Musicians, Local 802, *Minutes of the Trial Board, 1922–1966*. Reel Nos. 5257–5335.

American Federation of Musicians, Local 802, *Phonograph Recording Contract Form*. Microfiche Nos. 84466–486584.

BMG Archives, 1540 Broadway, New York, New York

Cristobal Díaz Ayala

Rigler & Deutsch Record Index of Pre-LP Commercial Discs Held by the Associated Audio Archives. NYPL for the Performing Arts, 521 West 43rd Street, New York, New York

Radames Giro

Tico Label Discography (online at bsnpubs.com/tico.html)

This discography consists of five parts: (1) 78 rpm recordings by Arsenio Rodríguez's Conjuntos, 1940–56 and 1960; (2) LPs recorded by Arsenio Rodríguez's conjuntos, 1957–68; (3) CD collections of 78 rpms recorded by Arsenio Rodríguez y Su Conjunto; (4) noncommercial recordings by Arsenio Rodríguez archived at the Center for Folklife Programs and Cultural Studies Archive, Smithsonian Institution; and (5) a selected discography of contemporaneous recordings of other Latin music artists. In the first section the order of the information listed is as follows: title of the song, genre (as indicated on the actual record label), composer, catalog number, and the serial number of the CD on which the recording has been rereleased. Finally, the musicians who participated in the recordings, where known, are listed after each recording date. (Raúl Travieso and Israel Berrios were my main sources in identifying these musicians.)

78 rpm Recordings by Arsenio Rodríguez's Conjuntos, 1940–56, 1960

El pirulero no vuelve más (pregón), A. Rodríguez, 83314-A, CUCD 1703
Yo 'ta namorá (afro), A. Rodríguez, 83314-B, CUCD 1703

Recorded on September 12, 1940, for RCA Victor in Havana. Pedro Luís Sarracent, first voice and clave; Miguelito Cuní, first voice and maracas; Marcelino Guerra, second voice and guitar; Rubén "El Sentímental" Calzado, first trumpet and arranger; Miguel

Molinet, second trumpet; Lino Frías, piano; Arsenio Rodríguez, tres; Nilo alfonso, contrabass; Israel "Kiki," Rodríguez, tumbadora; Antolín Suárez Fierro "Papa Kila," bongó.

Corazón de hielo (bolero), A. Rodríguez, 83530-A, CUCD 1703
Yo tuve la culpe (bolero), A. Rodríguez, 83562-A, CUCD 1703
No hace na' la mujer (guaracha), B. J. Gutiérrez, 83562-B, CUCD 1703
Todos seguimos la conga (conga), A. Rodríguez, 83530-B, CUCD 1703

Recorded on March 31, 1941, for RCA Victor in Havana. Conrado Cepero, first voice and clave; Pedro Luís Sarracent, first voice and clave; Miguelito Cuní, first voice and maracas; Marcelino Guerra, second voice and guitar; Rubén Calzado, first trumpet and arranger; Miguel Molinet, second trumpet; René Hernández or Adolfo "Panasea" O'Reilly, piano; Arsenio Rodríguez, tres; Nilo Alfonso, contrabass; Kiki, tumbadora; Papa Kila, bongó.

Llora timbero (rumba), A. Rodríguez, Co 30789
El dulcero de Güines (pregón), A. Rodríguez, Co 30795
Si volvieras (bolero son), LF, Co 30794
Triste soledad (bolero son), G. García, Co 30790

Recorded on May 16, 1941, for Columbia in Havana. Probably the same personnel as March 31, 1941. On "Llora timbero," Israel Rodríguez Scull is listed as composer on the Library of Congress copyright card dated June 7, 1941. Arsenio Rodríguez and Tata Gutiérrez (director of Septeto Bolero) are listed as co-composers on the current BMI song catalog.

Sediento de amor (bolero son), Jacinto Scull, 83948-A
Como traigo la yuca (guaracha), A. Rodríguez, 83948-B, HQ CD 64
Con un solo pie (conga), B. J. Gutiérrez, 83963-A

Recorded on June 18, 1942, for RCA Victor in Havana. Probably the same personnel as March 31, 1941.

Intranquilidad, Mercedes Valdés, 83963-B, HQ CD 64

Recorded on June 24, 1942, for RCA Victor in Havana. Probably the same personnel as March 31, 1941.

Sin tu querer (bolero son), Pablo Cairo, 23-0050-A, CUCD 1703
Sandunguera (guaracha), Luís Piedra & M. Guerra, 23-0050-B, CUCD 1703
Triste lucha (bolero son), A. Rodríguez, 23-0061-A

Recorded on September 14, 1943, for RCA Victor in Havana. Pedro Luís Sarracent, first voice and clave; Miguelito Cuní, first voice and maracas; Marcelino Guerra, second voice and guitar; Rubén Calzado, first trumpet and arranger; Benetín Bustillo, second trumpet; Panasea, piano; Nilo Alfonso, contrabass; Arsenio Rodríguez, tres; Kiki, tumbadora; Papa Kila, bongó.

Ñaña seré (guaracha), A. Rodríguez and Guillermo Valdés, 3-0061-B

Recorded on September 21, 1943, for RCA Victor in Havana. Probably the same personnel as September 14, 1943.

Camina a trabajá, Haragón (son montuno), A. Rodríguez, 23-0082-B
¿Quién será mi amor? (bolero son), Mercedes Valdés, 23-0078-B, CUCD 1703

Recorded on November 16, 1943, for RCA Victor in Havana. Pedro Luís Sarracent, first voice and clave; Miguelito Cuní, first voice and maracas; Orlando "Güichichi" Sirial, second voice and guitar; Rubén Calzado, first trumpet and arranger; Benetín Bustillo, second trumpet; Panasea, piano; Nilo Alfonso, contrabass; Arsenio Rodríguez, tres; Kiki, tumbadora; Papa Kila, bongó.

A buscar camarón (son montuno), A. Rodríguez, 23-0076-B
Pilla con pilla, Guillermo Valdés, 23-0082-A
Oye como dice, F. Chapotín, 23-0078-A, CUCD 1703

Recorded on November 29, 1943, for RCA Victor in Havana. Probably the same personnel as November 16, 1943.

¡So caballo! (son montuno), A. Rodríguez, 23-0076-A

Recorded on December 7, 1943, for RCA Victor in Havana. Probably the same personnel as November 16, 1943.

Quien ama no traiciona (bolero son), A. Rodríguez, 23-0173-B, CUCD 1703
Mi chinita me botó (son guajiro), A. Rodríguez, 23-0173-A
Oye mi consejo (bolero son), A. Rodríguez, 23-0193-A
Estás equivocada (bolero son), Osvaldo Farrés, 23-0182-A
Mujeres, enamórenme (guaracha), A. Rodríguez, 23-0182-B
Yo no como corazón de chivo (guaracha son), 23-0193-B

Recorded on July 6, 1944, for RCA Victor in Havana. Probably the same personnel as November 16, 1943.

Tú no eres culpable (bolero), Pepe Robles and M. Guerra, 23-0362-A
Mi guane (guajira), Rafael López, 23-0350-B
Nadie más que tú (bolero), Jacinto Scull, 23-0373-B
Timbilla (rumba de cajón), A. Rodríguez, 23-0362-B
Agonía (bolero), A. Rodríguez, 23-0373-A
Yeyey (pregón), Emilio Sanso and O. Gainza, 23-0350-A

Recorded on July 5, 1945, for RCA Victor in Havana. Pedro Luís Sarracent, first voice and clave; Miguelito Cuní, first voice and maracas; Güichichi, second voice and guitar; Terry "Mapi," first trumpet; Benetín Bustillo: second trumpet; Rubén González

"El Bonito," piano and arranger; Nilo Alfonso, contrabass; Arsenio Rodríguez, tres; Kiki, tumbadora; Papa Kila, bongó.

No hay yaya sin guayacán (son montuno), A. Rodríguez, 23-0401-B, CUCD 1703
Ya lo verás (bolero), A. Rodríguez, 23-0401-A
Inspiración (bolero), Pablo Pérez Chorot, 23-0428-A
El último amor (bolero), A. Rodríguez, 23-0428-B

Recorded on November 27, 1945, for RCA Victor in Havana. Joseíto Nuñez, first voice and clave; Miguelito Cuní, first voice and maracas; Güichichi, second voice and guitar; Terry "Mapi," first trumpet; Benetín Bustillo, second trumpet; Rubén Gonzalez "El Bonito," piano and arranger; Nilo Alfonso, contrabass; Arsenio Rodríguez, tres; Kiki, tumbadora; Papa Kila, bongó.

Deuda (bolero), L. Marquetti, 23-0452-A, TCD-043
Canta, Montero (son montuno), A. Rodríguez, 23-0452-B, TCD-031

Recorded on May 20, 1946, for RCA Victor in Havana. René Álvarez, first voice and clave; Miguelito Cuní, first voice and maracas; Güichichi, second voice and guitar; Terry "Mapi," first trumpet; Benetín Bustillo, second trumpet; Arsenio Rodríguez, tres; Rubén Gonzalez "El Bonito," piano and arranger; Nilo Alfonso, contrabass; Kiki, tumbadora; Papa Kila, bongó.

Chicharronero (son), Luís Martínez, 23-0492-A, TCD-031
Una experiencia más (bolero), A. Rodríguez, 23-0519-B
Dame un cachito pa' huelé (son montuno), A. Rodríguez, 23-0492-B, TCD-031
El reloj de pastora (son), A. Rodríguez, 23-0470-B, TCD-031
Cero guapos en Yateras (son), Luís Martínez, 23-0519-A
Cangrejo fué a estudiar (son), A. Rodríguez, 23-0470A, TCD-031

Recorded on June 21, 1946, for RCA Victor in Havana. René Álvarez, first voice and clave; René Scull, first voice and maracas; Güichichi or Carlos Ramírez, second voice and guitar; Terry "Mapi," first trumpet; Guillermo Fellové or Domingo Corbacho, second trumpet; Juan "El Gordo" Rogert, third trumpet; Luís "Lilí" Martínez Griñan, piano and arranger; Nilo Alfonso, contrabass; Arsenio Rodríguez, tres; Kiki, tumbadora; Papa Kila, bongó.

Tengo que olvidarte (bolero son), Jacinto Scull, 23-0755-B, TCD-043
Celos de mujer (guaracha), A. Rodríguez, 23-0655-A
Juventud amaliana (guaguancó), A. Rodríguez, 23-0655-B, TCD-031
Semilla de caña brava (guaracha), Luís Martínez, 23-0755-A, TCD-031
¿Por qué la trajiste? (bolero son), A. Rodríguez, 23-0734-B

Recorded on December 13, 1946, for RCA Victor in Havana. René Scull, first voice and clave; Pedro Luís Sarracent, first voice and maracas; Güichichi or Carlos Ramírez, second voice and guitar; Terry "Mapi," first trumpet; El Gordo, second trumpet;

Domingo Corbacho, third trumpet; Lilí, piano; Lázaro Prieto, contrabass; Arsenio Rodríguez, tres; Kiki, tumbadora; Papa Kila, bongó.

Mi convicción (bolero son), Luís Martínez, 23-0766-A, TCD-043
Adivínalo (guaracha), José L. Forest, 23-0766-B, TCD-031
Soy el terror (son), A. Rodríguez, 23-0734-A

Recorded on January 10, 1947, for RCA Victor in Havana. René Scull, first voice and clave; Pedro Luís Sarracent, first voice and maracas; Güichichi or Carlos Ramírez, second voice and guitar; Domingo Corbacho, first trumpet; Terry "Mapi," second trumpet; El Gordo, third trumpet; Lilí, piano; Lázaro Prieto, contrabass; Arsenio Rodríguez, tres; Félix "Chocolate" Alfonso, tumbadora; Papa Kila, bongó.

Porque tu sufres (guaracha), Chano Pozo, 5057-A, TCD-017
Rumba en swing (guaracha), Chano Pozo, 5057-B, TCD-017
Cometelo tú (guaracha), Chano Pozo, 5053-A, TCD-017
Pasó en Tampa (guaracha), A. Rodríguez, 5053-B, TCD-017

Orquesta Chano Pozo con Tito Rodríguez. Recorded in July 1947 for Coda in New York City. Tito Rodríguez, first voice; Machito, maracas; Mario Bauza, trumpet and bass clarinet; Frank Davila, trumpet; Bobby Woodlen, trumpet; Fred Skerrit, alto saxophone; Eugene Johnson, alto saxophone; José "Pin" Madera, tenor saxophone; René Hernández, piano and arranger; Julio Andino, bass; Arsenio Rodríguez, tres; Ubaldo Nieto, timbales; Chano Pozo, tumbadora; José Mangual, bongó.

Contestame (bolero), A. Rodríguez, 5061-A
Sacale brillo al piso (son montuno), A. Rodríguez, 5061-B, TCD-307

Chano Pozo y su Conjunto con el Mago del Tres. Recorded in July 1947 for Coda in New York City. Panchito Riset, first voice; Jorge Alonso "Candy Store," vocal; Marcelino Guerra, vocals and clave; Mario Cora, trumpet; Frank Gilberto Ayala, piano; Julio Andino, bass; Arsenio Rodríguez, tres; Chano Pozo, tumbadora; Bilingüe, bongó.

Serende (guaguancó), Chano Pozo, 5059-A, TCD-017
Seven, Seven (son montuno), Chano Pozo, 5059-B, TCD-017

Chano Pozo y su Conjunto. Recorded in July 1947 for Coda in New York City. Panchito Riset, first voice; Jorge "Candy Store" Alonso, vocal; Marcelino Guerra, vocals and clave; Mario Cora, trumpet; Frank Gilberto Ayala, piano; Julio Andino, bass; Arsenio Rodríguez, tres; Chano Pozo, tumbadora; Bilingüe, bongó.

Lo dicen todas (guaracha), A. Rodríguez, 23-0828-B
La vida es un sueño (bolero), A. Rodríguez, 23-0828-A, TCD-031

Recorded on February 27, 1948, for RCA Victor in Havana. René Scull, first voice and clave; Pedro Luís Sarracent, first voice and maracas; Carlos Ramírez, second voice and guitar; Guillermo Fellové, first trumpet; Terry "Mapi," second trumpet; El Gordo, third trumpet; Lilí, piano and arranger; Lázaro Prieto, contrabass; Arsenio Rodríguez, tres; Chocolate, tumbadora; Papa Kila, bongó.

Yo no engaño a las nenas (son montuno), A. Rodríguez, 1205-A, TCD-017
Tocoloro (son montuno), A. Rodríguez, 1205-B, TCD-017
Tumba palo cucuye (son montuno), A. Rodríguez, 1206-A, TCD-017
Tintorera ya llegó (son montuno), A. Rodríguez, 1206-B, TCD-017

Recorded in March 1948 for Spanish Music Center (SMC) in Havana under the name Estrellas de Ritmo. Personnel probably the same as February 27, 1948.

El tabernero (bolero), Rafael Ortíz, 23-0888-B, TCD-043
El Cerro tiene la llave (guaracha), Fernando Noa, 23-0888-A, TCD-031
Te esperaré (bolero son), L. M. Griñan, 23-0897-A
No vuelvo a Morón (son montuno), Otilio del Portal, 23-0897-B

Recorded on April 8, 1948, for RCA Victor in Havana. Personnel same as February 27, 1948.

Esa china tiene coimbre (son montuno), A. Rodríguez, 23-0946-B, TCD-031
Soy tu destino (bolero), Isolina Carrillo, 23-0946-A, TCD-043

Recorded on March 26, 1948, for RCA Victor in Havana. Personnel probably the same as February 27, 1948.

Sacando candela (guaracha), Gervacio Kessell, 23-0995-B

Recorded on June 1, 1948, for RCA Victor in Havana. Personnel probably the same as February 27, 1948.

A Puerto Rico (bolero), A. Rodríguez, 23-0995-A
No toque el guao (son montuno), A. Rodríguez, 23-0975-B
Me siento muy solo (bolero), A. Rodríguez, 23-0975-A, TCD-043

Recorded on June 22, 1948, for RCA Victor in Havana. René Scull, first voice and clave; Pedro Luís Sarracent, first voice and maracas; Carlos Ramírez, second voice and guitar; Domingo Corbacho, first trumpet; Terry "Mapi," second trumpet; El Gordo, third trumpet; Lilí, piano and arranger; Lázaro Prieto, contrabass; Arsenio Rodríguez, tres; Chocolate, tumbadora; Papa Kila, bongó.

Monte adentro (son montuno), A. Rodríguez, 1209-A, TCD-017
Apurruñenme mujeres (son montuno), A. Rodríguez, 1209-B, TCD-017
Ya me lo dio (son montuno), A. Rodríguez, 1210-A
Masango (son montuno), A. Rodríguez, 1210-B

Recorded in July 1948 for SMC in Havana under the name Estrellas del Ritmo. Personnel probably the same as June 22, 1948.

A Belén le toca Ahora (guaguancó), A. Rodríguez, 23-1072-A, TCD-031
Los tres Juanas (bolero), B. J. Gutierrez, 23-1072-B, CUCD 1703

Recorded on October 19, 1948, for RCA Victor in Havana. Personnel probably the same same as June 22, 1948.

Luna al amanecer (bolero), L. M. Griñan, 23-1105-A
Dame un besito (son montuno), A. Rodríguez, 23-1130-B, CUCD 1703
Orgullo inútil (bolero), Rosendo Ruíz Jr., 23-1130-A

Recorded on October 27, 1948, for RCA Victor in Havana. Personnel same as June 22, 1948.

Lo que dice VD. (son montuno), Jesús Guerra, 23-1105-B, TCD-031

Recorded on October 28, 1948, for RCA Victor in Havana. Personnel probably the same as June 22, 1948.

Feliz viaje (bolero), A. Rodríguez, 23-1147-A
No me llores más (son montuno), L. M. Griñan, 23-1147-B, TCD-043

Recorded on January 12, 1949, for RCA Victor in Havana. René Scull, first voice and clave; Carlos Ramírez, second voice and guitar; Lilí, piano and arranger; Lázaro Prieto, contrabass; Arsenio Rodríguez, tres; Chocolate, tumbadora; Papa Kila, bongó.

Flor del fango (bolero), Cristóbal Doval, 23-1171-A
Que cosas tendran las mujeres (son montuno), L. M. Griñan, 23-1171-B

Recorded on January 28, 1949, for RCA Victor in Havana. Personnel probably the same as January 12, 1949.

En su partir (bolero), Jacinto Scull, 23-1180-B, TCD-043
Pueblo Nuevo se paso (guaguancó), L. M. Griñan, 23-1180-A
Llévatelo todo (son montuno), L. M. Griñan, 23-1194-A, TCD-043
Mírame más (bolero), Enrique Hernández, 23-1194-B

Recorded on February 19, 1949, for RCA Victor in Havana. Personnel probably the same as January 12, 1949.

Me boté de guano (montuno), Alfredo Armenteros, 23-1336-A, TCD-031
Es mejor olvidarte (bolero), René Scull, 23-1336-B

Recorded on August 2, 1949, for RCA Victor in Havana. René Scull, first voice and clave; Carlos Ramírez, second voice and guitar; Alfredo "Chocolate" Armenteros, second trumpet; Lilí, piano and arranger; Lázaro Prieto, contrabass; Arsenio Rodríguez, tres; Chocolate, tumbadora; Papa Kila, bongó.

El palo tiene curujey (son montuno), Pascuel Bueno Griñan, 23-1367-B, CUCD 1703
Finaliza un amor (bolero), Raúl Díaz, 23-1367-A, CUCD 1703

Recorded on August 19, 1949, for RCA Victor in Havana. René Scull, first voice and clave; Conrado Cepero, first voice and maracas; Carlos Ramírez, second voice and guitar; Rafael Corbacho, first trumpet; Chocolate, second trumpet; Lilí, piano and arranger; Lázaro Prieto, contrabass; Arsenio Rodríguez, tres; Chocolate, tumbadora; Papa Kila, bongó.

Los Sitios aceré (guaguancó), Silvio A. Pino, 23-1382-A, TCD-043
Sagrado amor (bolero), Lázaro Prieto, 23-1382-B, TCD-043

Recorded on September 6, 1949, for RCA Victor in Havana. René Scull, first voice and clave; Conrado Cepero, first voice and maracas; Carlos Ramírez, second voice and guitar; Félix Chappotín, first trumpet; Chocolate, second trumpet; Oscar "Florecita" Velazco, third trumpet; Lilí, piano and arranger; Lázaro Prieto, contrabass; Arsenio Rodríguez, tres; Chocolate, tumbadora; Papa Kila, bongó.

Dundumbanza (son montuno), A. Rodríguez, 23-1488-A/51-5022-A, TCD-043
Flor de canela (bolero), A. Rodríguez, 23-1488-B/51-5022-B, CUCD 1703

Recorded on December 29, 1949, for RCA Victor in Havana. Personnel probably the same as September 6, 1949.

Pero yo no se (bolero), F. Chappottín, 23-1504-A/51-5029
Juventud de Colón (guaguancó), Federico Gayle Suárez, 23-1504-B/51-5029

Recorded on January 13, 1950, for RCA Victor in Havana. Personnel probably the same as September 6, 1949.

No puedo comer vistigacha (guaracha), A. Rodríguez, 23-1518-A, TCD-043
Por tu bien (bolero), L. M. Griñan, 23-1518-B, CUCD 1703

Recorded on January 26, 1950, for RCA Victor in Havana. Personnel probably the same as September 6, 1949.

Kila, Quique y Chocolate (son montuno), I. Rodríguez, 3/29/50, 23-1583-A, TCD-031
Vuelvo a la vida (bolero), A. Rodríguez, 23-1583-B, TCD-043

Recorded for RCA Victor in Havana. René Scull, first voice and clave; Conrado Cepero, first voice and maracas; Carlos Ramírez, second voice and guitar; Félix Chappotín, first trumpet; Carmelo Alvarez, second trumpet; Florecita, third trumpet; Lilí, piano and arranger; Lázaro Prieto, contrabass; Arsenio Rodríguez, tres; Kiki or Chocolate, tumbadora; Papa Kila, bongó.

El rumbón de Luyanó (guaguancó), Lázaro Prieto, 23-1591-A/51-5093-A, TCD-043
Recuerda aquella noche (bolero), A. Rodríguez, 23-1591-B/51-5093-B

Recorded on April 19, 1950, for RCA Victor in Havana. Personnel probably the same as March 29, 1950.

El rincón caliente (son), A. Rodríguez, 23-1604-A/51-5106-A, TCD-031
Qué susto (bolero), A. Rodríguez, 23-1604-B/51-5106-B, CUCD 1703

Recorded on April 24, 1950, for RCA Victor in Havana. Personnel probably the same as March 29, 1950.

La sandunga del son (son montuno), Raúl Díaz, 23-5205-A
Con reciprocidad (bolero), B. J. Gutiérrez, 23-5205-B

Recorded on June 29, 1950, for RCA Victor in Havana. Personnel probably the same as 29 March 1950.

Anabacoa (guaracha), J. Ramírez, 23-5209-A
Cárdenas (bolero), A. Rodríguez, 23-5209-B

Recorded on August 8, 1950, for RCA Victor in Havana. Personnel probably the same as March 29, 1950.

Todo terminó (bolero), I. Rodríguez, 23-5219-A
Juventud de Cayo Hueso (guaguancó), A. Rodríguez, 23-5219-B, TCD-031
Con un amor se borra otro amor (son montuno), A. Rodríguez, 23-5237-A, TCD-043
Ten valor (bolero), A. Rodríguez, 23-5237-B

Recorded on September 12, 1950, for RCA Victor in Havana. Personnel probably the same as March 29, 1950.

Ta benito (afro), A. Rodríguez, 23-5299-A, TCD-043
Aquí como allá (lamento), A. Rodríguez, 23-5299-B, TCD-031
Te mantengo y no quieres (son montuno), Rafael Ortíz, 23-5300-A
Cree lo que tú quierás (bolero), J. Rodríguez, 23-5300-B

Recorded on November 9, 1950, for RCA Victor in Havana. Estella Rodríguez, first voice on "Ta Benito" and "Aquí como allá"; René Scull, first voice and clave; Conrado Cepero, first voice and maracas; Carlos Ramírez, second voice and guitar; Félix Chappottín, first trumpet; Florecita, second trumpet; Carmelo Alvarez, third trumpet; Arsenio Rodríguez, tres; Kiki or Chocolate, tumbadora; Papa Kila, bongó; Lilí, piano; Lázaro Prieto, bass.

El que no tiene no vale (bolero son), F. Chapottin, 23-5304-A
Quizás con los años (bolero), Lazaro Prieto, 23-5304-B

Recorded on November 15, 1950, for RCA Victor in Havana. Personnel probably same as November 9, 1950.

Me dijo que sí y le dije que no (son montuno), A. Rodríguez, 23-5365-A
Falso desprecio (bolero), Antonio Alonso, 23-5365-B

Recorded on February 13, 1951, for RCA Victor in Havana. Personnel probably same as November 9, 1950.

Caminante y Laborí (son montuno), A. Rodríguez, 23-5383-A
Jamás te perdonaré (bolero), Enrique Pérez Poey, 23-5383-B

Recorded on March 6, 1951, for RCA Victor in Havana. Personnel probably same as November 9, 1950.

Tu faz morena (bolero), Juan Limonta, 23-5405-A
Jumba (son montuno), A. Rodríguez, 23-5405-B

Recorded on April 3, 1951, for RCA Victor in Havana. Personnel probably same as November 9, 1950.

Murumba (rizo negro), F. Chappottín, 23-5432-B
Negrita (guajira son), M. Guerra, 23-5432-A

Recorded on May 1, 1951, for RCA Victor in Havana. Miguelito Cuní, first voice and clave; René Scull, first voice and maracas; Carlos Ramírez, second voice and guitar; Félix Chappottín, first trumpet; Florecita, second trumpet; Carmelo Alvarez, third trumpet; Arsenio Rodríguez, tres; Kiki or Chocolate, tumbadora; Papa Kila, bongó; Lilí, piano; Lázaro Prieto, bass.

Amores de Verano (guaguancó), A. Rodríguez, 23-5461-A
Te contaré (bolero), A. Rodríguez, 23-5461-B

Recorded on May 29, 1951, for RCA Victor in Havana. Personnel probably the same as May 1, 1951.

Amor en cenizas (bolero), A. Rodríguez, 23-5481-A
Mira . . . cuidadito (son montuno), A. Rodríguez, 23-5481-B

Recorded on June 22, 1951, for RCA Victor in Havana. Personnel probably the same as May 1, 1951.

A Graciela (bolero), A. Rodríguez, 23-5520-B
Mira que soy chambelón (son montuno), A. Rodríguez, 23-5520-A

Recorded on August 14, 1951, for RCA Victor in Havana. Personnel probably the same as May 1, 1951.

Pobre mi Cuba (lamento guajiro), A. Rodríguez, 23-5593, TCD-043
Guaraguí (son montuno), A. Rodríguez, 23-5593, TCD-043

Recorded on October 25, 1951, for RCA Victor in Havana. Personnel probably same as May 1, 1951.

Ya se fué (bolero), M. Guerra, 23-5624
Amor a mi patria (lamento), A. Rodríguez, 23-5624

Recorded on December 11, 1951, for RCA Victor in Havana. Personnel probably the same as on May 1, 1951.

Esclavo triste (lamento), A. Rodríguez, 10-040-A
Mulence (guaguancó), A. Rodríguez, 10-041-B
Pa' que gozen (mambo son), A. Rodríguez, 10-041-A
La gente del Bronx (guaguancó), A. Rodríguez, 10-040-B

Recorded ca. 1951 for Tico in New York City. Released in 1955 on the ten-inch LP *Authentic Cuban Mambo's: Arsenio Rodriguez and his Orchestra* (LP-135) and re-released on the CD *Arsenio Rodríguez y su Conjunto: "Como se goza en el Barrio"* (TCD-022). René Scull, first voice; Manolo "El Barroso" Morales, first voice; Candido Antomattei, second voice and guitar; Edil Rivera, trumpet; Luís Berríos Serralta, trumpet; Héctor "Venezuela" Vidal, trumpet; René Hernández, piano and arranger; Arsenio Rodríguez, tres; Lázaro Prieto, bass; Raúl Travieso, bongó; Kiki, tumbadora.

Jaguey (son montuno), A. Rodríguez, 10-074-A
Meta y guaguancó (guaguancó), A. Rodríguez, 10-074-B
Esas no (son montuno), A. Rodríguez, 10-075-A
Como se goza en el barrio (guaguancó), A. Rodríguez, 10-075-B

Recorded c. 1951 for Tico in New York City. Released in 1955 on the ten-inch LP *Authentic Cuban Mambo's: Arsenio Rodriguez and his Orchestra* (LP-135) and re-released on the CD *Arsenio Rodríguez y su Conjunto: "Como se goza en el Barrio"* (TCD-022). Personnel same as above, except René Scull replaced by Juán Olano, first voice.

Burundanga (montuno afro), F. Chappottín, 23-5644
Injusta duda (bolero canción), Enrique González, 23-5644

Recorded on January 22, 1952, for RCA Victor in Havana. Personnel probably the same as May 1, 1951.

Mi conoco (guajira son), A. Rodríguez, 23-5694
Pogolotti (guaguancó), Eloy Oliva, 23-5694

Recorded on March 18, 1952, for RCA Victor in Havana. Personnel probably same as May 1, 1951.

Swing y son (swing-son), A. Rodríguez, 10-121-A
Oiga mi guaguancó (guaguancó), A. Rodríguez, 10-122
Ahora capetillo (son capetillo), A. Rodríguez, 10-123-B
Oye mi cantar (guajira), A. Rodríguez, 10-123-A
Yo soy chambelon (son montuno), A. Rodríguez, 10-120-A
Maye santa (son montuno), A. Rodríguez, 10-121-B
Arpegio por Arsenio (solo de tres), A. Rodríguez, 10-120-B
Se va el comparsa (conga), A. Rodríguez, 10-122

Recorded c. 1952 for Tico in New York City. Released in 1955 on the ten-inch LP *Authentic Cuban Mambo's: Arsenio Rodriguez and his Orchestra*, vol. 2 (LP-136) and rereleased on the CD *Arsenio Rodríguez y su Conjunto: "Como se goza en el Barrio"* (TCD-022). Personnel same as above, except Ray Coen replaces René Hernández on piano.

No quiero (son capetillo), I. Rodríguez, Ex 20-334, TRLP 5005/SCCD 9352
Si me voy (bolero), I. Rodríguez, Ex 20-334/SCCD 9352
Besarte quisiera (bolero rítmico), A. Rodríguez, Ex 20-335/SCCD 9352
Se formo el bochinche (son montuno), I. Rodríguez, Ex 20-335/SCCD 9352

Recorded on April 9, 1952, for Seeco (Exito) in New York City. Released in 1958 on the LP *Exitos de Arsenio Rodríguez y su Conjunto* (TRLP-5005). René Scull, first voice; El Barroso, first voice; Candido Antomattei, second voice and guitar; Edil Rivera, trumpet; Luís Berríos Serralta, trumpet; Venezuela, trumpet; Arsenio Rodríguez, tres; Ray Coen, piano and arranger; Lázaro Prieto, bass; Raúl Travieso, bongó; Kiki, tumbadora. Sources: RDRI, CDA

Solo fué un sueño (bolero), Felipe Goyco "Don Felo," Ex 20-347, TRLP 5005/SCCD 9352
El dolorcito de mi china (son capetillo), I. Rodríguez, Ex 20-347, TRLP 5005/SCCD 9352
Hipocresía (bolero), I. Rodríguez, Ex 20-348, TRLP 5005/SCCD 9352
Cambia el paso (son capetillo), I. Rodríguez, Ex 20-348, TRLP 5005/SCCD 9352

Recorded on June 27, 1952, for Seeco (Exito) in New York City. Released in 1958 on the LP *Exitos de Arsenio Rodríguez y su Conjunto* (TRLP-5005). Personnel same as April 9, 1952.

Juégame limpio (son capetillo), A. Rodríguez, Ex 20-369, TRLP 5005/SCCD 9352
Vive en el recuerdo (bolero), A. Rodríguez, Ex 20-369, TRLP 5005/SCCD 9352
Ya voló (conga), Neno González, Ex 20-370
Se ama una vez (bolero), A. Rodríguez, Ex 20-370

Recorded on September 12, 1952, for Seeco (Exito) in New York City. Ex 186 and 187 released in 1958 on the LP *Exitos de Arsenio Rodríguez y su Conjunto* (TRLP-5005). Personnel probably the same as on April 9, 1952, except René Scull replaced by Juán Olano, first voice.

Que me mande la niña (son mambo), I. Rodríguez, Ex 20-386, ESCD-4218
Pimienta (son capetillo), I. Rodríguez, Ex 20-386, ESCD-4218
Pobre chinito (mambo), I. Rodríguez, Ex 20-385, ESCD-4218
Baila Simón (son montuno), I. Rodríguez, Ex 20-385, ESCD-4218

Recorded on April 2, 1953, for Seeco (Exito) in New York City. Personnel probably the same as on September 12, 1952. Source: CDA.

Mambo abacua (mambo), A. Rodríguez, 23-6696
Mi primer cariño (cha-cha), A. Rodríguez, 23-6696
Acerca el oido (bolero), A. Rodríguez, 23-6734
Mambo en la cueva (mambo), Tata Gutiérrez, 23-6734

Recorded on March 16, 1955, for RCA Victor in New York City. Güito, first voice; El Barroso, first voice; Candido Antomattei, second voice; Edil Rivera, first trumpet; Luís Berrios Serralta, second trumpet; Venezuela, third trumpet; Arsenio Rodríguez, tres; Israel Berrios, guitar; El Látigo, piano and arranger; Cuajarón, bass; Raúl Travieso, bongó; Kiki Travieso, tumbadora; José Valiente, timbales.

Me estoy comiendo un cable (guaracha), A. Rodríguez, 23-6811
Cuba cha cha cha (cha-cha), A. Rodríguez, 23-6811
Sobre el arco iris (cha-cha), E.Y. Harburg and H. Arlen 23-6840
Conformate (guaguancó), A. Rodríguez, 23-6840

Recorded on June 21, 1955, for RCA Victor in New York City. Personnel probably the same as March 16, 1955.

Lo sabía (bolero), A. Rodríguez, 23-6970
Que negra pa' acelerá (rumba), A. Rodríguez, 23-6985
Me quedé sin ti (bolero), A. Rodríguez, 23-7000
Titi, tu kundungo quiere papa (cha-cha), A. Rodríguez, 23-6970
Ayaca de maiz (son pregón), Silvano Schueg "Chori," 23-7000

Graciela, tú lo sabes (cha-cha), A. Rodríguez, 23-6985

Recorded on April 16, 1956, for RCA Victor in Havana. Güito, first voice; Estela Rodríguez, first voice; Orlando "Wichi" Sirial, second voice. Other musicians are unknown.

Triste lucha (bolero), A. Rodríguez, 23-7129
Dame tu yoyo Ma Belén (son montuno), A. Rodríguez, 23-7129
Contigo no soy feliz (bolero), Jacinto Scull, 23-7140
Casera mire que caña (son pregón), A. Rodríguez, 23-7140
Adios Roncona (columbia matancera), A. Rodríguez, 23-7120
Con flores del matadero (guaguancó), A. Rodríguez, 23-7120

Recorded on October 5, 1956, for RCA Victor in Havana. Probably the same personnel as April 16, 1956.

Curazao (bolero-cha), A. Rodríguez, 45-6008-A
Son montuno en Curazao (son montuno), A. Rodríguez, 45-6008-B

Recorded in June 1960 for Grabaciones Angel Job in Curaçao. Jose Casseres (vocals), Frank Sufrón (vocals), Macucho (piano), Luís Berrios Seralta (trumpet), Raúl Travieso (bongo and timbales), and Kiki (tumbadora).

LPs Recorded by Arsenio Rodríguez's Conjuntos, 1957–68

Montunos cubanos: Estrellas del Ritmo (SMC Pro Arte C-508). Recorded as a ten-inch LP for SMC in New York City. Reissued on CD *Legendary Sessions: Chano Pozo & Arsenio Rodríguez* (TCD-017). René Scull, first voice; Marcelino Guerra, second voice; René Hernández, piano; Arsenio Rodríguez, tres; Lázaro Prieto, bass; Raúl Travieso, bongó; Kiki, tumbadora. Other musicians are unknown. According to Radames Giro, these recordings were made on May 10, 1950; according to the liner notes to CD TCD-017 these recordings were made in 1953. It is more likely that the 1950 date is accurate, based on the musicians who appear on these recordings (i.e., by 1952 Marcelino Guerra and René Hernández had been replaced, the latter by Ray Coen) and the fact that between 1952 and 1953 Arsenio was recording new songs he was marketing as capettilos (see Exito recordings, 1952–53). Furthermore, in 1950, Arsenio was still under contract with RCA, hence the surreptitious name Estrellas del Ritmo for the SMC recordings. His contract with RCA ended by June 1952 and did not resume until 1955.

Palo congo (Blue Note LP-1561). Recorded for Blue Note in New York City. Released on LP in 1957 and reissued on CD (Blue Note TOCJ-1561) in 1998. Sabu L. Martínez, tumbadora and vocal; Arsenio Rodríguez, tres, tumbadora, and vocal; Raúl Travieso, bongó; Kiki, tumbadora; Ray Romero, tumbadora; Evaristo Baro, bass; Willie Capo, vocal; Sarah Baro Martínez, vocal.

Sabroso y caliente con Arsenio Rodríguez y su Conjunto (Puchito 586). Recorded for Puchito in New York City. Released on LP c. 1957 and rereleased on CD Antilla 586. Luís "Güito" Kartwrite, first voice; Julian Llanos, first voice; Candido Antomattei, second voice; Gilberto Valdés, flute; Pedro Luís Jackson, trumpet; Luís Berrios Serralta, trumpet; Mario Cora, trumpet; René "El Latigo" Hernández, piano; Evaristo "Cuajarón" Baro, contrabass; Arsenio Rodríguez, tres; Francisco Angel "Kako" Bastar, timbal; Raúl Travieso, bongó; Kiki, tumbadora.

Primitivo (RST-2261). Recorded for Roost in New York City in 1958. Released in 1965; rereleased as *Arsenio y Kike: canta Monguito* (Tico LP-1173) in 1968 and *Primitivo* on CD (Tico SLP-1173) in 1999. Ramón "Monguito" Quián, first vocal; Davy González, first vocal; Candido Antomattei, second voice; Israel Berrios, second voice and guitar; Agustin Caraballoso, trumpet; Johnny Malco, trumpet; Arsenio Rodríguez, tres; Abelardo Chacón, timbal; Kiki, tumbadora. Source: Both Sides Now Stereo Newsletter (bsnpubs.com).

Cumbanchando con Arsenio (Fiesta en Harlem) (SMC-1074). Recorded in New York City in 1960. Rosalia Montalvo, vocal; Israel Berrios, second voice and guitar; Alfredo Valdés Jr., piano; Arsenio Rodríguez, tres; Raúl Travieso, bongó and vocal; Kiki, tumbadora. Other musicians are unknown.

Arsenio Rodríguez y Su Conjunto vol. 1 (ALP 1337). Recorded for Ansonia in New York City, c. 1959–60. Released c. 1964. Reissued on CD HGCD 1337. Chewi Rivera, first voice; Candido Antomattei, second voice; Israel Berrios, second voice and guitar; Alfredo "Chocolate" Armenteros, trumpet; Victor Paz, trumpet; Agustin Caraballoso, trumpet; Arsenio Rodríguez, tres; Alfredo Valdés Jr., piano and arranger; Raúl Díaz, bass; Evelio Quintero, timbal; Raúl Travieso, bongó; Kiki, tumbadora.

Arsenio Rodríguez y Su Conjunto vol. 2 (Ansonia 1418). Recorded for Ansonia in New York City, c. 1960–62. Reissued on CD HGCD 1337 and Ansonia CD-1418. Santiago Cerrón, first voice; Marcelino Guerra, second voice; Israel Berrios, second voice and guitar; Alfredo "Chocolate" Armenteros, trumpet; Victor Paz, trumpet; Agustin Caraballoso, trumpet; Johnny Marco, trumpet; José "Bebo" Peréz Cedeño, tenor saxophone; Arsenio Rodríguez, tres; René "El Látigo" Hernández, piano; Alfonso "El Panameño" Joseph, bass; Evelio Quintero, timbal; Kiki, tumbadora.

La pachanga (Tico Records TRSLP-1092). One LP, 1963. Reissued on Tico CD TRSLP-1092. One CD, 1999. Chewi Rivera, first voice; Israel Berrios, second voice and guitar; Alfredo Valdés Jr., piano; Arsenio Rodríguez, tres; Kiki, tumbadora. Other musicians are unknown.

Quindembo: Afro Magic La Magia de Arsenio Rodríguez (CLT 7049). Recorded for Columbia Records in New York City, 1963. Reissued as *Leyendas/Legends: Quindembo: Afro Magic La Magia de Arsenio Rodríguez* (CDL 81534/2-469742) by Sony Tropical, 1995. Arsenio Rodríguez, tres, vocals, and percussion; Kiki, percussion; Evaristo Baro, bass; Mauricio Smith, flute, tenor saxophone, and arranger; Gene Jefferson, alto saxophone; José Valiente, percussion; Evelio Quintero, trap set and percussion.

Patato & Totico (Verve V6-5037). One LP, 1967. Reissued on Mediterraneo MCD-10065. One CD, n.d., and Verve POCJ-2777. One CD, 1999. Carlos "Patato" Valdés, quinto; Eugenio "Totico" Arango, vocal; Juan "Curba" Dreke, vocal; Hector Cadavieco, vocal; Mario Cadavieco, vocal; Tony Mayarí, vocal; Virgilio Martí, vocal; Arsenio Rodríguez, tres; Israel "Cachao" López, bass; Papaito, clave; Francisco "Panchin" Valdés, palitos.

Viva Arsenio! Arsenio Rodriguez & the Afro-Cubano Sound (BLPS-216). Recorded for Bang Records in New York City in 1966 and released in 1967. Arsenio Rodríguez, tres, vocals, and director; Marcelino Guerra, second voice; Israel Berríos, second voice; Anita Delgado, voice; Israel "Cachao" López, contrabass; Evelio Quintero, timbal and drums; Kiki, tumbadora; José Mangual, bongó.

Arsenio Dice (Tico LP 1175). Reissued on Tico SLP 1175. One CD, 1998. Recorded for Tico in New York City in 1968. Julian Llanos, first voice; Israel Berrios, second voice and guitar; Marcelino Guerra, second voice; Victor Paz, trumpet; Agustín Caraballoso, trumpet; José "Bebo" Peréz Cedeño, tenor saxophone; René "El Látigo" Hernández, piano and arranger; Arsenio Rodríguez, tres and director; Kiki, tumbadora; Alfonso "El Panameño" Joseph, bass.

CD Collections of 78 rpms Recorded by Arsenio Rodríguez y Su Conjunto

A todos los barrios: Arsenio Rodríguez. Cariño Records DBM1-5803. One LP, 1974. Reissued BMG Music 3336-2-RL. One CD, 1992.

Arsenio Rodríguez y Su Conjunto: Oye como dice. Cubanacán CD 1703. One CD, 1997.

Arsenio Rodríguez y Su Conjunto: Tocoloro. Música Latina Nostalgia 55006. One CD, 1999.

Como se Goza en el Barrio. Tumbao Cuban Classics TCD-022. One CD, 1992.

Cuban Classics vol. 8: Arsenio/Chano/Estrellas. WS Latino. WSCD-4218. One CD, 2001.

Dundunbanza 1946–1951. Tumbao Cuban Classics. TCD-043. One CD, 1994.

Exitos de Arsenio y Su Conjunto. Tropical. Reissued as *Arsenio Rodríguez: Clasicas de un Sonero.* Seeco SCCD 9352. One CD, 1998.

Montunos Cubanos. SMC. 1950. Rereleased as *Legendary Sessions: Chano Pozo & Arsenio Rodriguez with Machito and his Orchestra.* Tumbao Cuban Classics TCD-017. One CD, 1992.

Montuneando con Arsenio Rodríguez y su Conjunto 1946–1950. Tumbao Cuban Classics TCD-031. One CD, 1993.

Noncommercial Recordings by Arsenio Rodríguez Archived at the Center for Folklife Programs and Cultural Studies Archive, Smithsonian Institution

Festival Recordings: First Church of Christ Choir; Jimmy Driftwood; Eva and Clarence Girvin; Rodriguez Brothers (Festival of American Folklife. 69.101.11. 10RR. FP-1969-10RR-011).

Festival Recordings: Mono Dub of 1969-0012: Rodriguez Brothers; Moving Star Hall Singers; Ola Belle Reed, Alec (Festival of American Folklife. 69.101.67. 7RR. FP-1969-7RR-0067). Recorded in Washington, DC, at the Festival of American Folklife, July 6, 1969. Festival Recordings, morning.

Festival Recordings: Mono Dub of 69-0007: Rodriguez Brothers; Moving Star Hall Singers (Festival of American Folklife. 69.101.55. 7RR. FP-1969-7RR-0055). Recorded in Washington, DC, at the Festival of American Folklife, July 5, 1969. Festival Recordings, evening, Departmental Auditorium/Main Stage (Center of Mall). "Black Music through Languages of the New World," Bernice Reagon, MC.

Festival Recordings: Rodriguez Brothers (Festival of American Folklife. 69.101.49. 7RR. FP-1969-7RR-0049). Recorded in Washington, DC, at the Festival of American Folklife, July 5, 1969. Festival Recordings, afternoon, Toby Show Tent, Bernice Reagon, MC.

Festival Recordings: Rodriguez Brothers; Moving Star Hall Singers (Festival of American Folklife. 69.101.07. 10RR. FP-1969-10RR-0007).

Festival Recordings: Rodriguez Brothers; Moving Star Hall Singers; Ola Belle Reed, Alec Campbell (Festival of American Folklife. 69.101.12. 10RR. FP-1969-10RR-0012).

Rinzler Fieldwork: Arsenio Rodriguez (7RR. FP-RINZ-7RR-0813). Recorded in New York City in May 1964 for Ralph Rinzler.

Selected Discography

Abelardo Barroso con la Orquesta Sensación, 1954–1956: No hay como mi son. Caney CCD 514. One CD, 1996.

Antología integral del son vol. 1, *Bases históricas: Familia Valera Miranda.* Siboney/EGREM LD-286 and LD-287. Two LPs, n.d.

Antonio Arcaño y sus Maravillas: Danzón mambo, 1944–1951. Tumbao Cuban Classics TCD-029. One CD, 1993.

The Best of René Touzet. GNP/Crescendo Record. GNPD 2000. One CD, 1994.

The Best of Tito Puente and his Orchestra vol. 1, *1950–1960*. BMG Music 3369-2-RL. One CD, 1992.

The Best of Tito Rodríguez and his Orchestra vol. 1, *1955–1956*. BMG Music 3419-2-RL. One CD, 1992.

The Best of Tito Rodríguez and his Orchestra vol. 2, *1953–1955*. BMG Music 74321-15944-2. One CD, 1993.

Boogaloos con el Gran Combo. Cantan Pellín Rodríguez y Andy Montañez. Gema 3044. One LP, n.d.

Buena Vista Social Club Presents Manuel "Guajiro" Mirabal. World Circuit/Nonesuch 79810-2. One CD, 2004.

Cañonazo: Johnny Pacheco. Fania SLP 325. One CD, 1972. Originally recorded c. 1964.

Celia Cruz con La Sonora Matancera en vivo C.M.Q. (1951–1952). Barbaro Records B230. One CD, 1995.

Celia, Johnny, Justo and Papo: Recordando el ayer. Fania Records VS-52. One Cd, 1976.

Chappotin y sus Estrellas. Panart Records 4072. One CD, 1994.

Chappotín y Sus Estrellas. Antilla CD-107. One CD, n.d.

Chappottin y sus Estrellas. Bongo Latino CDB-010. One CD, 1994.

Chappottin y sus Estrellas. Antilla Records CD-594. One CD, n.d.

Conjunto Casino vol. 2. Panart Records 5169. One CD, 1994.

Conjunto Casino "En cumbanchoa." Discmedi Blau DM 058CD. One CD, n.d.

Conjunto Casino: Rumba quimbumba, 1941–1946. Tumbao Cuban Classics TCD-030. One CD, 1993.

Conjunto Kubavana de Alberto Ruíz: Rumba en el Patio. Tumbao Cuban Classics TCD-034. One CD, 1994.

Conjunto Modelo: Guaguancó en La Habana. Tumbao Cuban Classics TCD-059. One CD, 1995.

Cortijo en New York: Cortijo y su Combo con Ismael Rivera. Rumba Records CD 55515. One CD, n.d.

Cortijo y su Combo: "El alma de un pueblo." Seeco SCCD-9326. One CD, 1999.

Cuando suenan los tambores: Tito Puente y su Orquesta, 1949–1951. BMG Music 3226-2-RL. One CD, 1992.

Cuban Big Bands 1940–1942. Harlequin HQ CD 63. One CD, 1995.

Cuban Counterpoint: History of the Son Montuno. Rounder Records CD 1078. One CD, 1992.

Cuban Sextetos & Conjuntos. Harlequin HQ CD 64. One CD, 1996.

Eddie Palmieri: Echando pa'lante (Straight Ahead). Tico SLP 1113. One CD, n.d. Originally recorded in 1964.

Eddie Palmieri: Lo que traigo es sabroso. Alegre LPA 8320. One CD, 1996. Originally recorded in 1964.

Eddie Palmieri and His Orchestra: Super-Imposition. Tico SLP 1194. One CD, n.d. Originally recorded in 1970.

Eddie Palmieri y su Conjunto "La Perfecta" vol. 2, *El molestoso*. Alegre LPA 8240. One CD, 1996. Originally recorded in 1962.

Go Go Mambo!: Pérez Prado and his Orchestra. Tumbao Cuban Classics TCD-013. One CD, 1992.

Guaguancó a todos los barrios: Conjunto Estrellas de Chocolate. Antilla Records CD-15. One CD, n.d.

Güiro, bongó y maracas: Cuban Dance Bands in New York, 1931–1938. Harlequin HQ CD 126. One CD, 1999.

Hot Music from Cuba, 1907–1936. Harlequin HQ CD 23. One CD, 1993.

Ismael Rivera con Cortijo y su Combo: Con todos los hierros/Everything but the Kitchen Sink! Tico TSLP 1158. One CD, 1971.

Johnny Pacheco: Viva Africa. Fania Records SLP 330. One CD, 1972.

José Curbelo and his Orchestra: "Live at the China Doll" New York, 1946. Tumbao Cuban Classics TCD-074. One CD, 1995.

Julio Cueva y su Orquesta: La butuba cubana. Tumbao Cuban Classics TCD-032. One CD, 1994.

La Gloria Matncera: El limoncito. Tumbao Cuban Classics TCD-071. One CD, 1995.

La Sonora Matancera: Se formo la rumbantela. Tumbao Cuban Classics TCD-045. One CD, 1994.

Las muchas Celias. Cubanacán CUCD 1710. One CD, 1998.

Los ineditos "en vivo" de Estrellas de Chocolate. DC Productions CD 9205. One CD, n.d.

Lo mejor de La Sonora Ponceña. Inca I 1045. One CD, 1975.

Mariano Mercerón y sus Muchachos Pimienta: "Negro ñañamboro." Tumbao Cuban Classics TCD-050. One CD, 1994.

Memories of Cuba: Orquesta Casino de la Playa (1937–1944). Tumbao Cuban Classics TCD-003. One CD, 1991.

Mi diario musical: Celia Cruz acompañada de la Sonora Matancera. Polydor 314 529 813-2. One CD, 1992.

Miguelito Valdés with the Orquesta Casino de la Playa. Harlequin HQ CD 39. One CD, 1994.

More than Mambo: the Introduction to Afro-Cuban Jazz. Verve 314 527 903-2. One CD, 1995.

Musicalidad en sepia: Cuní con Chappottin y sus Estrellas. Maype CD-110. One CD, n.d.

Orchestra Harlow: Tribute to Arsenio. Fania SLP 00404. One CD, 1972.

The Original Mambo Kings: An Introduction to Afro-Cubop. Verve 314 513 876-2. One CD, 1993.

Orlando Guerra "Cascarita" con la Orquesta Casino de la Playa, 1944–1946: El guarachero. Tumbao Cuban Classics TCD-033. One Cd, 1994.

Orquesta Casino de la Playa. Harlequin HQ CD 51. One CD, 1995.

Orquesta Casino de la Playa. Tumbao Cuban Classics TCD-037. One CD, 1994.

Orquesta Casino de la Playa: Fufuñando. Tumbao Cuban Classics TCD-054. One CD, 1995.

Pachanga with Barretto. Riverside 7506. Reissued in *Ray Barretto*. Fantasy PR 24713. 2 LPs, 1973.

Pacheco Presents Monguito. Fania Records SLP-341. One CD, 1971.

Pacheco y Su Charanga. Alegre LPA 801. One LP, 1960.

Quitate de la vía, Perico: Cortijo y su Combo con Ismael Rivera. Rumba RLP 55548. One LP, n.d.

Ray Barretto: The Message. Fania Records SLP 00403. One LP, 1972.

Recordando a Arsenio. Tico Records TRSLP 1231. One CD, 1971.

René Álvarez y su Conjunto Los Astros: Yumbale. Tumbao Cuban Classics TCD-062. One CD, 1995.

Reunion: Miguelito Valdes with Machito and His Orchestra (Tico 1098).

Sexteto Cubanos vol. 1, *Sones 1930: Sexteto Munamar, Sexteto Machin, Sexteto Nacional, Sexteto Matancero*. Arhoolie Productions. ARH CD 7003. One CD, 1991.

Sexteto Cubanos vol. 2, *Sones 1926–1928: Sexteto Boloña, Sexteto Occidente, Sexteto Nacional, Sexteto Matancero*. Arhoolie Productions. ARH CD 7006. One CD, 1995.

Sexteto Nacional: "Cubaneo": Primeras Grabaciones, 1927–1928. Tumbao Cuban Classics TCD-097. One CD, 1999.

Sexteto y Septeto Habanero: Grabaciones Completas vol. 1, *1925–1927*. Tumbao Cuban Classics TCD-301. One CD, 1998.

Sexteto y Septeto Habanero: Grabaciones Completas vol. 2, *1927*. Tumbao Cuban Classics TCD-302. One CD, 1998.

Sexteto y Septeto Habanero: Grabaciones Completas vol. 3, *1928*. Tumbao Cuban Classics TCD-303. One CD, 1998.

Sexteto y Septeto Habanero: Grabaciones Completas vol. 4, *1928–1931*. Tumbao Cuban Classics TCD-304. One CD, 1998.

Top Percussion: Tito Puente. BMG Music 3264-2-RL. One CD, 1992.

Tremendo Cumban: Machito and His Afro-Cuban Orchestra. Tumbao Cuban Classics TCD-004. One CD, 1991.

Tribute to Arsenio Rodríguez: Orquesta Harlow. Fania Records SLP 00404. One LP, 1972.

Viva África. Fania Records SLP 330. One LP, 1966.

Willie Rosario: Más ritmo. Inca LP 1025. One CD, 1972.

Notes

Introduction

1. I refer to Arsenio by his first name because his closest friends and relatives use it out of affection, and it is the name used by almost everyone else to distinguish him from other artists named Rodríguez, a surname that is very common in Latin America.

2. All translations from Spanish are the author's.

3. *Marc Ribot y Los Cubanos Postizos* (The Prosthetic Cubans) (Atlantic 83116-2) and *¡Muy Divertido!* (Very Entertaining) (Atlantic 83293-2).

4. See liner notes to *Salsa Africa: Afro-Cuban Salsa Music* (Candela Records 42859442).

5. Performance techniques and repertories associated with jazz have been particularly effective in rendering musical styles as "modern" and "progressive." In Africa, Latin America, and the United States since at least the 1930s, aspects of big band swing music and jazz have been fused with local forms, resulting in styles considered "progressive" and cosmopolitan (see Austerlitz 1997, pp. 56–59; Erlmann 1991, pp. 43–62; Turino 2000, pp. 559–71; Wade 2000, pp. 87, 124).

6. Pam Sporn's video documentary *Cuban Roots/Bronx Stories* is a wonderful exception to the otherwise lack of documentation on the black Cuban immigrant experience after 1959. It highlights the historical journey of a black Cuban family, revealing that the Cuban American experience (post-1959) is more diverse racially and ideologically than is popularly understood. See *Cuban Roots/Bronx Stories*(2000), produced and directed by Pam Sporn; 57 min., Third World Newsreel, videocassette.

7. Steven Loza points out that the convergence of performance practices between Latin and African American musical repertories has characterized the emergence of various Latin music styles and genres beginning with mambo and Latin jazz in the 1950s through hip hop in the 1980s (Loza 1999, pp. 222–23; see also Flores 2000).

8. Paul Gilroy describes this defining condition of the African diaspora as the "changing same" (Gilroy 1993, pp. 101, 122, 127, 198).

Chapter One

1. Read also Guillén's "Balada de los dos abuelos" (Ballad of the Two Grandfathers, White 1993, pp. 60–61).

2. The information in the following outline of Arsenio's youth, except where indicated, was collected from several interviews with Raúl Travieso in addition to two other sources (Nieves Rivera 1952; Carbo Menéndez 1971).

3. In 1919 the population of Güira de Macuriges was only 1,333, and the population of the entire municipality was 12,516 (Cuba, Dirección General del Censo 1919, p. 396).

4. I use the Spanish spelling to denote the province of La Habana and the English spelling to denote the city of Havana.

5. Official concern in the improvement of either housing or public hygiene was almost nonexistent in most rural parts of Cuba (Grupo Cubano de Investigaciones Económicas 1963, p. 397).

6. The law that abolished slavery in Cuba finally took effect on July 29, 1880, but the eight-year tutelage it established set the terminal date for slavery in 1888 (Knight 1970, p. 177).

7. It has been estimated that in 1857 Matanzas had 6,208 urban slaves compared to 38,468 rural slaves. Güines, considered a province in the mid-nineteenth century, had 645 urban slaves compared to 15,885 rural slaves (Knight 1970, p. 135).

8. For explanations of these names see Brandon (1993), Castellanos and Castellanos (1987, 1992), Guanche (1996), Howard (1998), and Knight (1970).

9. The name Congo was used to designate peoples coming from the wide cultural area sometimes referred to as Lower Guinea, which roughly encompasses modern southern Cameroon down to southern Angola, the Central African Republic, and the Democratic Republic of the Congo. All of these peoples spoke Bantu languages belonging to the Bantoid group, Benue-Congo subfamily. In Cuba, however, the terms *Congo* and *Bantú*, when referring to culture, have become interchangeable (see Castellanos and Castellanos 1987, pp. 101–5). In addition, studies have focused on compiling the Congo lexicon as spoken in Cuba and comparing it etymologically and orthographically with words in languages such as Kikongo, Lari, Monokotuba, and Lingala, which are spoken in Lower Guinea (see González Huguet and Baudry 1967; de Granda 1973).

10. One published account identified Arsenio's great-grandfather as his nearest African-born ancestor (Salazar 1994, p. 12). This has yet to be documented.

11. The central aspect of palo monte is the invocation of ancestral spirits. "Biyumba," which was recorded for *Palo Congo* (Blue Note LP-1561) in 1957, is an example of a palo monte ritual song, in which Arsenio invokes the spirits of his mother, Dorotea, his father, Bonifacio, and Justo Trava, the father of Arsenio's older half-brothers.

12. Malanga (also known as José Rosario Oviedo) died tragically and mysteriously in the 1930s (Martínez Rodríguez 1995, p. 144). Arsenio and Tata Gutiérrez commemorated his death in "Llora timbero," which Arsenio recorded on May 16, 1941, and published on June 7, 1941. It remains a standard in the Cuban and salsa music repertoires to this day. Arsenio also commemorated Mulence in "Mulence" (rec. 1953) and Roncona in "Adiós Roncona" (rec. October 5, 1956).

13. León states that the marímbula derived from the smaller zanzaor mbila (lamellaphone) of the Congos (see León 1984, pp. 120, 122, 139, 240).

14. Oviedo had formed his sexteto in the city of Matanzas in early 1926 and moved the group to Marianao later that year.

15. Arsenio's performances at this festival were recorded, the tapes of which are archived at the Center for Folklife Programs and Cultural Studies Archive,

Smithsonian Institution. This quote was transcribed from *Festival Recordings: Rodriguez Brothers* (Festival of American Folklife. 69.101.49. 7RR. FP-1969-7RR-0049).

16. In his book *Nationalizing Blackness: Afrocubanismo and Artistic Revolution in Havana, 1920–1940*, Robin Moore (1997) discusses the various artistic facets and goals of the afrocubanismo period, focusing on its contradictory and ambivalent relationships with the social reality of many musicians, entertainers, and, in general, Cubans of color. For instance, he shows that afrocubanismo composers such as Amadeo Roldán, Alejandro García Caturla, Ernesto Lecuona, Gilberto Valdés, and others were white from a middle- and upper-class background and had little personal understanding of black rural and urban working-class culture from which they nevertheless drew much of the inspiration for their symphonic compositions and theatrical works. Moore also explains that working-class Afro-Cuban musicians' participation in the afrocubanismo movement was largely relegated to the sphere of popular entertainment.

17. In 1940 Ortiz substituted the ajiaco metaphor with his theory of transculturation (Ortiz 1995).

18. At this time Casino de la Playa's instrumentation was violin, two alto saxophones, tenor saxophone, two trumpets, trombone, piano, guitar, bass, and lead vocals doubling on clave and maracas. Casino de la Playa eventually recorded ten of Arsenio's songs between 1937 and 1940, all of which have been rereleased on CD compilations of Casino de la Playa's recordings (see Discography).

19. Slaves in nineteenth-century Cuba were divided into bozales, those recently brought from Africa; *ladinos*, those who were imported before the passage of the law in 1821, prohibiting the slave trade; and *criollos*, those born on the island (Wurdeman 1844, p. 249).

20. The following translations into Spanish of Arsenio's afrocubanos are Felipe García Villamil's, a high-ranking practitioner of Palo Monte, Santería, and Abakuá.

21. Cuban folklorist Lydia Cabrera provided ample ethnographic descriptions of the uses of a palero's ganga and its contents, which include sticks and roots of various types of trees, herbs, dirt, animals, and other natural elements (Cabrera 1992, pp. 118–38).

22. Interestingly, the "monkey" in this passage may refer to the Pan-African figures Esu-Elegbara and the Signifying Monkey, the myths of which inscribe the nature and function of formal language use and its interpretation (see Gates 1988, 21–2, 42).

23. Fernando Ortiz explains that the word "caravela" is Congo and was commonly used during the nineteenth century among African-born Congo priests of the Kindembo sect to refer to each other as sworn brothers (i.e., "caravelas") (Ortiz 1952, p. 423). García Villamil explained that in the past the decomposed body of a caravela or "kimbisa" (e.g., a sworn brother from the same religious sect) was kept in a sack and used as a spiritual source, which would then be called interchangeably "caravela," "kimbisa," or "ganga."

24. In 1937 *Adelante* published several essays in response to an inquiry put forward by the editors into the problem of racial divisions between blacks and

mulattos (particularly in the eastern province of Oriente). According to at least two of the respondents, the social and ideological implications of mestizaje were at the core of this division. Ernesto Pinto Interián (1937) believed that the source of the problem was the inculcation of feelings of "superiority over blacks" by parents of mixed marriages into their children. Similarly, Gustavo Urrutia (1937) explained that the social ramifications of superación and "mejoramiento" among Cubans of color included skin color hierarchies, in which lighter-skinned Cubans were often regarded as *adelantados* (advanced) and darker-skinned Cubans were regarded as *atrasados* (backward).

25. *Rinzler Fieldwork: Arsenio Rodriguez* (7RR. FP-RINZ-7RR-0813).

26. At that time Rinzler was working for the Newport Festival Foundation as director of Field Research. In addition, he was also working as an impresario and agent for Doc Watson, a blind old-time musician. Having made many contacts with booking agents and concert producers in the late 1950s and early 1960s, Rinzler actively promoted musicians such as Doc Watson and Bill Monroe, with whom he had come into contact in the field.

27. Distinguished Professor Emerita Bernice Reagon received her doctorate in African American history and culture in 1975 from Howard. In 1973 Reagon founded Sweet Honey in the Rock, the renowned and Grammy Award–winning African American women's a cappella ensemble. She is also curator emeritus at the Smithsonian Institution.

28. *Festival Recordings: Rodriguez Brothers* (Festival of American Folklife. 69.101.49. 7RR. FP-1969-7RR-0049).

29. For example, in 1932, composer Eliseo Grenet was exiled to Spain by government authorities who perceived his "Lamento cubano" as subversive (Moore 1997, p. 78).

30. Pedro Ferro, who managed Arsenio's conjunto in Los Angeles in the mid-1960s, remembers reading books on Cuban independence fighters to Arsenio. Ferro also recounts that Arsenio was "an extraordinary lover of black Cuban *mambises*" (Ferro interview 2000).

31. See also Leonardo Acosta's discussion of a rumba composed by Gonzalo Asencio Hernández or Tío Tom, which criticizes the same event (Acosta 1991, pp. 63–65).

32. My use of the idea of double consciousness is inspired by the following two observations: (1) Paul Gilroy's suggestion that Du Bois produced the notion of double consciousness "not just to express the distinctive standpoint of black Americans but also to illuminate the experience of post-slave populations in general" (Gilroy 1993, p. 126); and (2) Ronald Radano's suggestion that Du Bois employed this notion as an ideological strategy for contending with the powerful forces of racism (Radano 2003, p. 279).

Chapter Two

1. Cuban musicologists Odilio Urfé (in Orovio 1992), Argeliers León (1984), and Jesus Gómez Cairo (1995) have included the Cuban son as part of a broader Caribbean "*son* complex."

2. Cousins Jacinto Scull and Esteban Reguira Dovigny sang first and second voice, respectively. "Curiquito," who also sang second voice, was a childhood friend of Arsenio's from Güines. Mario Agudín, who played trumpet, lived in Los Hornos, and was an army sergeant stationed in the nearby fort of Columbia in Marianao. He was later replaced by Serafín Terry, who was also from Güines. Even Arsenio's oldest brother, Julio, briefly played bass. At this time Arsenio was living in the working-class barrio of Pogolotti.

3. This septeto is not to be confused with the all-white big band Orquesta Bellamar, which was active in the major tourist cabarets in the late 1930s and early 1940s.

4. The core members and associates, who had approved the group's bylaws on August 10, 1936, were now Esteban Regueira Dovigny (president, director, guitarist, and second voice), José Ramón Ortíz (secretary and treasurer), Luís Regatillo (bassist), Mario Carballo (*bongosero*), Arsenio Rodríguez (*tresero*), Manuel Manrique (first voice and clave player), and Oscar Velazco O'Farrill (voting member). The septeto's headquarters was on Gervasio no. 132, just west of downtown Havana (Archivo Nacional de Cuba. *Registro de Asociaciones*. Fondo 54, legajo 206).

5. Despite popular belief, Arsenio's conjunto was probably not the first to incorporate a second trumpet, piano, or tumbadora. Raúl Travieso asserted that Arsenio began to use a tumbadora around 1935, but on other occasions he suggested that this addition did not occur until after 1941. According to other sources, other son groups before 1940 had attempted to incorporate at least one of these three instruments. For instance, La Sonora Nacional de Piñón was advertised as "el Dúo de Trompetas del Sexteto Sonora Nacional de Piñón" for their program on radio CMCG in May 1938 (*Hoy*, May 31, 1938). Here, "sexteto" refers to this son group's instruments (i.e., two vocals with maracas and clave, guitar, tres, bass, and bongó), not including the two trumpets. Evidently, in addition to La Sonora Nacional de Piñón, Carabina de Ases and several other son groups were regularly using a two-trumpet format and, in the case of Sexteto Gloria Cubana, a piano by 1938 (Blanco Aguilar 1992, p. 34; Collazo 1987, pp. 177–78; López interview 1995; Moore 1997, p. 155). Some have credited Sexteto Afrocubano with incorporating the tumbadora in 1936, but others have credited Conjunto La Llave with being the first to do this in 1940 (Blanco Aguilar 1992, p. 125; Mongo Santamaría in Fernández 1998, p. 125). Nevertheless, through the end of 1942, while Arsenio was establishing his new conjunto format and son montuno style, other son groups such as Septeto Sonora Matancera and Septeto Casino, who had been performing for elite sociedades since the 1930s, continued to use the septeto format for their public performances (see *Diario de la Marina*, November 1940 through June 1942; *Hoy*, December 1941 through April 1943).

6. See *Diario de la Marina* December 1940 through February 1941. According to Raúl Travieso, the name of Arsenio's septeto that played at Sans Souci was Segundo Conjunto de Arsenio (see also Fernández 1998, pp. 124–25). His group was referred to as a septeto in at least one advertisement put out by Sans Souci (*Diario de la Marina*, January 3, 1941).

7. The only one of the conjunto's recordings from 1940 and 1941 in which a tumbadora is audible is the conga "Todos seguimos la conga" (Everyone Follows the Conga).

8. Elpidio y Margot were replaced by Estela y René, the internationally famous *pareja de rumba* (rumba couple), on the night of January 4 (*Diario de la Marina*, January 7, 1941).

9. Some statistics show that tourism declined from 127,000 visitors in 1940 to 12,000 in 1943 (Pérez 1995a, p. 283).

10. See *Diario de la Marina*, December 31, 1940, and *Hoy*, December 28, 1941.

11. The owners of Cuba's two largest beer factories maintained outdoor dance floors on their factory grounds. La Tropical (est. 1888) was the oldest and largest of Cuba's beer companies. It was located in the barrio of Ceíba, Marianao. By 1929 the factory complex consisted of the actual breweries and warehouses, an office building, a 15,000-seat baseball stadium, and outdoor dance facilities. La Polar, whose parent company was Compañía Cervecera Internacional (est. 1911), was the second largest beer manufacturer in Cuba. It also was also located in Marianao. Some of the most popular dance floors included Mamoncillo, Ensueño, and Tropical in La Tropical, and Merendero Criollo, Patio Sevillano, Polar, Terraza China, and Trimalta in La Polar. Sociedades españolas, white upper-class social clubs, as well as middle- and working-class social clubs all utilized the facilities at these beer gardens for their social functions. Accordingly, the ensembles they hired were the same charangas, big bands, and son groups that they hired to perform in their private ballrooms (Inclán Lavastida 1943, p. 190; República de Cuba 1943, p. 455; Otero et al. 1954, pp. 765–70).

12. For instance, as early as 1944, Joaquín Ordoqui, Lázaro Peña, Blas Roca, and other key associates of both the Communist Party and Mil Diez were under surveillance by operatives working for the U.S. State Department. The surveillance involved covert operations as well as listening to speeches given by party and union leaders on Mil Diez (U.S. Diplomatic Post 1940–45). In a State Department memorandum, a "Mr. O'Connor" wrote: "Since . . . CMX is entitled to use a power as high as 50 kilowatts, the possibility exists of this station, at some time in the future, making ideological broadcasts to the United States. Mr. McNaughten [an FCC employee] said that when he was in Cuba recently, the Cuban officials [of the Ministry of Communications] told him that they were trying to do something about the situation, but he is not certain that they really mean to do anything" (U.S. State Department 1945–49).

13. The day after the communist newspaper *Hoy* declared that the Ministry of Communications had ordered the closure of Mil Diez because it had allegedly used a signal power exceeding its authorized amount, which was 10,000 watts (*Hoy*, May 2, 1948). Others believe that the Minister of Labor, and the subsequent Cuban president, Dr. Carlos Prío Socarrás, ordered the closure of Mil Diez (García Montes and Alonso Avila 1970, p. 383).

14. The similar nicknames "El Ciego Prodigioso" and "El Ciego Extraordinario" were used by Mil Diez in their initial advertisements (see *Hoy*, March 21, 28, 1943).

15. The guaracha originated in the nineteenth century and was popularized in Cuban *bufos* (comic operas). By the 1930s big bands and septetos had started to perform guarachas in a faster tempo and with an added, son-influenced, montuno section. What remained of the nineteenth-century guaracha was its typically playful, roguish, and sometimes bawdy lyrics (see León 1984, pp. 166–84, and Moore 1997). Guaguancó is one of the three principal song and dance forms of rumba (the other two are *yambú* and *columbia*). The traditional instrumentation used to perform guaguancó includes claves and a set of three tumbadoras (or congas, from lowest to highest: *tumba*, *llamadora*, and *quinto*).

16. Many of these two- and four-bar harmonic cycles involve the alternation of tonic and dominant chords or two chords a whole step apart. Although both types of harmonic patterns are common among older styles of son music, the latter (two chords a whole step apart) is particularly noteworthy of Arsenio's recordings because of its rarity in pre-1940 commercially recorded son music. See *Antología integral del son* (EGREM LD-286 and LD-287) for examples of *nengón*, *montuno-cruzado*, and other older styles of son music that use these cyclic-harmonic structures.

17. "Guía" has been defined as an improvised text sung by the first voice in alternation with the coro or chorus during the montuno section (e.g., Galán 1983, p. 307; Robbins 1990, p. 190). Others have used the name *pregón* (which is also the name for a style of son music) in referring to the lead, improvised vocal (e.g., Mauleón 1993, p. 186, 191). In the context of salsa music, however, *guía* is another name for the verse section (e.g., Gerard with Sheller 1988, p. 34). I use *guía* to mean the solo vocal part that alternates with the coro during the montuno section, as it is used by Peer International, the copyright owner of most of Arsenio's catalog, in his lead sheets.

18. In pre-1940 commercially recorded son music, the two-part son form was far more common than the one-part. In many cases, the verse section of the two-part *sones* was extended, resulting in brief montunos (for example, the sones recorded by Sexteto Boloña between 1926 and 1928, ARH CD 7006). In contrast, the one-part form rarely appears in pre-1940 son recordings. Two rare examples include "Tribilín cantore," recorded by Septeto Habanero (TCD-303), and "Bururú barará," recorded by Sexteto Nacional (TCD-097). These particular examples are based entirely on a two-bar cyclic tonic-dominant harmonic pattern.

19. The defining performative procedures that Ortiz identifies in Afro-Cuban and African music include *dialogismo* (dialogue among musicians and dancers), *remplissage* (filling up of musical textures), *odium vacui* (hatred or avoidance of emptiness in musical textures), *entretejedura* (interweaving of musical parts), and *embriaguez* (intoxication and climactic rapture in a musical performance) (Ortiz 1993).

20. Paul Austerlitz provides a very insightful approach in conveying the "feel" of West African and Caribbean music through his use of "textiling notation," which though not implemented here nevertheless does highlight the procedures of hocketing, sonic and bodily interactivity, cyclic time, and climax that are especially at work in Arsenio's music (Austerlitz 2003).

21. I base my transcriptions of the son footwork pattern from several demonstrations, including one executed by Arsenio's niece Mercedes "Cheché" Scull in Havana, which I recorded on video, and another executed by son dancers in the video *Ignacio Piñeiro* (dir. Luís Felipe Bernaza, Jorge Haydu, Dolores Calviño, Ricardo Istueta, Alberto Menéndez, Barbara Hernández, and Joaquin Moreno; dist. El Instituto Cubano del Arte e Industria Cinematograficos, Havana, Cuba. Videocassette, about 20 minutes).

22. The conjunto's first six recordings, made in 1940 and 1941, do not reflect the use of contratiempo in the bass lines. Specifically, Nilo Alfonso, who was Arsenio's first steady bass player (1940–46), plays the "anticipated bass" pattern and other, less syncopated patterns. By 1942 Alfonso's patterns began to change with the appearance of accents on the offbeats. In addition, his bass lines began to follow the melodic content of the sung refrains, such as in "Como traigo la yuka" (How I Bring the Yuka; rec. June 18, 1942) and "Camina a trabajá, Haragón" (Go to Work, Lazy; rec. November 16, 1943) as well as "Mi chinita me botó" (rec. July 6, 1944).

23. For examples of this bass line listen to "Mi china sí" (rec. c. 1948) by René Álvarez y Su Conjunto "Los Astros" (TCD-062), "Rompe saraguey" (rec. c. 1952) by Chappottín y Sus Estrellas (Antilla Records CD-107) and "Fania" (rec. c. 1960) by Conjunto Estrellas de Chocolate (Antilla Records CD-15).

24. The martillo is a one-bar repeating pattern that consists of a sequence of left-hand fingertip and palm touches (slashes) and right-hand fingertip strokes (filled-in notes) on the *macho* or smaller drum (upper ledger line in the musical examples), and one strike on beat four on the hembra or larger drum (lower ledger line). The tumbadora also plays a repeating one-bar pattern that consists of a sequence of palm and fingertip strikes (slashes) as well as a slap on beat two (notated with X) and an opened-tone attack on beat four (notated with notehead).

25. From 1940 to 1952, Antolín "Papa Kila" Suárez Ferro was Arsenio's steady bongó player. Originally from Los Palacios, Pinar del Río, Papa Kila moved to the barrio of El Cerro, Havana, shortly after 1933. He played the bongó with various septetos, including the official septeto of the military quarters in Columbia, Marianao, before joining Arsenio's newly formed conjunto in 1940. Arsenio had two steady tumbadora players in Cuba. His original tumbadora player, brother Kiki, played with the conjunto from its formation until 1945. Félix "Chocolate" Alfonso replaced Kiki, and remained with the group until 1950, when Kiki rejoined the conjunto. The conjunto's regular bassists were Nilo Alfonso (1940–46) and Lázaro Prieto (1946–52) (Raúl Travieso interviews, August 3, 1998, and February 7, 2000; Pedro Ferro interview, October 20, 2000).

26. Cuban musicians had indeed been playing figures similar to those notated in Example 2.4 not only in rural styles of son music, as performed on the tres, but also in urban styles since at least the late 1920s. For example, trumpet player Félix Chappottín, a member of Arsenio's conjunto from 1949 to 1952, plays off-beat accenting patterns on the trumpet during the fifth and sixth refrain of "Tribilín cantoré," recorded by Septeto Habanero in 1928 (TCD-303).

27. According to some sources the word *cocimiento* is a Cubanism, from the rural parts of the island, which means "a kick in the ass," such as in the phrase, "Dale cocimiento de zapatón" (Give him a kick in the ass) (Sánchez-Boudy 1999, p. 195).

28. Other examples with ternary phrased cierres include "No vuelvo a Morón" (1948), "Lo dicen todas" (1948), "Llevatelo todo" (1949), "El rincón caliente" (TCD-031; 1950), and "Te mantengo y no quieres" (1950).

29. See note 20.

30. For example, listen to "A la United Café" (TCD-032), recorded in 1945 by Orlando "Cascarita" Guerra with Bebo Valdés's big band, and "Algo nuevo" (TCD-104), recorded in 1946 by Miguelito Valdés.

31. The guaracha's popularization in tourist and theatrical entertainment of the afrocubanismo period (late 1920s to 1930s) in Havana might have factored into the dominance of this genre in the repertories of those white style conjuntos and big bands, which continued to perform regularly in tourist cabarets in addition to touring Latin America throughout the 1940s. More important, its association with black character types of Cuba's blackface theater of the nineteenth century, in addition to popular music of the afrocubanismo period, must have played a role in the perception of the guaracha, as played in a fast tempo by conjuntos, as indicative of white- and tourist-style music (see Moore 1997).

32. Archivo Nacional de Cuba. *Registro de Asociaciones*. Libro 22, folio 235, número 13232.

33. Only after Arsenio's conjunto had gained national popularity through its performances in the provinces of Havana and Matanzas and its daily live presentations on Radio Mil Diez did some sociedades españolas hire his conjunto. For example, Arsenio and Arcaño performed for Centro Asturiano in their *palacio* (palace) on September 6, 1947, and Club Deportivo Candado on January 22, 1949. Arsenio also performed for Centro Gallego in its palacio on at least six occasions between 1947 and 1950, including its 1949 carnival celebrations (*Diario de la Marina*, March 1, 1947, August 10, 14, 17, 22, 1947, September 3–5, 1947, December 27, 1950; *Hoy*, April 28, 1948, May 13, 1948, December 10, 1948, January 22, 1949, February 1, 1949).

34. Before "Juventud amaliana," Arsenio's conjunto had recorded "Pilla con Pilla" (1943), which reflected some of the features that would characterize his conjunto-style guaguancós. They had also recorded "Timbilla" (1945), and later recorded "Anabacoa" (1950), both of which consist of the traditional guaguancó pattern played by the tumbadora.

35. In addition he composed "Amores de verano" (Summer Lovers) at the request of Vicente Amores, a local dance impresario, to publicize one of his summer dance festivals (Valdés Ginebra interview 1999).

36. The traditional form of guaguancó consists of three parts. In the diana, or introduction, the lead vocalist sings a relatively short phrase consisting of nonsense syllables, and the rhythm parts establish their two-bar interlocking patterns. For transcriptions of these patterns see Gerard and Sheller 1988, pp. 62–68. Following the diana is the extended canto or inspiración in which the lead vocalist (sometimes improvising) sings a long narrative in one of many variations of the

décima form (see Pasmanick 1997). The guaguancó concludes with a climactic montuno, which consists of alternations between a chorus and the lead vocalist and lively couple dancing.

37. Although blacks and whites lived together in lower-class barrios, the high-income residential areas were almost completely white (Masferrer and Mesa-Lago 1974, p. 372).

38. See also Butterworth (1980, pp. 5–17) for a description of Las Yaguas, a squatter settlement in Luyanó that developed in the early 1930s and continued to grow through the 1950s.

Chapter Three

1. The following information in this section (except where indicated) was collected over many interviews with Raúl Travieso.

2. Raúl Travieso suspected that Arsenio's association with the communist-owned Radio Mil Diez played a role in customs' decision to keep them in Tampa for several days.

3. See Grillo (2000) for a firsthand account of race relations among white and black Cubans and African Americans in pre–World War II Tampa, Florida.

4. One afternoon, Arsenio called Raúl to his room and told him to write down the lyrics he had just composed, which described the following humorous incident. That morning, Raúl tried to order coffee with milk for himself and Arsenio, but none of the hotel employees spoke Spanish. He tried asking one employee, who responded by asking, "What are you saying? What are you saying?" Raúl resorted to giving him physical gestures, after which the employee brought him a glass of milk instead of coffee with milk and sugar. Then Raúl tried in vain asking the receptionist, who decided to call their travel agency for a Spanish interpreter. The agency sent over a Cuban, who when he arrived was enthusiastically greeted by Raúl and Arsenio. Raúl told him what had happened, after which the interpreter explained that "café con leche" in English is "coffee and milk," hence the lyric in the verse of "Pasó en Tampa."

5. According to John Storm Roberts the formation of Coda in 1945 and the Spanish Music Center (SMC) in 1948 by local dance promoter, record producer, and record store owner Gabriel Oller was an important development in the spread and diversity of Latin music, particularly the less commercial styles compared to those which were largely disseminated by American-owned companies (Roberts 1999, pp. 112–13, 120–21).

6. Despite (or because of) being blind, Arsenio was prone to getting into arguments and even physical confrontations, especially when he felt he was being belittled. On June 14, 1945, Arsenio's conjunto, with Kiki playing tumbadora, performed in Los Sitios, a rough barrio in Havana, where an altercation ensued between Arsenio and several men, including Wilfredo Mayo, who were in the audience. Mayo struck Arsenio with his fist and knocked him to the ground, at which point, according to Raúl Travieso, Mayo pulled out a knife. At that moment Kiki struck Mayo over the head with his tumbadora, knocking the knife out of his hands. Kiki then picked up the knife and chased after Mayo who had proceeded to

run away. When Kiki caught up to Mayo, he stabbed him. Mayo continued to run, and eventually he bled to death near the corner of Reina and Lealtad, not too far from Los Sitios. Kiki was charged with murder and initially sentenced to fourteen years, which he began to serve in 1945 at the Castillo del Principe jail in Havana. After several appeals Kiki was released in early 1950, having served five years in prison. According to friend Pedro Luís Ferro, Kiki harbored regret and repentance for the rest of his life, even to the extent of writing letters to Mayo's family asking for their forgiveness (*Diario de la Marina*, March 15, 1946; Raúl Travieso interview, October 12, 1998; Ferro interview, October 20, 2000).

7. The bass pattern in "Ran kan kan" can also be heard in Machito's "Barbara batibiri," "Tumba el quinto," and "Vive como yo" (Verve 314 527 903-2), all of which were recorded in 1950.

8. The mambo dance repertory and stylistic development are areas that have not been comprehensively documented and analyzed. For a brief description of the interinfluences between Afro-Cuban and jazz dancing styles during the 1940s and 1950s in New York, see Stearns (1979, pp. 360–61). For a brief explanation of the origin of the mambo dance style in New York, see Byrnes and Swanson (1951). For contemporary descriptions of mambo dance styles, see Luis (1958), Ohl (1958), and Thompson (1958, 1959).

9. Alava was a photographer in New York from 1953 to 1960; he attended and photographed several of Arsenio's performances.

10. By 1952 Héctor Pellot had returned to Puerto Rico to join Moncho Leña and Mon Rivera in forming Los Ases del Ritmo, who soon after popularized the conjunto-style *plena* (Carp 1996, pp. 4–6).

11. In September 1950 his conjunto performed for his daughter Regla María's *quinceñera*, which took place in Pogolotti, Marianao. For this special occasion he composed the bolero "Si me voy" (If I Go; SCCD 9352) and performed it in dedication to his daughter (Travieso Montecino interview, June 25, 1999). The lyrics poignantly express Arsenio's feelings over his impending departure from his beloved daughter. He later recorded it on April 9, 1952, with his Conjunto de Estrellas in New York. Between 1950 and 1952 Arsenio continued to perform and record in Havana, participating in at least sixteen recording sessions and performing at various social clubs with his Havana conjunto.

12. See *La Prensa*, January 1951 to March 1952.

13. In actuality, Pérez Prado had already performed (as El Rey del Mambo) at the Teatro Puerto Rico and the St. Nicholas Ballroom in April 1951 (see *El Diario de Nueva York*, April 13, 14, 20, 1951).

14. In the Minutes of the Executive Board of the American Federation of Musicians Local 802, Candido appears as Arsenio's contractor.

15. Before joining Arsenio's new orchestra, Castillo, Agüigui, and Álvarez were members of José Luís Moreno's orchestra, which also performed regularly at the Tropicana Club in the South Bronx.

16. The Mambo U.S.A. tour only made it to about ten cities, including Chicago (October 23), Pittsburgh (October 29), Washington, DC (October 31), and Cleveland (November 4) (Riambau interview 2003; see *Down Beat*, October through December 1954).

17. The recordings in these LPs were originally recorded by Arsenio's conjunto in 1951 and 1952 and later released on CD (TCD-022) in 1992 (see Tico Label Discography, online at http://bsnpubs.com/tico.html).

18. See *El Diario de Nueva York*, May 21, 1957.

19. The Park Palace was the second-story hall, and the Park Plaza was the somewhat smaller hall underneath.

20. In the contract Arsenio signed with Peer International in 1958, his address is listed as 152 East 116th Street, whereas in Local 802's 1957 directory of musicians his address is listed as 151 East 116th Street.

21. The following data on the Park Palace/Plaza is taken from Carp 1999b (except where indicated).

22. By 1960 the Club Caborrojeño had transformed from a social club to a dance hall, the new owner of which discontinued its past discriminatory policies (David Carp, personal communication).

23. During the 1930s in Havana Gilberto Valdés contributed to the afrocubanismo movement by composing Afro-Cuban-inspired popular and art music. But he was best known for introducing Afro-Cuban sacred and secular percussion instruments to the symphonic orchestra for a series of concerts in 1937 (see Moore 1997).

24. Gilberto Valdés also played flute on John "Dizzy" Gillespie's *Afro* (Norgran MGN-1003), which was recorded in 1954.

25. *La Prensa*, January 1, 1955.

Chapter Four

1. For example, see the liner notes to *Arsenio Rodríguez y Su Conjunto: "Como se goza en el barrio"* (TCD-022), *Arsenio Rodríguez y Su Conjunto: 24 exitos originales* (Ansonia CD HGCD 1337), and *Buena Vista Social Club Presents Manuel "Guajiro" Mirabal* (World Circuit/Nonesuch 79810-2).

2. According to Fernando Ortiz, *quindembo* was the name of a pre–twentieth-century sacred Congolese drum and the name of an old secret brotherhood of African-born *congo* priests (Ortiz 1952, pp. 423–24).

3. Reig was also responsible in bringing Arsenio to participate in the recording of Patato Valdés's 1967 LP *Patato & Totico* (Verve V6-5037), which was a very influential record for some early salsa musicians (see Singer 1982, p. 148).

4. Ansonia's catalog included well-known artists and groups from Cuba (e.g., La Sonora Matancera), Puerto Rico (e.g., Daniel Santos and Ramito), and the Dominican Republic (e.g., Joseíto Mateo and Luís Quintero).

5. Hòfi (or "hof" in Dutch) is Papiamento, the local language of the Netherlands Antilles, which is a composite of Portuguese, Spanish, English, Dutch, and African elements.

6. The most comprehensive history of popular music in Curaçao to date is S. "Yapi" Martijn (1991).

7. Jose Casseres joined Arsenio's conjunto and returned with the group to New York, where he eventually formed his own group (Martijn 1991, pp. 155–56).

8. Significant concentrations of predominately Mexicans and Mexican Americans existed in various areas of the city, particularly the East Los Angeles area, encompassing Boyle Heights, East Los Angeles proper, and City Terrace (Western Economic Research 1972; Fair Employment Practice Commission 1966). In contrast, relatively small concentrations of Cubans and Puerto Ricans existed throughout the city. For example, according to the 1970 U.S. Census, Cubans and Puerto Ricans living in East Los Angeles totaled about 600, compared to this area's estimated 57,000 Mexicans and Mexican Americans. Somewhat larger concentrations of Cubans were reported in Glendale (1,800) and Pasadena (700), north and northeast of Los Angeles (U.S. Department of Commerce 1973) (see also Modares 1994, p. 49).

9. Cuban bandleaders who were active at this time included Rolando Lozano, "Mazacote," Marianao Mercerón, Albertico Pérez, and Dandy Beltrán. The most popular group, however, was led by Cuban pianist René Touzet, who began his career in Havana in the late 1930s leading an all-white jazz band at the Casino Nacional and Montmartre, both of which were first-tier cabarets. Through the 1960s Touzet's conjunto, which at various times included such notables as Francisco Aguabella, recorded at least eleven LPs for GNP/Crescendo, while performing regularly for Latin social clubs as well as at the popular Crescendo and Casa Escobar on the Sunset Strip and the Hollywood Palladium (Touzet imterview 2000).

10. As Héctor Ramírez Bedoya notes, La Sonora Matancera's style was emulated by dozens of popular "conjuntos" that formed in the 1950s and 1960s in countries such as Mexico, Venezuela, Peru, and especially Colombia (Ramírez Bedoya 1998, 107–8).

11. Cesar Miguel Rondón's book *El libro de la Salsa: Crónica de la música del Caribe urbano* (1980) continues to be the only source on salsa's development in New York City in the 1960s.

12. Aguire cites Nicholas and Prohias (1973), whose conclusions are similar. As documented in Pam Sporn's video documentary *Cuban Roots/Bronx Stories*, the Fosters, a black Cuban family, left Havana in 1962 and arrived in Miami where they stayed in the segregated section of the city. Soon after, they moved to the South Bronx.

13. By 1974, Johnny Pacheco established Vaya Records for Cruz and transformed her into the queen of salsa.

14. At the African Roots, Latino Rhythms conference in East Harlem on November 13, 1999, bandleader Johnny Colón confirmed that Curbelo deliberately "kept certain musicians out of the business."

15. Flautist, saxophonist, and arranger Mauricio Smith was a Panamanian of color, whose musical career in New York began in the early 1960s.

16. Most of these dances were not publicized in *El Diario-La Prensa*. See Club Cubano Inter-Americano 1946–96.

17. The following performances are advertised in *La Opinion*, October 7, 1969, through November 27, 1970.

18. The following information on Arsenio's death is taken from an official copy of his death certificate from the County of Los Angeles (no. 7097-054578).

Chapter Five

1. Contrary to what some have stated (e.g., Waxer 2002b, p. 11, and Berríos-Miranda 2002, p. 25), neither the history of salsa's New York, Puerto Rican, or Cuban roots nor the musical and stylistic development of salsa in New York have been comprehensively documented or subjected to serious musical analysis, at least in terms of examining and comparing recordings and other primary sources of early salsa performance (e.g., film) in conjunction with oral testimony. Instead, an overwhelming majority of the writings on salsa derives from historical, sociological, and cultural studies perspectives that focus on issues concerning salsa and the commercial music industry and Puerto Rican and pan-Latino identity as these have prevailed in New York and Puerto Rico. See Rondón (1980), Boggs (1992), and Padura Fuentes (1997) for historical narratives. See Baron (1977), Cortes, Falcón, and Flores (1976, pp. 124–33), Blum (1978), Singer (1982), and Manuel (1991) concerning the salsa industry. See Duany (1984), Padilla (1989, 1990), and Manuel (1994) concerning salsa and identity. See the essays in Waxer (2002a) concerning salsa and its various contemporary local and global sites. See also Waxer (2002a, pp. 19–24) and Washburne (1999, pp. 25–29) for more detailed reviews of the state of research of salsa. More recent studies on salsa have focused on its emergence in other regions and as a global phenomenon in addition to issues concerning gender, race, and class, thus broadening the geographical and theoretical terrain of the study of salsa. See Aparicio (1998, 2002) for analyses on the issues of identity, race, and gender in salsa; Waxer (2002a) for a social history of salsa, including all-women salsa groups, in Cali, Colombia; and the various essays in Waxer (2002b) dealing with salsa in its local and global manifestations.

2. See also Thompson (1983, p. 48) and Gelb (1961) for concise histories of the pachanga's interrelated yet distinct developments in Cuba and New York.

3. Other young musicians including Pacheco, Charlie Palmieri, Eddie Palmieri, and Barry Rogers participated in after-hours jam sessions every Tuesday night at the club. In addition, Eddie Palmieri's conjunto La Perfecta originated from these jam sessions at the Tritons, thus ushering in the trombone sound that would largely define salsa music (Carp 1998, pp. 15–16).

4. For example, Machito had released the Afro-Cuban jazz classic *Kenya: Afro-Cuban Jazz* LP in 1957 before releasing *The New Sound of Machito* in 1963. Tito Puente had released jazz-influenced LPs such as *Night Beat* in 1958 and *The Revolving Bandstand Sessions* in 1960 before releasing *Pachanga con Puente* in 1961.

5. Flores explains that Latin boogaloo took its name and direct crossover impulse from its immediate source, black boogaloo, which was the foremost name for R&B and soul music through the mid-1960s (Flores 2000, p. 92).

6. The following documentation on *Viva Arsenio!* and Bang Records is from American Federation of Musicians, Local 802, *Phonograph Recording Contract Form*, Microfiche Nos. 97376, 97378, and 223329; "A Stereo Retrospective on Bang/Shout Records," *Both Sides Now: The Story of Stereo Rock and Roll* 15 (June 1990): 151, 156–60; and "Bob Feldman, Erstwhile Australian," *Both Sides Now: The Story of Stereo Rock and Roll* 15 (June 1990): 154–55.

7. The first five LPs released by Bang between 1965 and 1967 were recorded by the Strangeloves, the McCoys, and Neil Diamond.

8. Apparently, the dance footwork and style of the Latin version of the boogaloo was similar to the African American version. For documentation on the latter see Butler and Butler (1975).

9. This is not counting Harlow's *Tribute to Arsenio Rodríguez* LP (Fania 404, 1972), five of the six numbers of which were originally recorded by Arsenio's conjuntos.

10. Although the mambo on two pattern has been favored by mambo and salsa dancers, particularly from New York, the on one pattern was also used by mambo dancers in the 1950s and continues to be used by contemporary salsa dancers (see Bamford 1995; Terrace 1995; Navarro 2000).

11. Other examples in which the original bass lines in contratiempo are substituted include Pacheco's rerecording of "El kikiriki" (originally recorded by Conjunto Estrellas de Chocolate in the early 1950s), in which the anticipated bass pattern is used in the diablo section, and Willie Rosario's version of "Con un amor se borra otro amor" (With One Love You Forget Another Love, originally recorded by Arsenio's conjunto in 1950), in which the guaracha pattern is used in the diablo section.

12. Weinstein arranged for and performed and recorded with Larry Harlow and Eddie Palmieri in the 1960s. Arsenio's diablos, however, were not the only source from which Rogers drew. Carp notes that in addition to Cuban music Rogers studied and in fact began his professional career performing R&B music, such as with the Hugo Dickens Group, in New York in the 1950s (Carp 1999a). According to Rogers himself, "When I came out of [the Dickens Group] I ran into Eddie [Palmieri] and I just threw in there what I had learned in the past three or four years with Hugo's group" (ibid., p. 7). This of course included what in salsa parlance became known as moñas.

13. In the contemporary salsa arrangement, according to Christopher Washburne, the moña typically occurs toward the end, following the mambo and montuno sections and preceding a repetition of the montuno before the final coda (Washburne 1999).

14. *Our Latin Thing (Nuestra Cosa)*. 1993. Produced by Jerry Masucci and directed by Leon Gast. Movies & Pictures International, videocassette.

Bibliography

Primary Sources

Interviews Conducted by the Author

Aguilar, Pedro "Cuban Pete." Interview with author. Manhattan, NY. December 8, 2002.

Alava, Silvio (Las Vegas, NV). Interview via the Internet. March 2000.

Alvarado, Melba. Interview. Tape recording. Manhattan, NY. March 3, 2000.

Antomattei, Candido (San Juan, P.R). Interview via telephone. November 4, 1998.

Armenteros, Alfredo. "Chocolate" (East Harlem, NY). Interview via telephone. January 19, 1997.

———. Interview. Tape recording. East Harlem, NY. January 25, 2000.

———. Interview. Tape recording. East Harlem, NY. February 18, 2000.

Beltrán, Dandy. Interview. Tape recording. Torrence, CA. September 11, 1996.

Bernadina, Edwin "Basilel" and Pacheco Statie. Interview. Tape recording. Curaçao. December 6, 2003.

Berrios, Israel (Carolina, P.R.). Interview via telephone. Tape recording. October 11, 1998.

———. Interview via telephone. Tape recording. October 15, 1998.

———. Interview via telephone. Tape recording. January 13, 2000.

———. Interview via telephone. Tape recording. May 20, 2002.

Boulong, Pedro (Manhattan, NY). Interview via telephone. Tape recording. January 24, 2000.

Cabrera, Julián. Interview. Tape recording. Manhattan, NY. June 27, 1998.

Calzado, Rudy. Interview. Tape recording. Manhattan, NY. June 27, 1998.

Cané, Humberto. Interview. Tape recording. Monterey Hills, CA. August 28, 1996.

———. Interview via telephone. March 8, 1999.

Caraballoso, Augustín (Manhattan, NY). Interview via telephone. March 16, 1998.

———. Interview via telephone. April 7, 1998.

———. Interview via telephone. December 11, 1999.

Carbó Menéndez, José. Interview. Tape recording. Union City, NJ. March 6, 1998.

———. Interview. Tape recording. Union City, NJ. April 5, 1998.

Coén, Ray (Río Piedras, P.R.). Interview via telephone. April 26, 2000.

Díaz, Julio "Tito" (Chicago). Interview via telephone. September 10, 2004.

———. Interview via telephone. September 27, 2004.

Ferro, Pedro (Miami, FL). Interview via telephone. September 2, 1997.

———. Interview via telephone. September 4, 1997.
———. Interview. Tape recording. Miami, FL. October 20, 2000.
Frías, José. Interview. Tape recording. Queens, NY. July 9, 2000.
García Villamil, Felipe. Interview. Tape recording. Bronx, NY. November 26, 1997.
———. Interview. Tape recording. Bronx, NY. January 30, 1998.
———. Interview. Video tape recording. Bronx, NY. May 1, 1998.
Giro, Radamés. Interview. Marianao, La Habana, Cuba. June 30, 1999.
Golden, Gene. Interview. Palisades Park, NJ. March 14, 2001.
Hierrezuelo Ruíz, Eulalio H. Interview. Tape recording. Lincoln Heights, CA. November 2, 1997.
Jansen, Richard. Interview. Tape recording. Willemstad, Curaçao. December 8, 2003.
Joseph, Alfonso "El Panameño" (Gaylordsville, CT). Interview via telephone. November 29, 2001.
Kortwrite, Luís "Wito" (Bronx, NY). Interview via telephone. January 25, 1999.
Leicea, Calixto. Interview. Tape recording. Manhattan, NY. October 24, 2000.
Levine, Mark (San Francisco, CA). Interview via telephone. March 31, 1997.
Liman, Abby (Manhattan, NY). Interview via telephone. January 6, 1999.
López, Oscar (Los Angeles). Interview via telephone. Tape recording. March 30, 2000.
López, Paul. Interview. Tape recording. Lincoln Heights, CA. August 22, 1996.
López, René. Interview via telephone. Tape recording. Feburary 8, 2004.
Macías, Rudy. Interview. Tape recording. Whittier, CA. August 16, 1999.
Marin, Orlando. Interview. Tape recording. Queens, NY. January 20, 2000.
Martínez, Johnny. Interview. Video tape recording. Burbank, CA. August 11, 1998.
———. Interview. Tape recording. Burbank, CA. January 3, 2000.
Martínez Baro, Sarah. Interview. Tape recording. East Harlem, NY. February 19, 2000.
Montecino Herrera, Manuela. Interview. Tape recording. Barrio Obrero, La Habana, Cuba. June 25, 1999.
Moran, Rocky. Interview. Tape recording. Monrovia, CA. May 25, 1997.
Newsum, Phil. Interview. Tape recording. Manhattan, NY. 2001.
Oliva, Juan. Interview. Tape recording. Los Angeles, CA. November 9, 1996.
Palmieri, Eddie (New York, NY). Interview via telephone. Tape recording. February 26, 2002.
Pérez, Graciela (New York, NY). Interview via telephone. Tape recording. September 26, 1998.
Rabora (Thorne), Jackie (Los Angeles). Interview via telephone. Tape recording. April 6, 2000.
Reagon, Bernice (Washington, DC). Interview via telephone. Tape recording. May 3, 2004.
Riambau, Horatio. Interview. Tape and video recording. Manhattan, NY. June 23, 2003.
Rivera, Edil (Mayagüez, P.R.). Interview via telephone. Tape recording. January 14, 2000.

———. Interview via telephone. Tape recording. January 21, 2000.
———. Interview via telephone. Tape recording. January 28, 2000.
———. Interview via telephone. Tape recording. February 26, 2000.
Roma, Benny. Interview. Tape recording. Manhattan, NY. June 27, 1998.
Romero, Ray. Interview. Leonia, NJ. June 25, 2000.
Rosa, Ken "Leo" (Bronx, NY). Interview via telephone. Tape recording. December 1, 1999.
———. Interview via telephone. Tape recording. December 8, 1999.
Rubalcava, Alfred R. Interview. Hollywood, CA. July 31, 2001.
Sabatar, Jimmy. Interview. Tape recording. Manhattan, NY. June 27, 1998.
Sánchez, David. Interview. Tape recording. Sun Valley, CA. August 11, 1999.
Santos, John. Interview. Tape recording. Oakland, CA. February 14, 1997.
Sesma, Lionel "Chico." Interview. Tape recording. Los Angeles. 27, March 1997.
Smith, Mauricio. Interview. Tape recording. Brooklyn, NY. April 30, 1999.
Suárez, Manolo. Interview. Tape recording. Los Angeles. July 31, 1996.
———. Interview. Tape recording. Los Angeles. September 11, 1996.
Suárez, Norman. Interview. Tape recording. Willemstad, Curaçao. December 10, 2003.
Torres, Joe (Las Vegas, NV). Interview via telephone. Tape recording. February 17, 2000.
Touzet, René (Miami, FL). Interview via telephone. Tape recording. March 6, 2000.
Travieso, Mercedes. Interview. Tape recording. Lawton, La Habana, Cuba. July 8, 1999.
Travieso Montecino, Regla María. Interview. Tape recording. Barrio Obrero, La Habana, Cuba. June 25, 1999.
———. Interview. Tape recording. Lawton, La Habana, Cuba. July 8, 1999.
Travieso, Raúl. Interview. Tape recording. Los Angeles. June 19, 1996.
———. Interview. Tape recording. Los Angeles. July 31, 1996.
———. Interview. Tape recording. Los Angeles. February 8, 1997.
———. Interview via telephone. February 17, 1997.
———. Interview. Tape recording. Los Angeles. April 5, 1997.
———. Interview. Tape recording. Los Angeles. April 15, 1998.
———. Interview. Video tape recording. Los Angeles. August 3, 1998.
———. Interview via telephone. October 12, 1998.
———. Interview via telephone. March 15, 1999.
———. Interview via telephone. December 13, 1999.
———. Interview via telephone. February 7, 2000.
———. Interview via telephone. February 17, 2000.
———. Interview via telephone. June 26, 2000.
Travieso, Xiomara. Interview. Tape recording. Bronx, NY. June 14, 1999.
Valdés, Alfredo Jr. Interview. Tape recording. Manhattan, NY. October 18, 1997.
———. Interview. Tape recording. Queens, NY. December 4, 1999.
———. Interview via telephone. August 19, 2001.
Valdés Ginebra, Fidel Aldo. Interview. Tape recording. Centro Habana, La Habana, Cuba. July 10, 1999.

Valiente, José. Interview. Tape recording. Queens, NY. July 9, 2000.

———. Interview via telephone. March 28, 2001.

Villareal, Reginald. Interview. Tape recording. Willemstad, Curaçao. December 7, 2003.

Interviews Conducted by Others

Álvarez, René. Interview by Robin Moore. Tape recording. La Habana, Cuba. April 4, 1994.

Arcaño, Antonio. Interview by Jesús Blanco and René López. Video Recording. La Habana, Cuba. November 21, 1988.

———. Interview by Robin Moore. Tape recording. La Habana, Cuba. July 16, 1992.

Armenteros, Alfredo "Chocolate." Interview by Smithsonian Institution: Jazz Oral History Program. Tape recording. East Harlem, NY. February 8–9 and July 6, 1996.

Berrios, Israel with Riverita. Interview by Jaime Jaramillo. Video recording. San Juan, P.R. July 26, 1996.

Berrios, Israel. Interview by Cristóbal Díaz Ayala. Tape recording. Carolina, P.R. June 13, 1997.

Flores, Luís "Maquina." Interview with David Carp. Riverdale, NY. October 22, 1993.

Harlow, Larry. Interview by David Carp. Tape recordings. Manhattan, NY. December 2, 1997.

Lima, Abe. Interview by David Carp. Tape recording. Manhattan, NY. August 26, 1994.

López, Israel "Cachao." Interview by Smithsonian Institution: Jazz Oral History Program. Tape recording. Miami, FL. January 24–25, 1994.

López, René. Interview by Jaime Jaramillo. Video recording. San Juan, P.R. February 11, 1995.

Pacheco, Johnny. Interview by David Carp. Tape recording. Manhattan, NY. April 2, 1997.

Rivera, Hector. Interview with Henry Medina. New York City. September 25, 1993.

Rodríguez, Arsenio. Interview by Radio Caracol Colombia. Tape recording. Los Angeles. 1964.

Valdés, Bebo. Interview by Smithsonian Institution: Jazz Oral History Program. Tape recording. September 20–21, 2000.

Valdés, Carlos "Patato." Interview by Smithsonian Institution: Jazz Oral History Program. Tape recording. September 17–18, 1995.

Secondary and Other Sources

Abler, Ronald and John S. Adams. 1976. *A Comparative Atlas of America's Great Cities: Twenty Metropolitan Regions*. Minneapolis: Association of American Geographers and University of Minnesota Press.

Abrahams, Roger D. 1995. "Ralph Rinzler (1934–1994)." *Journal of American Folklore* 108/429: 325–27.

Acosta, Leonardo. 1982. *Música y descolonización*. La Habana: Editorial Arte y Literatura.

———. 1983. *Del tambor al sintetizador*. La Habana: Editorial Letras Cubanas.

———. 1991. "The Rumba, the Guaguancó, and Tío Tom." *Essays on Cuban Music: North American and Cuban Perspectives*. Edited by Peter Manuel. Lanham: University Press of America.

———. 1993a. *Elige tú, que canto yo*. La Habana: Editorial Letras Cubanas.

———. 1993b. "¿Quién inventó el mambo?" In *El mambo*. Edited by Radamés Giro. La Habana: Editorial Letras Cubanas. First published in *Revolución y Cultura* 42 (febrero de 1976).

———. 1993c. "Reajustes, aclaraciones y criterios sobre Dámaso Pérez Prado." In *El mambo*. Edited by Radamés Giro. La Habana: Editorial Letras Cubanas. First published in *Bohemia* 39 (29 de septiembre de 1989).

———. 1998. "Música y cultura popular cubana." *La gaceta de Cuba* 36/5: 12–14.

Acosta, Leonardo, Olivier Cossard, René Espí, and Helio Orovio. 1999. *Fiesta Havana, 1940–1960: L'âge d'or de la musique cubaine*. Paris: Vade Retro.

Aguire, Benigno E. 1976. "Differential Migration of Cuban Social Races." *Latin American Research Review* 11/1: 103–24.

Amaro, Nelson and Carmelo Mesa-Lago. 1971. "Inequality and Classes." In *Revolutionary Change in Cuba*. Edited by Carmelo Mesa-Lago. Pittsburgh: University of Pittsburgh Press.

Ames, David W. 1950. "Negro Family Types in a Cuban Solar." *Phylon: The Atlanta University Review of Race and Culture* 11/2: 159–63.

Aparicio, Frances R. 1998. *Listening to Salsa: Gender, Latin Popular Music, and Puerto Rican Cultures*. Hanover: Wesleyan University Press.

———. 2002. "La Lupe, La India, and Celia: Toward a Feminist Genealogy of Salsa Music. In *Situating Salsa: Global Markets and Local Meanings in Latin Popular Music*. Edited by Lise Waxer. New York: Routledge.

Archivo Nacional de Cuba. *Registro de Asociaciones*. Indice 1, 2, 3.

Arredondo, Alberto. 1937. "El arte negro a contrapelo." *Adelante* (August): 5–6, 20.

———. 1938. "Eso que llaman afrocubanismo musical." *Adelante* (April): 5.

Austerlitz, Paul. 2003. "Mambo Kings to West African Textiles: A Synesthetic Approach to Black Atlantic Aesthetics." In *Musical Migrations, Vol. 1: Transnationalism and Cultural Hybridity in Latin/o America*. New York: Palgrave.

Ávalos, Michael Iván. 1991. Linear notes to *Sexteto Cubanos* vol. 1, *Sones 1930: Sexteto Munamar, Sexteto Machin, Sexteto Nacional, Sexteto Matancero*. Arhoolie Productions, CD 7003. One CD, 1991.

———. 1995. Linear notes to *Sextetos Cubanos* vol. 2, *Sexteto Boloña, Sexteto Occidente, Sexteto Nacional, Sexteto Matancero*. Arhoolie Productions, CD 7006. One CD, 1995.

Bamford, LeAnn. 1995. "Salsa Nightclub Style: Originally Called Mambo." *Dancing USA* 13/4 (July/August): 4–5.

"Ban by Church Is Beaten in Peru." 1951. *Ebony*, September.

Baron, Robert. 1977. "Syncretism and Ideology: Latin New York Salsa Musicians." *Western Folklore* 36/3: 209–25.

Bender, Lynn Darrel. 1973. "The Cuban Exiles: An Analytical Sketch." *Journal of Latin American Studies*. 5/2: 271–78.

Benítez-Rojo, Antonio. 1996. *The Repeating Island: The Caribbean and the Postmodern Perspective,* 2nd ed. Translated by James Maraniss. Durham, NC: Duke University Press.

Benjamin, Alan F. 2002. *Jews of the Dutch Caribbean: Exploring Ethnic Identity on Curaçao*. London: Routledge.

Berríos-Miranda, Marisol. 2002. "Is Salsa a Musical Genre?" In *Situating Salsa: Global Markets and Local Meanings in Latin Popular Music*. New York: Routledge.

———. 2003. "'Con Sabor a Puerto Rico': The Reception and Influence of Puerto Rican Salsa in Venezuela." In *Musical Migrations: Transnationalism and Cultural Hybridity in Latin/o America,* vol. 1. Edited by Frances R. Aparicio and Cándida F. Jáquez with María Elena Cepeda. New York: Palgrave Macmillan.

Betancourt, Lino. 1984. "Miguelito Cuní: Ese sonero impecable." *Bohemia* 76/11: 23–24.

Betancur Álvarez, Fabio. 1999. *Sin clave y bongó no hay son: Música afrocubana y confluencias musicales de Colombia y Cuba,* 2nd ed. Medellín: Editorial Universidad de Antioquia.

Blanco Aguilar, Jesús. 1992. *Ochenta años del son y los soneros de Caribe, 1909–1989*. Caracas: Fondo Editorial Tropykos.

Blum, Joseph. 1978. "Problems of *Salsa* Research." *Ethnomusicology* 22/1: 137–49.

Blum, Stephen. 1992. "Analysis of Musical Style." In *Ethnomusicology: An Introduction*. New York: Norton.

Boggs, Vernon W. 1992. *Salsiology: Afro-Cuban Music and the Evolution of Salsa in New York City*. New York: Excelsior Music.

Boswell, Thomas D. and James R. Curtis. 1984. *The Cuban-American Experience: Culture, Images, and Perspectives*. New Jersey: Rowman and Allanheld.

Boudet, Ileana. 1974. "Arcaño y sus Maravillas." *Revolución y cultura* 25: 32–35.

Brandon, George. 1993. *Santeria from Africa to the New World: The Dead Sell Memories*. Bloomington: Indiana University Press.

Brock, Lisa. 1998. "Introduction: Between Race and Empire." In *Between Race and Empire: African-Americans and Cubans before the Cuban Revolution*. Edited by Lisa Brock and Digna Castañeda Fuertes. Philadelphia: Temple University Press.

Browning, Barbara. 1995. *Samba: Resistance in Motion*. Bloomington: Indiana University Press.

Bryce-Laporte, Roy Simon. 1972. "Black Immigrants: The Experience of Invisibility and Inequality." *Journal of Black Studies* 3/1: 29–56.

Butler, Albert and Josephine Butler. 1975. *Encyclopedia of Social Dance*. New York: Albert Butler Ballroom Dance Service.

Butterworth, Douglas. 1980. *The People of Buena Ventura: Relocation of Slum Dwellers in Postrevolutionary Cuba.* Urbana: University of Illinois Press.

Byrnes, Don and Alice Swanson. 1951. "Mambo: A Vest Pocket Analysis." *Dance Magazine* 25/10 (October): 29, 36, 38.

Cabrera, Lydia. 1992. *El monte,* 7th ed. Miami: Ediciones Universal.

———. 2000. *Vocaulario congo (El Bantú que se habla en Cuba).* Miami: Ediciones Universal.

Carbo Menéndez, José. 1971. "Arsenio Rodríguez." *El diario-La prensa* (January 12): 26–27.

Carp, David. 1996. "Profile: Who Is Moncho Leña?" Online document available at www.descarga.com

———. 1997. "Interview: A Visit with Maestro Johnny Pacheco." Online document available at www. descarga. com.

———. 1998. "Profile: Eddie Palmieri: Form and Substance." Online document available at www.descarga.com.

———. 1999a. "Barry Rogers: Salsero, Searcher, World Musician." Online document available at www. descarga.com.

———. 1999b. "Report on Field Work for Place Matters/City Lore, South Bronx Latin Music Project." Unpublished manuscript.

Carreras, Julio Angel. 1989. *Esclavitud, abolición y racismo.* La Habana: Editorial de Ciencias Sociales.

Castellanos, Jorge and Isabel Castellanos. 1987. "The Geographic, Ethnologic, and Linguistic Roots of Cuban Blacks." *Cuban Studies* 17: 95–110.

———. 1988. *Cultura Afrocubana.* Vol. 1, *El negro en Cuba, 1492–1844.* Miami: Ediciones Universal.

———. 1990. *Cultura Afrocubana.* Vol. 2, *El negro en Cuba, 1845–1959.* Miami: Ediciones Universal.

———. 1992. *Cultura Afrocubana.* Vol. 3, *Las religiones y las lenguas.* Miami: Ediciones Universal.

———. 1994. *Cultura Afrocubana.* Vol. 4, *Letras, Música, Arte.* Miami: Ediciones Universal.

Castillo, A. 1961. "Gilberto Valdés: Un interprete de los ritmos afrocubanos." *Bohemia* 53/44 (October): 120–21.

Chernoff, John Miller. 1981. *African Rhythm and African Sensibility: Aesthetics and Social Action in African Musical Idioms.* Chicago: University of Chicago Press.

Chinchilla, Norma, Nora Hamilton, and James Loucky. 1993. "Central Americans in Los Angeles: An Immigrant Community in Transition." In *In the Barrios: Latinos and the Underclass Debate.* Edited by Joan Moore and Raquel Pinderhughes. New York: Russell Sage Foundation.

Chomsky, Aviva, Barry Carr, and Pamela Maria Smorkaloff. 2003. *The Cuba Reader: History, Culture, Politics.* Durham, NC: Duke University Press.

Clarke, Donald. 1989. *The Penguin Encyclopedia of Popular Music.* Edited by Donald Clarke. New York: Viking.

Clifford, James. 1978. "'Hanging Up Looking Glasses at Odd Corners': Ethnobiographical Prospects." In *Studies in Biography.* Edited by Daniel Aaron. Harvard English Studies 8. Cambridge, MA: Harvard University Press.

Club Cubano Inter-Americano. 1941–95. *Club Cubano Inter-Americano Photograph Collection.* 3 Boxes. Schomburg Center for Research in Black Culture, New York Public Library.

———. 1946–96. *Club Cubano Inter-Americano Records.* 2 Boxes. Schomburg Center for Research in Black Culture, New York Public Library.

Colectivo de Autores. 1990. *Barrio de Cayo Hueso.* La Habana: Editorial de Ciencias Sociales.

Collazo, Bobby. 1987. *La última noche que pasé contigo.* Puerto Rico: Editorial Cubanacan.

Colón, Willie and John Storm Roberts. 1976. "Salsa." In *Dancing Madness.* New York: Anchor Books.

Cortés, Carlos E., ed. 1980. *The Cuban Minority in the U.S.* 2 vols. New York: Arno Press.

Cortes, Felix, Angel Falcón, and Juan Flores. 1976. "The Cultural Expression of Puerto Ricans in New York: A Theoretical Perspective and Critical Review." *Latin American Perspectives* 3/2: 117–52.

Courlander, Harold. 1944. "Abakuá Meeting in Guanabacoa." *The Journal of Negro History* 29/4: 461–70.

Cuba, Dirección General del Censo. 1919. *Census of the Republic of Cuba 1919.* Havana: Maza, Arroyo y Caso, S. en C.

Cubillas, Vicente Jr. 1952. "Habla Arsenio Rodríguez: ¡Ese maldito mambo!" *Bohemia* 44 (49): 24–25.

Cuéllar Vizcaíno, Manuel. 1993. "La revolución del mambo." In *El mambo.* Edited by Radamés Giro. La Habana: Editorial Letras Cubanas. First published in *Bohemia* 40/22 (May 30, 1948): 20–21, 97–99.

Daniel, Yvonne. 1995. *Rumba: Dance and Social Change in Contemporary Cuba.* Bloomington: Indiana University Press.

Davies, Richard Arthur. 1999. *Cuban Trumpet Playing: The Solo Performance Style of Alfredo "Chocolate" Armenteros.* Ph.D. diss., New York University.

de Granda, Germán. 1973. "Materiales léxicos para la determinación de la matriz africana de la 'lengua congo' de Cuba." *Revista Española de Lingüística* 3: 55–79.

de la Fuenta, Alejandro. 1995. "Race and Inequality in Cuba, 1899–1981." *Journal of Contemporary History* 30: 131–68.

———. 1999. "Myths of Racial Democracy: Cuba, 1900–1912." *Latin American Research Review* 34/3: 39–73.

de Posada, Luís. 1954. "Clubes sociales y deportivos." In *Libro de Cuba: Una enciclopedia ilustrada que abarca las artes, las letras, las ciencias, la economía, la política, la historia, la docencia y el progreso general de la nación cubana.* Edición Conmemorativa del Cincuentenario de la Independencia, 1902–1952 y del Centenario del Nacimiento de José Martí, 1853–1953. Edited by Juan Joaquín Otero et al. Habana: Publicaciones Unidas.

Della Corte, A. and G. M. Gatti. 1949. *Diccionario de la música.* Translated by M. Ferraria and N. Lamuraglia. Buenos Aires: Ricordi Americana S. A. Originally published as *Dizionario de musica.*

Depestre Catony, Leonardo. 1989. *Homenaje a la música popular cubana*. Santiago de Cuba: Editorial Oriente.

Diamante, Carlos. 1948. *Arranging Latin American Music Authentically*. New York: King Brand.

Díaz Ayala, Cristóbal. 1993. *Música cubana del areyto a la nueva trova*, 3rd edition. San Juan: Editorial Cubanacan. Originally published 1981.

———. 1988. *Si te quieres por el pico divertir... (Historica del pregón musical latinoamericano)*. San Juan: Editorial Cubanacan.

———. 1994. *Cuba canta y baila—discografía de la música cubana* vol. 1: *1898–1925*. San Juan: Fundación Musicalia.

———. 1998. *Cuando salí de La Habana: 1898–1997 Cien años de música cubana por el mundo*. Puerto Rico: Fundación Musicalia.

Dollero, Adolfo. 1919. *Cultura cubana (La provincia de Matanzas y su evolución)*. Habana: Imp. Scoaney Fernández.

Duany, Jorge. 1984. "Popular Music in Puerto Rico: Toward an Anthropology of *Salsa*." *Latin American Music Review* 5/2: 186–216.

———. 1990. "Review-Essay." *Latin American Music Review* 11/2: 286–96.

Dudley, Shannon. 1996. "Judging 'By the Beat': Calypso versus Soca." *Ethnomusicology* 40/2: 269–98.

Dufrasne-Gonzalez, J. Emanuel. 1985. *La homogeneidad de la másica caribena: Sobre la música comercial y popular de Puerto Rico*. Ph.D. diss., University of California, Los Angeles.

Dworkin y Méndez, Kenya. 2000. "Introduction." In *Black Cuban, Black American: A Memoir*. Houston: Arte Público Press.

Eastman, Ralph. 1998. "'Pitchin' up a Boogie': African-American Musicians, Nightlife, and Music Venues in Los Angeles, 1930–1945." In *California Soul: Music of African Americans in the West*. Edited by Jacqueline Cogdell DjeDje and Eddie S. Meadows. Berkeley: University of California Press.

Echevarría, Luís Alfaro and Juan Francisco de la Paz Pérez. 1981. "Elementos lexicales del Español en los rituales afrocubanos." *Islas* 68: 177–209.

Ellis, Keith. 1998. "Nicolás Guillén and Langston Hughes: Convergences and Divergences." In *Between Race and Empire: African-Americans and Cubans before the Cuban Revolution*. Edited by Lisa Brock and Digna Castañeda Fuertes. Philadelphia: Temple University Press.

Erlmann, Veit. 1991. *African Stars: Studies in Black South African Performance*. Chicago: University of Chicago Press.

———. 1996. *Nightsong: Performance, Power, and Practices in South Africa*. Chicago: University of Chicago Press.

Fabian, Johannes. 1983. *Time and the Other: How Anthropology Makes Its Object*. New York: Columbia University Press.

Fair Employment Practice Commission. 1966. *Negroes and Mexican Americans in South and East Los Angeles: Changes between 1960 and 1965 in Population, Employment, Income, and Family Status: An Analysis of a U.S. Census Survey of November 1965*. California: Division of Fair Employment Practices.

Fanon, Frantz. 1968. *The Wretched of the Earth*. New York: Grove Press.

Feather, Leonard. 1952. "Percy: No Faith in Phony Latins!" *Down Beat* (November 19): 12.

Fernández, María Antonia. 1985. *Bailes populares cubanos*. La Habana: Editorial Pueblo y Educación.

Fernández, Raúl A. 1997. "Celia Cruz: Artista de América Latina." *Deslinde* 21: 103–21.

———. 1998. "'Mongo' Santamaría: soñando en cubano." *Deslinde* 23: 121–33.

Fernández Robaina, Tomás. 1994. *El negro en Cuba 1902–1958: apuntes para la historia de la lucha contra la discriminación racial*. La Habana: Editorial de Ciencias Sociales.

———. 1998. "Marcus Garvey in Cuba: Urrutia, Cubans, and Black Nationalism." In *Between Race and Empire: African-Americans and Cubans before the Cuban Revolution*. Edited by Lisa Brock and Digna Castañeda Fuertes. Philadelphia: Temple University Press.

Figueroa, Frank M. 1995. *Encyclopedia of Latin American Music in New York*. St. Petersburg: Pillar Publications.

Flores, Juan. 2000. *From Bomba to Hip-Hop: Puerto Rican Culture and Latino Identity*. New York: Columbia University Press.

———. 2004. "Creolité in the 'Hood: Diaspora as Source and Challenge." *CENTRO Journal* 16/2: 282–93.

Floyd, Samuel A. Jr. 1995. *The Power of Black Music: Interpreting Its History from Africa to the United States*. New York: Oxford University Press.

Fogelson, Robert M., comp. 1969. *The Los Angeles Riots. Mass Violence in America*. Edited by Robert M. Fogelson and Richard E. Rubenstein. New York: Arno Press and *New York Times*.

Freire Díaz, Joaquín. 1985. *Historia de los municipios de Cuba*. Miami: La Moderna Poesia.

Gagné, Richard. 1996. "Ralph Rinzler, Folklorist: Professional Biography." *Folklore Forum* 27/1: 20–49.

Galán, Natalio. 1983. *Cuba y sus sones*. Valencia: Artes Gráficos Soler.

García, Armando and Ana María García. 1976. "El sentimiento de la música cubana." *Joven Cuba* (April): 14–17, 31–33.

García Montes, Jorge and Antonio Alonso Avila. 1970. *Historia del partido comunista de Cuba*. Miami: Ediciones Universal.

Gates, Henry Louis. Jr.1988. *The Signifying Monkey: A Theory of African-American Literary Criticism*. New York: Oxford University Press.

Gelb, Arthur. 1961. "La Pachanga Is New Dance Craze: Cuban Step Sweeps El Morocco and the Palladium but Versions Differ in Fad Inspired by Song Hit." *New York Times* (May 9).

Gerard, Charley with Marty Sheller. 1988. *Salsa! The Rhythm of Latin Music*. Tempe, AZ: White Cliffs Media.

Gilroy, Paul. 1993. *The Black Atlantic: Modernity and Double Consciousness*. Cambridge, MA: Harvard University Press.

Giro, Radamés. 1993. "Todo lo que usted quiso saber sobre el mambo . . ." In *El mambo*. Edited by Radamés Giro. La Habana: Editorial Letras Cubanas. First published in *La gaceta de Cuba* (October-November-December 1992).

———. 1995a. *Panorama de la música popular cubana*. Edited by Radamés Giro. La Habana: Editorial Letras Cubanas.

———. 1995b. "Los motivos del son: Hitos en su sendero caribeño y universal." In *Panorama de la música popular cubana*. Edited by Radamés Giro. La Habana: Editorial Letras Cubanas. First published in *La gaceta de Cuba* (abril-mayo-junio 1994).

Glasser, Ruth. 1995. *My Music Is my Flag: Puerto Rican Musicians and their New York Communities, 1917–1940*. Berkeley: University of California Press.

Gleason, Ralph J. 1951. "Swingin' the Golden Gate: Prado's West Coast Tour Proving a Huge Success." *Down Beat*, October 5.

———. 1952. "Miguelito Valdes Makes Mighty Pitch for Progress." *Down Beat*, August 13.

Godfried, Eugène. 2000. "Buena Vista Social Club: Critics, Self-Criticism, and the Survival of Cuban *Son*." *AfroCubaWeb* (www.afrocubaweb.com/eugenegodfried/buenavistacritics).

Gómez Cairo, Jesús. 1995. "Acerca de la interacción de géneros en la música popular cubana." In *Panorama de la música popular cubana*. Edited by Radamés Giro. La Habana: Editorial Letras Cubanas. First published in *Boletín de música* 83–84 (julio–octubre 1980).

González Huguet, Lydia and Jean René Baudry. 1967. "Voces 'Bantú' en el vocabulario 'Palero'." *Etnologia y Folklore* 3: 31–64.

Greenbaum, Susan D. 1986. "Afro-Cubans in Ybor City: A Centennial History." Unpublished manuscript.

Grenet, Emilio. 1995. "Música cubana: Orientaciones para su conocimiento y estudio." In *Panorama de la música popular cubana*. Edited by Radamés Giro. La Habana: Editorial Letras Cubanas. First published in *Popular Cuban Music: 80 Revised and Corrected Compositions Together with an Essay on the Evolution of Music in Cuba*. Havaná: Carasa y Cía, 1939.

Grillo, Evelio. 2000. *Black Cuban, Black American: A Memoir*. With an introduction by Kenya Dworkin y Méndez. Houston: Arte Público Press.

Grupo Cubano de Investigaciones Economicas and José R. Álvarez Díaz. 1963. *Un estudio sobre Cuba; colonia, republica, experimento socialista: estructura economica, desarrollo institucional, socialismo y regresion*. Coral Gables: University of Miami Press.

Guanche, Jesús. 1996. *Componentes étnicos de la nación cubana*. Ciudad de La Habana: Fundación Fernando Ortiz.

Guevara, Gema R. 2003. "'La Cuba de Ayer/La Cuba de Hoy': The Politics of Music and Diaspora." In *Musical Migrations: Transnationalism and Cultural Hybridity in Latin/o America*, vol. 1. Edited by Frances R. Aparicio and Cándida F. Jáquez with María Elena Cepeda.

Guillén, Nicolás. 1931. *Sóngoro cosongo: poemas mulatos*. La Habana: Ucar, García y Cia.

Gutiérrez Serrano, Raúl. 1947. "The Radio in Cuba." *International Journal of Opinion and Attitude Research* 1/2: 62–70.

Hagedorn, Katherine J. 2001. *Divine Utterances: The Performance of Afro-Cuban Santería*. Washington, DC: Smithsonian Institution Press.

Haslip-Viera, Gabriel. 1993. "The Evolution of the Latino Community in New York City: Early Nineteenth Century to the Present." In *Latinos in New York*. Edited by Gabriel Haslip-Viera and Sheri Bauer. Indiana: Notre Dame Press.

Hassan, Salah D. 2002. "Introduction: 'Origins' of Postmodern Cuba." *New Centennial Review* 2/2: 1–17.

Helg, Aline. 1995. *Our Rightful Share: The Afro-Cuban Struggle for Equality, 1886–1912*. Chapel Hill: University of North Carolina Press.

Hentoff, Nat. 1954. "The Mambo!! They Shake A-Plenty with Tito Puente." *Down Beat*, October 6.

Hernández, Erena. 1986. *La música en persona*. La Habana: Editorial Letras Cubanas.

———. 1993a. "Conversación con Pérez Prado." In *El mambo*. Edited by Radamés Giro. La Habana: Editorial Letras Cubanas. First published in *La música en persona*. La Habana: Editorial Letras Cubanas, 1986.

———. 1993b. "Orestes López responde a Pérez Prado." In *El mambo*. Edited by Radamés Giro. La Habana: Editorial Letras Cubanas. First published in *La música en persona*. La Habana: Editorial Letras Cubanas, 1986.

Hiraldo, Carlos. 2003. *Segregated Miscegenation: On the Treatment of Racial Hybridity in the U.S. and Latin American Literary Traditions*. New York: Routledge.

Howard, Philip A. 1998. *Changing History: Afro-Cuban Cabildos and Societies of Color in the Nineteenth Century*. Baton Rouge: Louisiana State University Press.

Hutchinson, Sydney. 2004. "Mambo on 2: The Birth of a New Form of Dance in New York City." *Centro Journal* 16/2: 108–37.

Iglesias, César Andreu, ed. 1984. *Memoirs of Bernardo Vega: A Contribution to the History of the Puerto Rican Community in New York*. Translated by Juan Flores. New York: Monthly Review Press.

Inclán Lavastida, Fernando. 1943. *Historia de Marianao: De la epoca indigena a los tiempos actuales*. Prologo por el Dr. Ruben Alfonso Quintero. Marianao: Editorial "El Sol."

Jonnes, Jill. 1986. *We're Still Here: The Rise, Fall, and Resurrection of the South Bronx*. Boston: Atlantic Monthly Press.

Keil, Charles. 1994a. "Motion and Feeling through Music." In *Music Grooves: Essays and Dialogues*. Chicago: University of Chicago Press. First published in *Journal of Aesthetics and Art Criticism* 24 (1966): 337–49.

Knight, Franklin W. 1970. *Slave Society in Cuba during the Nineteenth Century*. Madison: University of Wisconsin Press.

Lachatañeré, Rómulo. 1950. "Rasgos 'bantú' en la santería." *Estudios Afro-Cubanos* 2 (1998): 183–91.

Lam, Rafael. 1996. "Arsenio: el corsario negro." *Tropicana Internacional* 2: 25–28.

Lenneberg, Hans. 1988. *Witnesses and Scholars: Studies in Musical Biography*. Musicology: A Book Series, vol. 5. New York: Gordon and Breach.

León, Argeliers. 1984. *Del canto y el tiempo*. La Habana: Editorial Letras Cubanas.

———. 1991. "Notes toward a Panorama of Popular and Folk Music." In *Essays on Cuban Music: North American and Cuban Perspectives*. Edited by Peter Manuel. Lanham: University Press of America.

Lezcano, José Manuel. 1991. "African-Derived Rhythmical and Metrical Elements in Selected Songs of Alejandro García Caturla and Amadeo Roldán." *Latin American Music Review* 12/2: 173–86.

Lipsitz, George. 1994. *Dangerous Crossroads: Popular Music, Postmodernism and the Poetics of Place*. London: Verso.

Lipski, John M. 1993. "On the Non-Creole Basis for Afro-Caribbean Spanish." University of New Mexico Latin American Institute Research Paper Series 24. Albuquerque: University of New Mexico.

Locke, David. 1982. "Principles of Offbeat Timing and Cross-Rhythm in Southern Eve Dance Drumming." *Ethnomusicology* 26/2: 217–46.

López, Oscar Luís. 1981. *La radio en Cuba: estudio de su desarrollo en la sociedad neocolonial*. Habana: Editorial Letras Cubanas.

López, René and Andy Kaufman. 1974. Linear notes to *Mano a Mano: Arsenio Rodríguez y Su Conjunto Orquestal Todos Estrellas y Antonio Arcaño y Sus Maravillas*. Cariño Records. DBM1-5800. One LP.

Loza, Steven. 1993. *Barrio Rhythm: Mexican American Music in Los Angeles*. Urbana: University of Illinois Press.

———. 1999. *Tito Puente and the Making of Latin Music*. Urbana: University of Illinois Press.

———, ed. 2003. *Musical Cultures of Latin America: Global Effects, Past and Present*. Proceedings of an International Conference, University of California, Los Angeles, May 28–30, 1999. Los Angeles: Department of Ethnomusicology and Systematic Musicology, University of California.

Luis, Robert. 1958. "Rumba's Anniversary." *Dance Magazine* 32/6 (June): 66–67.

———. 1959. "Evolution of Cha Cha." In *Dance Magazine* 33/10 (October): 69–70.

Luzón Benedicto, José Luis. 1987. *Economía, población y territorio en Cuba (1899–1983)*. Madrid: Ediciones Cultura Hispánica del Instituto de Cooperación Iberoamericana.

"Mambo, El." 1950. *Newsweek*, September 4.

"Mambo, The." 1951. *Time*, April 9.

Manuel, Peter. 1985. "The Anticipated Bass in Cuban Popular Music." *Latin American Music Review* 6/2: 249–61.

———. 1991. "Salsa and the Music Industry: Corporate Control or Grassroots Expression?" In *Essays on Cuban Music: North American and Cuban Perspectives*. Edited by Peter Manuel. Lanham: University Press of America.

———. 1994. "Puerto Rican Music and Cultural Identity: Creative Appropriation of Cuban Sources from Danza to Salsa." *Ethnomusicology* 38/2: 249–80.

———. 1998. "Improvisation in Latin Dance Music History and Style." In *In the Course of Performance: Studies in the World of Musical Improvisation*. Edited by Bruno Nettl and Melinda Russell. Chicago: University of Chicago Press.

Martijn, S. "Yapi." 1991. *Kòrsou musical: Un dokumentashon di nos historia musika popular entre 1930 i 1989*. Vol. 1 (1930–1950). Curaçao: Drukkerij Scherpenheuvel N.V.

Martínez, Mayra A. 1993. "Hacer el son como lo siento: Lilí Martínez." In *Cubanos en la música*. La Habana: Editorial Letras Cubanas.

Martínez Furé, Rogelio. 1991. "Tambor." In *Essays on Cuban Music: North American and Cuban Perspectives*. Edited by Peter Manuel. Lanham: University Press of America.

Martínez Rodríguez, Raúl. 1995. "La rumba en la provincia de Matanzas." *Panorama de la música popular cubana*. La Habana: Editorial Letras Cubanas.

Masferrer, Marianne and Carmelo Mesa-Lago. 1974. "The Gradual Integration of the Black in Cuba: Under the Colony, the Republic, and the Revolution." In *Slavery and Race Relations in Latin America*. Edited by Robert Brent Toplin. Westport, CT: Greenwood Press.

Masud-Piloto, Felix. 1996. *From Welcomed Exiles to Illegal Immigrants: Cuban Migration to the U.S., 1959–1995*. Lanham: Rowman and Littlefield.

Mauleón, Rebeca. 1993. *Salsa Guidebook: For Piano and Ensemble*. Petaluma: Sher Music.

McCall, John. 1998. "The Representation of African Music in Early Documents." In *Africa: The Garland Encyclopedia of World Music*, vol. 1. Edited by Ruth Stone. New York: Garland.

Menéndez, José Carbo. 1967. "Compositores Latinos: Arsenio Rodríguez." *Revista Zig-Zag* 12.

Méndez Bravet, Alina and Jorge Ignacio Pérez. 1991. *Arsenio Rodríguez: Del mito a las sombras*. La Habana: Universidad de la Habana.

Modares, Ali. 1994. *The Racial and Ethnic Structure of Los Angeles County: A Geographic Guide*. Los Angeles: Edmund G. "Pat" Brown Institute of Public Affairs.

Monson, Ingrid. 2000. *The African Diaspora: A Musical Perspective*. Edited by Ingrid Monson. New York: Garland.

Moore, Carlos. 2003. "Silence on Black Cuba." In *The Cuba Reader: History, Culture, Politics*. Edited by Aviva Chomsky, Barry Carr, and Pamela Maria Smorkaloff. Durham, NC: Duke University Press.

Moore, Robin. 1994. "Representations of Afrocuban Expressive Culture in the Writings of Fernando Ortiz." *Latin American Music Review* 15/1: 32–54.

———. 1995. "The Commercial Rumba: Afrocuban Arts as International Popular Culture." *Latin American Music Review* 16/2: 165–98.

———. 1997. *Nationalizing Blackness: Afrocubanismo and Artistic Revolution in Havana, 1920–1940*. Pittsburgh: University of Pittsburgh Press.

Moreno Fraginals, Manuel. 1977. "Africa in Cuba: A Quantitative Analysis of the African Population in the Island of Cuba." Translated by Jean Stubbs. *Annals of the New York Academy of Sciences* 292: 187–201. Comparative Perspectives on Slavery in New World Plantation Societies. Edited by Vera Rubin and Arthur Tuden.

Murphy, John P. 1991. "The Charanga in New York and the Persistence of the Típico Style." In *Essays on Cuban Music: North American and Cuban Perspectives*. Edited by Peter Manuel. Lanham: University Press of America.

Nasser, Amín E. 1994. *Benny Moré*. Ciudad de La Habana: Unión de Escritores y Artistas de Cuba.

Navarro, Mireya. 2000. "Mambo Dancers' Rift Leaves Stepped-On Toes." *New York Times Metro* (September 3): 1, 37.

Nelson, Lowry. 1950. "The Social Class Structure in Cuba." In *Materiales para el estudio de la clase media en la America latina*, vol. 2, *La clase media en México y Cuba: Cuatro Colaboraciones*. Edited by Theo R. Crevenna. Washington, DC: Union Panamericana, Departamento de Asuntos Cultuales.

Nieves Rivera, Rafael. 1952. "Cubiche en Borinquen: Arsenio Rodríguez dice es creador del mambo." *El Imparcial* (September 19): 26.

Nketia, J. H. Kwabena. 1981. "African Roots of Music in the Americas: An African View." In *International Musicological Society: Report of the Twelfth Congress Berkeley 1977*. Edited by Daniel Heartz and Bonnie Wade. Kassel: American Musicological Society.

Ohl, Dorothea Duryea. 1958. "Mambo not a Dance?" *Dance Magazine* 32/6 (June): 67–68.

Orovio, Helio. 1985. "Arsenio Rodríguez y el son cubano." *Revolución y Cultura* 7: 14–17.

———. 1992. *Diccionario de la música cubana: biografico y tecnico*, 2nd ed. La Habana: Editorial Letras Cubanas.

———. 2004. *Cuban Music from A to Z*. Durham, NC: Duke University Press.

Orozco González, Danilo. 1992. "Procesos socioculturales y rasgos de identidad en los géneros musicales con referencia especial a la música cubana." *Latin American Music Review* 13/2: 158–78.

Ortero González, Lisandro. 1953. "La comparsa en el ensayo: Lo que usted no ve en el Prado." *Bohemia* 45/8: 54–56, 81.

Otero, Juan Joaquín et al. 1954. *Libro de Cuba: Una enciclopedia ilustrada que abarca las artes, las letras, las ciencias, la economía, la política, la historia, la docencia y el progreso general de la nación cubana*. Edición Conmemorativa del Cincuentenario de la Independencia, 1902–1952 y del Centenario del Nacimiento de José Martí, 1853–1953. Habana: Publicaciones Unidas.

Ortiz Federico Jr. 1951. "El mambo y su influencia malsana." *La Opinion*, July 8.

Ortiz, Fernando. 1920. "La fiesta Afro-Cubana del 'Día de Reyes.'" *Revista bimestre cubana* 15/1: 5 26.

———. 1924. *Glosario de afronegrismos*. La Habana: Imprenta "El Siglo XX."

———. 1946. "Estudiemos la música afrocubana." *Estudios afrocubanos* 5: 7–18.

———. 1952. *Los instrumentos de la música afrocubana. III Los tambores xilofónicos y los membranófonos abiertos A a n*. La Habana: Publicaciones de la Dirección de Cultura del Ministerio de Educación.

———. 1965. *La africanía de la música folklórica de Cuba*. La Habana: Editora Universitaria.

———. 1992. *Los cabildos y la fiesta afrocubanos del Día de Reyes*. La Habana: Editorial de Ciencias Sociales.

———. 1993. *Los bailes y el teatro de los negros en el folklore de Cuba,* 3rd ed. La Habana: Publicaciones del Ministerio de Educacion, Dirección de Cultura. Originally published in 1951.

———. 1995. *Cuban Counterpoint: Tobacco and Sugar*. Translated by Harriet de Onís. Introduction by Bronislaw Malinowski. Prologue by Herminio Portell Vilá. New introduction by Fernando Coronil. Durham, NC: Duke University Press. Originally published in 1940.

Pabon, Tony. 1968. "The Night of the All-Stars." *Latin New York* 1/4 (March): 10–13.

Padilla, Felix M. 1985. *Latino Ethnic Consciousness: The Case of Mexican Americans and Puerto Ricans in Chicago*. Indiana: University of Notre Dame Press.

———. 1989. "Salsa Music as a Cultural Expression of Latino Consciousness and Unity." *Hispanic Journal of Behavioral Sciences* 11/1: 28–45.

———. 1990. "Salsa: Puerto Rican and Latino Music." *Journal of Popular Culture* 24/1: 87–104.

Padilla, Napoleón. 1983. "Anselmo Sacasas: La música cubana de ayer y la Orquesta 'Casino de la Playa.'" *Replica* 14/664.

Padura Fuentes, Leonardo. 1997. *Los rosotros de la salsa*. Ciudad de La Habana: Ediciones Unión.

Pasmanick, Philip. 1997. "*Décima* and *Rumba*: Iberian Formalism in the Heart of Afro-Cuban Song." *Latin American Music Review* 18/2: 252–77.

Pérez, Jr., Louis A. 1995a. *Cuba: Between Reform and Revolution,* 2nd ed. New York: Oxford University Press.

Pérez Firmat, Gustavo. 1994. *Life on the Hyphen: The Cuban-American Way*. Austin: University of Texas Press.

Phillips, R. Hart. 1945. "Cuba: Soviet Propaganda Center." *American Mercury* 60/258: 671–76.

———. 1959. *Cuba, Island of Paradox*. New York: McDowell, Obolensky.

Pinto, Angel C. 1937. "Una aclaración." *Adelante* (June): 10–11.

Pinto Interián, Ernesto. 1937. "Contestando nuestra encuesta." *Adelante* (March): 15.

Portell Vila, Herminio. 1953. "Barrio suburbano." *Bohemia* 45/11: 46–47, 114–15.

Poyo, Gerald E. 1991. "The Cuban Experience in the United States, 1865–1940: Migration, Community, and Identity." *Cuban Studies* 21: 19–36.

Quintero, Babby. 1952. "El mambo, el batanga." *La Prensa*, October 10.

Radano, Ronald and Philip V. Bohlman. 2000. "Introduction: Music and Race, Their Past, Their Presence." In *Music and the Racial Imagination*. Edited by Ronald Radano and Philip V. Bohlman. Chicago: University of Chicago Press.

Radano, Ronald. 2000. "Hot Fantasies: American Modernism and the Idea of Black Rhythm." In *Music and the Racial Imagination*. Edited by Ronald Radano and Philip V. Bohlman. Chicago: University of Chicago Press.

———. 2003. *Lying up a Nation: Race and Black Music*. Chicago: University of Chicago Press.

Ramírez Bedoya, Héctor. 1998. *Historia de la Sonora Matancera y sus estrellas*, 2nd ed. Medellín: Héctor Ramírez B. Original edition, 1996.

Ramos, Juan. 1950. "La virtud del mambo." *Diario de la Marina*, December 27.

Ramsey, Guthrie P. Jr. 2003. *Race Music: Black Cultures from Bebop to Hip-Hop*. Berkeley: University of California Press.

"RCA to Give Prado Push as Pop Artist." 1950. *Down Beat*, September 22.

Record Reviews. 1950. *Down Beat*, June 2.

Reig, Teddy with Edward Berger. 1990. *Reminiscing in Tempo: The Life and Times of a Jazz Hustler*. Studies in Jazz, no. 10. New Jersey: Scarecrow Press and the Institute of Jazz Studies, Rutgers University.

República de Cuba. 1943. *Dirección general del censo de 1943: Estados contentivos de habitantes y electores: Clasificados por provincias, municipios y barrios*. La Habana: Editorial Guerrero.

Reyes-Schramm, Adelaida. 1975. *The Role of Music in the Interaction of Black Americans and Hispanos in New York City's East Harlem*. Ph.D. diss., Columbia University.

Robbins, James. 1990. "The Cuban *Son* as Form, Genre, and Symbol." *Latin American Music Review* 11/2: 182–200.

Roberts, John Storm. 1975. "Salsa, the Sound of the City." *After Dark* (July): 50–55.

———. 1976. "Salsa's Prodigal Sun: Eddie Palmieri." *Down Beat* 43/8 (April 22): 21–22, 42–43.

———. 1999. *The Latin Tinge: The Impact of Latin American Music on the United States*, 2nd ed. New York: Oxford University Press. Originally published 1979.

Roca, Blas. 1960. *Los fundamentos del socialismo en Cuba*. La Habana: Ediciones Populares.

Roig de Leuchsenring, Emilio. 1939. *La Habana: Apuntes Históricos*. La Habana: Municipio de La Habana.

Roldan Viñas, Miguel. 1954. "Las sociedades españolas: solidos pilares de nuestra nacionalidad." In *Libro de Cuba: Una enciclopedia ilustrada que abarca las artes, las letras, las ciencias, la economía, la política, la historia, la docencia y el progreso general de la nación cubana*. Edición Conmemorativa del Cincuentenario de la Independencia, 1902–1952 y del Centenario del Nacimiento de José Martí, 1853–1953. Edited by Juan Joaquín Otero et al. Habana: Publicaciones Unidas.

Román-Velázquez, Patria. 2002. "Locating Salsa." In *Popular Music Studies*. Edited by David Hesmondhalgh and Keith Negus. London: Arnold.

Rondón, César Miguel. 1980. *El libro de la Salsa: Crónica de la música del Caribe urbano*. Caracas: Editorial Arte.

Ruf, Elizabeth. 1997. "Issues of Gender, Color, and Nationalism in Cuba's Tropicana Nightclub Performance." *Drama Review* 41/1: 86–105.

Ruíz, Gervasio G. 1949. "Los bailes cubanos." *Carteles* 30 (March 20): 28–31.

Ruíz, Rosendo, Vicente González-Rubiera, and Abelardo Estrada. 1995. "Los años treinta: núcleo central de la trova intermedia." In *Panorama de la música popular cubana*. Edited by Radamés Giro. La Habana: Editorial Letras Cubanas.

Salazar, Max. 1992. "Who Invented the Mambo?" *Latin Beat Magazine* 2/8: 9–14.

———. 1994. "Arsenio Rodríguez: Life Was Like a Dream." *Latin Beat Magazine* 4: 12–17.

———. 2002. *Mambo Kingdom: Latin Music in New York*. New York: Schirmer Trade Books.

Salwen, Michael B. 1994. *Radio and Television in Cuba: The Pre-Castro Era*. Ames: Iowa State University Press.

Sánchez, María Luisa. 1937. "Zafra y comparsas." *Adelante* (April): 13.

Sánchez-Boudy, José. 1999. *Diccionario mayor de cubanismos*. Miami: Ediciones Universal.

Sánchez Korrol, Virginia E. 1995. *From Colonia to Community: The History of Puerto Ricans in New York City*. Berkeley: University of California Press.

Santana Archibold, Sergio. 1992. *¿Que es la salsa? Buscando la melodía*... Medellín: Ediciones Salsa y Cultura.

Santana, Joaquin G. 1970. "Un son montuno para Benny Moré." *Bohemia* 62/39: 20–27.

Schwartz, Rosalie. 1998. "Cuba's Roaring Twenties: Race Consciousness and the Column 'Ideales de una Raza.'" In *Between Race and Empire: African-Americans and Cubans before the Cuban Revolution*. Edited by Lisa Brock and Digna Castañeda Fuertes. Philadelphia: Temple University Press.

Shemel, Sidney and M. William Krasilovsky. 1990. *This Business of Music*, 6th ed. New York: Billboard Books. Originally published 1964.

Singer, Roberta L. 1982. *My Music Is Who I Am and What I Do: Latin Popular Music and Identity in New York City*. Ph.D. diss., Indiana University.

Singer, Roberta L. and Robert Friedman. 1977. *Caliente—Hot: Puerto Rican and Cuban Musical Expression in New York*. New York: New World Records. CD NW 244-2.

Smith, Arnold Jay. 1976a. "Sounds from the Salsa Source: Tito and Machito." *Down Beat* 43/8 (April 22): 16, 42.

———. 1976b. "Ray Barretto's Crossover Crisis." *Down Beat* 43/8 (April 22): 17–18, 40.

Spottswood, Richard K. 1990. *Ethnic Music on Records: A Discography of Ethnic Recordings Produced in the United States, 1893 to 1942*, vol. 4. *Spanish, Portuguese, Phillipine, Basque*. Urbana: University of Illinois Press.

Stearn, Jess. 1956. "Las Vegas se vuelve hacia los trópicos: La Habana paraíso de jugadores." *Bohemia* 48/12 (18 marzo 1956): 38–39, 96–97.

Stearns, Marshall and Jean. 1979. *Jazz Dance: The Story of American Vernacular Dance*. New York: Schirmer Books.

Stock, Jonathan P. J. 2001. "Toward an Ethnomusicology of the Individual, or Biographical Writing in Ethnomusicology." *World of Music* 43/1: 5–20.

Terrace, Michael. 1995. "Mambo Camouflaged as Salsa." *Dancing USA* 13/4 (July/August): 5, 7.

Thompson, Robert Farris. 1958. "Mambo with Pantomime." *Dance Magazine* 32/6 (June): 68–69.

———. 1959. "Palladium Mambo I." *Dance Magazine* 23/9 (September): 73–75.

———. 1967. "New Voice from the Barrios." *Saturday Review* 50/43 (October 28): 53–55, 68.

———. 1983. "Portrait of the Pachanga: The Music, The Players, the Dancers." *Caribe* 7/1–2: 47–49. Reprinted from *Saturday Review* (October 28, 1961).

———. 1984. *Flash of the Spirit: African and Afro-American Art and Philosophy*. New York: Vintage Books.

———. 1990. "Kongo Influences on African-American Artistic Culture." In *Africanisms in American Culture*. Edited by Joseph E. Holloway. Bloomington: Indiana University Press.

———. 2002. "Teaching the People to Triumph over Time: Notes from the World of Mambo." *Caribbean Dance from Abakuá to Zouk: How Movement Shapes Identity*. Gainesville: University Press of Florida.

Torres, Dora Ileana. 1995. "Del danzón cantado al chachachá." In *Panorama de la música popular cubana*. Edited by Radamés Giro. La Habana: Editorial Letras Cubanas.

Turino, Thomas. 2000. "Race, Class, and Musical Nationalism in Zimbabwe." In *Music and the Racial Imagination*. Edited by Ronald Radano and Philip V. Bohlman. Chicago: University of Chicago Press.

Urfé, Odilio. 1977. "La música y la danza en Cuba." In *África en América Latina*. Edited by Manuel Moreno Fraginals. Mexico: UNESCO Siglo Veintiuno Editores.

———. 1979. "Danzón, mambo, y chachachá." *Revolución y Cultura* 1: 54–57.

———. 1982. "La música folklórica, popular, y del teatro cubano." *La cultura en Cuba socialista*. La Habana: Editorial Letras Cubanas.

———. 1993. "La verdad sobre el mambo." In *El mambo*. Edited by Radamés Giro. La Habana: Editorial Letras Cubanas. First published in *Inventario: Mensuario Polémico de Arte y Literatura* 1/3 (1948).

Urrutia, Gustavo. 1937. "Contestando nuestra encuesta." *Adelante* (June): 13.

U.S. Commission on Civil Rights, Western Regional Office. 1980. *Puerto Ricans in California: A Staff Report of the Western Regional Office, United States Commission on Civil Rights*. Washington, DC: Commission on Civil Rights.

U.S. Department of Commerce. 1973. *1970 Census of Population*, vol. 1, *Characteristics of the Population*, Part 6, *California*, Section 2. Washington, DC: Bureau of the Census.

U.S. Diplomatic Post. 1940–45. *Cuba*. Frederick: University Publications of America.

U.S. State Department. 1945–49. *Cuba: Internal Affairs and Foreign Affairs*. Frederick: University Publications of America.

Valdés Cantero, Alicia. 1988. *El músico en Cuba: Ubicación social y situatión laboral en el períoda 1939–1946*. La Habana: Editorial Pueblo y Educación.

Vélez, María Teresa. 1996. *The Trade of an Afro-Cuban Religious Drummer: Felipe García Villamil*. Ph.D. diss., Wesleyan University.

Verez de Peraza, Elena Luisa. 1954. *Publicaciones de las instituciones culturales cubanas*, 2nd ed. Habana: Ediciones Anuario Bibliográfico Cubano.

Wade, Peter. 1993. *Blackness and Race Mixture: The Dynamics of Racial Identity in Colombia*. Baltimore: Johns Hopkins University Press.

———. 2000. *Music, Race, and Nation: Música Tropical in Colombia*. Chicago: University of Chicago Press.

Washburne, Christopher. 1998. "Play It *Con Filin*!: The Swing and Expression of Salsa." *Latin American Music Review* 19/2: 160–85.

———. 1999. *Salsa in New York: A Musical Ethnography*. Ph.D. diss., Columbia University.

Waxer, Lise. 1994. *Cali Pachanguero: A Social History of Salsa in a Colombian City*. Ph.D. diss., University of Illinois at Urbana-Champaign.

———. 2002a. *The City of Musical Memory: Salsa, Record Grooves, and Popular Culture in Cali, Colombia*. Middletown: Wesleyan University Press.

———, ed. 2002b. *Situating Salsa: Global Markets and Local Meanings in Latin Popular Music*. New York: Routledge.

———. 2002c. "Situating Salsa: Latin Music at the Crossroads." In *Situating Salsa: Global Markets and Local Meanings in Latin Popular Music*. Edited by Lise Waxer. New York: Routledge.

———. 2002d. "Llegó la Salsa: The Rise of Salsa in Venezuela and Colombia." In *Situating Salsa: Global Markets and Local Meanings in Latin Popular Music*. Edited by Lise Waxer. New York: Routledge.

West, Cornel. 1999. *The Cornel West Reader*. New York: Basic Civitas Books.

Western Economic Research. 1971. *Negroes as a Percent of the Total Population in the Los Angeles Five County Area by Census Tracts, 1970 Census*. Sherman Oaks: Western Economic Research.

———. 1972. *Persons of Spanish Language and Surname as a Percent of the Total Population in the Los Angeles Five County Area by Census Tracts, 1970 Census*. Sherman Oaks: Western Economic Research.

White, Clement A. 1993. *Decoding the Word: Nicolás Guillén as Maker and Debunker of Myth*. Miami: Ediciones Universal.

Williams, Raymond. 1977. *Marxism and Literature*. Oxford: Oxford University Press.

Wurdeman, John G. 1844. *Notes on Cuba: Containing an Account of its Discovery and Early History; a Description of the Face of the Country, its Population, Resources, and Wealth; its Institutions, and the Manners and Customs of its Inhabitants; with Directions to Travellers Visiting the Island*. Boston: J. Monroe.

Wyndham, Marivic and Peter Read. 2003. "Buena Vista Social Club: Local Meets Global and Lives Happily Ever After." *Cultural Geographies* 10: 498–503.

Zaldívar, Mario. 1999. *El mito de la Sonora Matancera*. Costa Rica: Litografía IPECA.

Index

Page numbers in italics refer to figures and musical examples

About the Author

DAVID F. GARCÍA is Assistant Professor of Music at the University of North Carolina at Chapel Hill.